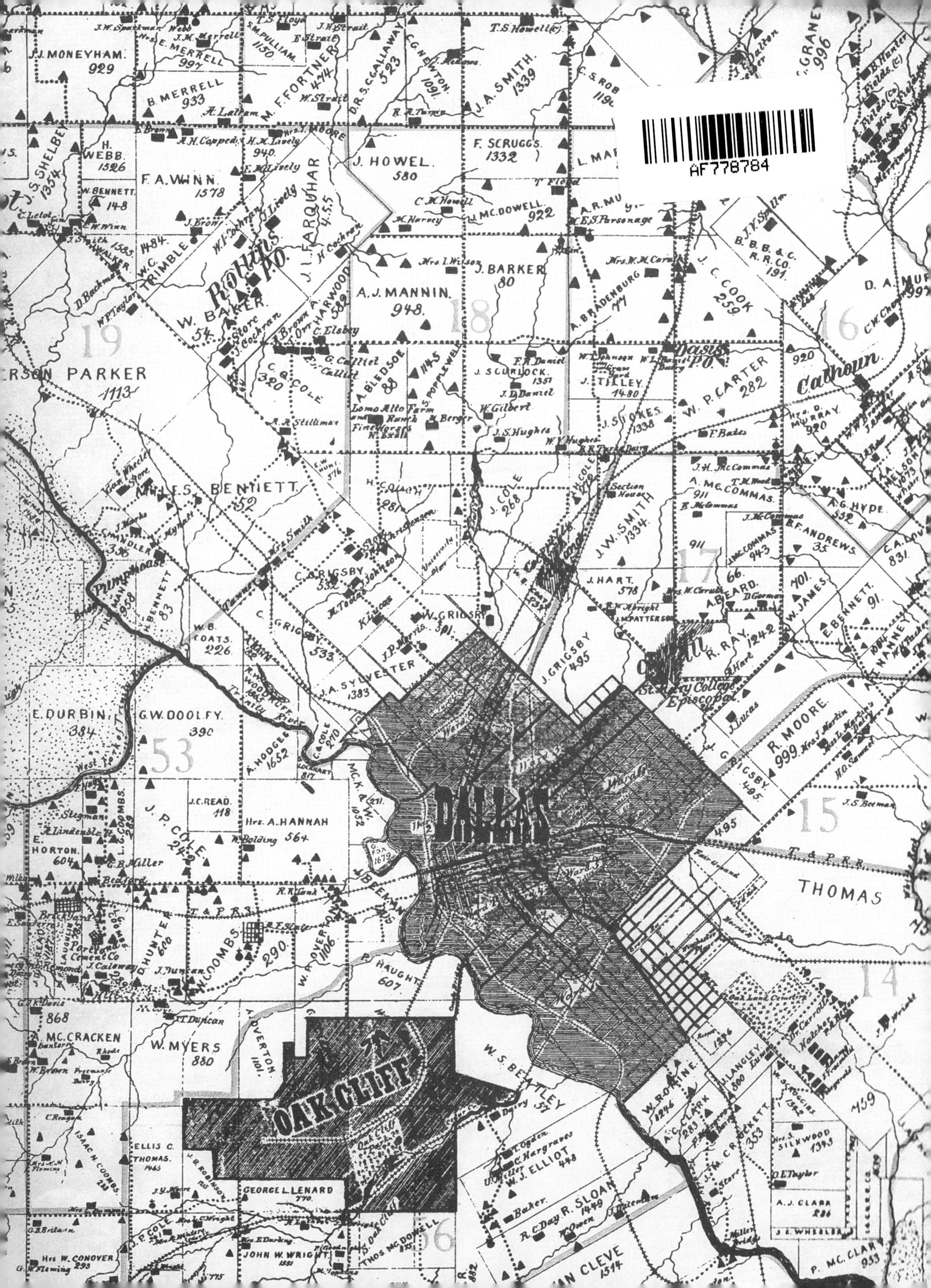

J. MONEYHAM 929
B. MERRELL 933
E. MERRELL 997
M. F. FORTNER 474
J. A. SMITH 1339
F. SCRUGGS 1332
J. HOWEL 580
F. A. WINN 1578
H. WEBB 1526
W. BENNETT 148
J. I. FARQUHAR 455
J. M. McDOWELL 922
J. BARKER 80
A. J. MANNIN 948
J. C. COOK 259
W. BAKER 54
Rollins P.O.
19
18
16
PARKER 1113
C. G. COLE 320
A. BLEDSOE 88
J. SCURLOCK 1351
J. TILLEY 1480
W. P. CARTER 282
Calhoun
J. STOKES 1338
MILES BENNETT 52
J. COLE 268
J. W. SMITH 1334
A. G. HYDE 332
B. F. ANDREWS 35
C. GRIGSBY 532
17
J. HART 578
A. BEARD 66
W. JAMES 701
E. BENNETT 91
W. B. COATS 226
J. GRIGSBY 495
R. RAY 1242
E. DURBIN 384
G. W. DOOLEY 390
53
J. A. SYLVESTER 1383
St. Mary College
Episcopal
R. MOORE 999
A. HODGES 1652
J. C. READ 118
Mrs. A. HANNAH 564
DALLAS
15
J. P. COLE 249
E. HORTON 604
T. & P. R.R.
THOMAS
W. R. OVERTON 1106
HAUGHT 607
14
A. McCRACKEN
W. MYERS 880
A. OVERTON 1101
OAK CLIFF
W. S. BEATTLEY
ISAAC N. COOMBS
ELLIS C. THOMAS 1465
GEORGE L. LENARD 770
W. J. ELLIOT 448
R. SLOAN 1449
W. H. SILKWOOD 1343
A. J. CLARK 286
JOHN W. WRIGHT 1551
THOS. McDOWELL 875
56
Mrs. W. CONOVER 293
VAN CLEVE 1514
P. McCLAR 933

IRVING

Joe Putnam
Mayor

Dear Friend,

Irving, Texas, is 100 years old, and our Centennial Celebration was exciting and memorable. We enjoyed a wonderful 15-month celebration to reminisce about our rich history, acknowledge our city's present-day attributes and anticipate an even greater future.

In keeping with the spirit of this significant anniversary, the Irving Centennial Celebration Task Force and the City of Irving are pleased to present this special pictorial history book.

We hope that you will enjoy these photographs and stories of Irving's first century.

Sincerely,

Joe Putnam
Irving Mayor

City of Irving
825 W. Irving Blvd. • Irving, Texas 75060 • 972.721.2410 • 972.721.2384 fax • www.ci.irving.tx.us

IRVING, TEXAS
From Rails to Wings

1903–2003

BY
NORMA STANTON

THE
DONNING COMPANY
PUBLISHERS

This pictorial book is dedicated to the people of Irving, Texas—
those who had the dream and built a prosperous town;
those who are carrying the vision forward;
and those who will lead Irving to even greater heights.

The Donning Company Publishers
184 Business Park Drive, Suite 206
Virginia Beach, VA 23462

Steve Mull, General Manager
Barbara B. Buchanan, Office Manager
Marshall McClure, Design Production Coordinator
Richard A. Horwege, Senior Editor
Joe Schnellmann, Graphic Designer
Mary Ellen Wheeler, Proofreader/Editorial Assistant
Daniel Carr, Imaging Artist
Barbara Bolton, Project Director
Pam Forrester, Project Research Coordinator
Scott Rule, Director of Marketing
Travis Gallup, Marketing Coordinator

Library of Congress Cataloging-in-Publication Data

Stanton, Norma, 1925–
Irving, Texas : rails to wings / by Norma Stanton.
p. cm.
Includes bibliographical references and index.
ISBN 1-57864-227-2 (alk. paper)
1. Irving (Tex.)—History. 2. Irving (Tex.)—Pictorial works. 3. Irving (Tex.)—Economic conditions.
4. Business enterprises—Texas—Irving. I. Title.
F394.I78S73 2003
976.4'531—dc22

2003062555

Printed in the United States of America

Contents

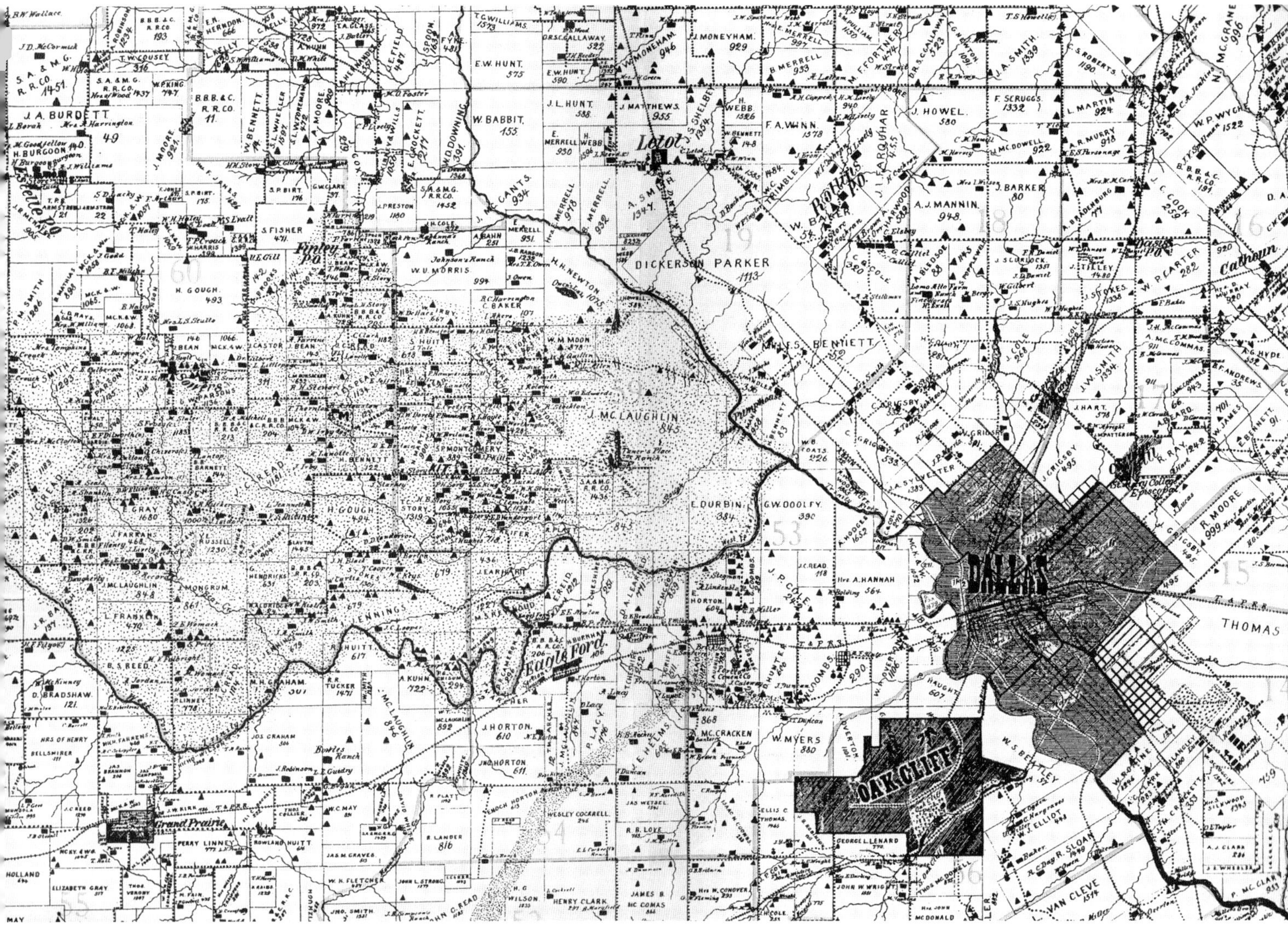

Portion of the Sam Street 1900 map.

Chapter I

Life before Irving

As of December 19, 2003, the city of Irving, Texas, is one-hundred years old. Of course there was life in the area long before there was a town or city of Irving. There had been Indian trails and Indian encampments. Cattle drives, stagecoaches, and wagon trains passed through. Several communities were scattered around this area between the Elm Fork and the West Fork of the Trinity River. This location affected the living conditions of the early settlers and created challenges to the future development of the city. The Elm Fork of the Trinity River formed a barrier to the east, while the West Fork impeded travel to the south. There were also many tributaries and several creeks that flowed through the area toward the river including Cottonwood Creek, Bear Creek, Hackberry Creek, and Delaware Creek. This was not always a big problem because much of the time, even before there were bridges, the river could be forded at certain crossings by horses, cattle, and wagons.

To citizens who have lived many years in the Dallas area, it is legend that at the time John Neely Bryan, who founded Dallas in 1841, stood at the site overlooking the Trinity River, he visualized a port city with boats coming in from the Gulf Coast. Through the years many serious attempts to make that vision a reality have raised hopes and then failed. In the mid-1800s several boats were built and launched with great fanfare bound for the coast, only to be grounded or destroyed. Hopes ran high for the *Sally Haynes* while it was being built in Dallas, but it sank about forty miles out. It wasn't until 1893 that a paddleboat named the *H. A. Harvey Jr.* actually made the trip from the coast and pulled in near Main Street in Dallas. The trip took sixty-seven days and excitement was so high that celebrations lasted four days. The great boat stayed in the Dallas area and for several years took passengers on pleasure outings on the water when conditions were favorable. The April 7, 1894 edition of the *Dallas Daily Times-Herald* reported: "If anybody doubts that Dallas is a big river town he should have been at the steamboat landing when the *Harvey* departed for McComas Bluff in the morning and returned in the evening yesterday. That prairie suburb, Fort Worth, would have died of envy could she have witnessed the sight."

Periodically the hope has been rekindled and projects launched, but at the end of the century the Trinity was still not dependable for navigation. Visitors who are acquainted with major rivers and who are in the area during dry weather sometimes laugh when we call it a river. But it was no laughing matter when the Trinity River rose and raged out of its banks. In the period before Irving was founded, floods were recorded in 1844, 1866, and 1871. In 1890 the river rose overnight and was two miles across by morning. Houses and businesses were under water, and people who were in Dallas from out of town were stranded for several days. The Commerce Street Bridge collapsed and railroad trestles were under water. Dallas reporters referred to the "Turbulent Trinity" as they described the dramatic scenes. There have been periodic recurrences of such flooding through the years, and the projects to tame the Trinity have been a major concern.

Indian George wore the dress of his Comanche ancestors when talking to Boy Scouts and other young people in Irving. He was scoutmaster for Troop 508, creator of an outstanding Indian Dance Team, and teacher of Indian culture and lore to both young people and senior citizens. Courtesy David Dunkley

George Alfred, a Comanche Indian known in Irving as "Indian George," worked with the Boy Scouts and talked to many students in Irving about the history of Indians. In recorded interviews, preserved in the City of Irving Archives, he tells us that several tribes passed through and the Comanche Tribe established an encampment in this area. He said that the "Great Camp" where the warrior Chief White Eagle lived was near the current location of the University of Dallas and that the "Warrior Camp" was at the current site of Irving City Hall. The Elm Fork of the Trinity River ran near the site of the present Texas Stadium where there were many tepees. In his words, "No Comanche will set up a tepee unless there is water." The creek that we know as Delaware Creek was once called Indian Run. *Delaware* was the name of an Indian tribe that hunted in the area and camped along the creek.

A map made of tiles on the floor of the South Irving DART Transit Center depicts the various Indian trails through what later became Irving. Jim Dunkley, the resident expert on these trails, was a strong influence, along with the Heritage Society, in the choice of this art project for the Irving station.

The Irving Parks Department has recently reclaimed an abandoned sand and gravel quarry and created the Shady Grove Trail Park on Vilbig Road east of MacArthur Boulevard and south of Shady Grove Road. The early map and history of the trails is displayed there. The site represents part of a trail that led from the Eagle Ford crossing toward Fort Worth. In 1887, Louis Caster deeded an acre for a church and school in a grove of post oaks. The settlement, which became known as Shady Grove, was between the West Fork of the Trinity and Rock Island with the Tarrant County line to the west and what later became Beltline Road on the east.

To help visualize what was in the area when the city of Irving was founded we have included a selected portion of the 1900 Sam Street Map of Dallas County (see page 6). We can see the town of Eagle Ford just south of the West Fork and the dotted lines representing the trails that were followed across the West Fork of the river up to and beyond the little community of Kit. Another dotted line branches off and goes west. Then looking along the Elm Fork there is a dotted line which comes north from Dallas, crosses to the west side of the river and proceeds due west. There were three main crossings where the river could most easily be forded from Dallas to enter the area that later became Irving. Eagle Ford, Record Crossing, and California Crossing are clearly depicted on the map. These river crossings were used by Indians, covered wagons, horseback riders, stagecoaches, and oxcarts and for cattle drives.

California Crossing got its name from the travelers who, hoping to find gold in California in 1849, followed trails through the area long before there were roads. A look at recent maps reveals a street in Dallas still called California Crossing. It crosses into Irving and extends to a point near the south end of Lake Carolyn in Las Colinas. A marker established by the Texas Historical Survey Committee is located on California Crossing Road west of the National Guard Armory and just north of Irving. The Dallas County Nature Park, in this area of the old river bottoms, preserves thousands of acres in a primitive state with paths and markers along trails much like early travelers experienced.

In the industrial area of Dallas there is a short segment of a street called Record Crossing which originates at Harry Hines Boulevard, crosses the old river channel, and ends at Stemmons Freeway and Highway 183. Before the river was moved and contained by levees, this would have been bottom land on the east and west sides of the river. Record Crossing was one of the original natural crossings where, in good weather, the Elm Fork of the river could be forded before there were any bridges, and it led to the area mentioned earlier where Indians camped beside the river. It continued to be one of the three main entries to the area even after the founding of Irving.

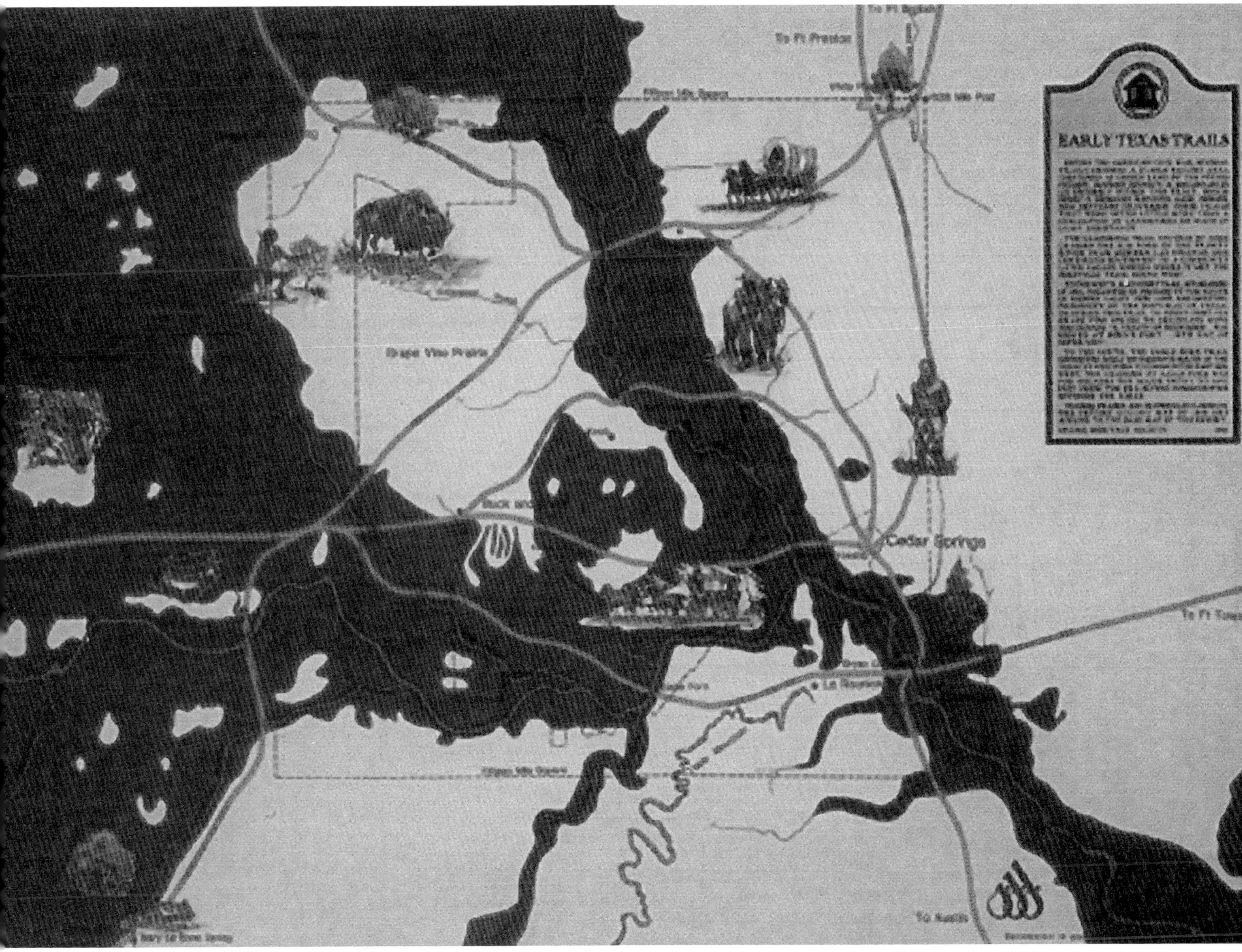

This map of the early trails through the "Forks" is displayed in Vilbig Park in South Irving.

On the 1900 map, we can locate, in the area that later became Irving, the communities of Kit, Sowers, Finley, and Estelle. The practical reason for naming a community had nothing to do with government or platting its boundaries. A settlement where several families lived, where there was a school, a church meeting, a store, or a landmark might be named on purpose or a name could just evolve. The main purpose of a more formal naming was to designate a post office. Communities, other than the four mentioned above, that existed before the founding of Irving were Union Bower, Hackberry, Shady Grove, and Bear Creek. They each have an interesting story, and they continued to exist for many years as part of the life of the town before gradually becoming officially a part of Irving by addition or annexation.

The little black rectangles scattered about the map represent houses belonging to residents in 1900. The triangles represent "rent" houses. The names of owner/residents are printed in small script. The larger block letters identify surveys and land claims. Many of these names can be recognized as people who made important contributions to life in the area and whose descendants continued to be very involved in shaping the city that Irving has become. Around Kit we see Britain, Lucas, King, Kitts, Worthington, Henry, Moreland, several Story family members, and others. Moving northwest there are homes with names Dorety, Lively, Joffre, Lanotte, and Thornton. Southwest of Kit and just north of the West Fork, we can see the residence of J. C. Looper and farther west, close to Bear Creek, two Smith homes. Follow Bear Creek to a point where it is fed by two tributaries, and lined up along a trail are the homes of Mrs. E. Rogers, O. Record Jr., Record, and Lively. Greene and Dilworth can be found on either side of the creek as we look farther north. These names, and several others in this area, are followed by a letter *C*, meaning "colored." Northeast of Kit and then following northwesterly there are more residences which belonged to pioneers whose names we still recognize in Irving. Among these are Edwards, Smith, Bodine, Voirin, Harrington, DeHaes, Lanotte, Clark, Ostrand, Beauford, and Harrington, and close to the Finley Post Office are Farine and Story. Between Finley and Estelle, F. P. Crouch, S. Ewalt, H. S. Ewalt, W. H. Haley, and T. Haley are shown as neighbors along a trail. And around Estelle, which is right at the Dallas/Tarrant County line, names of residents shown are Borah, Harrington, Goodfellow, Burgoon, Lucas, and Williams.

Notable around Sowers are the names of E. D. Sowers, Dr. Gilbert, L. Littlepage, W. A. Mitchell, Mrs. Burgoon, W. Haley, and C. E. Culberson. A large land grant to J. Caster is shown and a building captioned "store" is identified. Edmund Sowers arrived in a covered wagon in 1856 and claimed thirty-two acres of good land in the Parsons headright near what is now Pioneer and Beltline Roads. Good spring water was easily available there. He honored a gravesite that he found on the property marked with stones and subsequently provided a cemetery where he gave free plots to members of his community. This Sowers Cemetery is recognized with a Texas State Historic Marker.

Mr. Sowers continued to buy land and by 1876 he owned one thousand acres. He built a fine two-story house using lumber that he imported from Jefferson, Texas, which was the closest lumber mill. Hauling the materials by oxcarts over rough trails was neither easy nor swift. Each trip took three months. As more settlers gathered he opened a general store. There was a once-a-week mail stop there on the Dallas to Birdville route before the Civil War. It was discontinued for several years during the war. We are told that this was where the California Trail met the Birdville Trail going west. After the war Mr. Sowers reestablished a post office and served as postmaster for the Sowers area before giving it up to H. M. Lucas. The route was then Dallas to Grapevine, serving Sowers and Estelle.

When the house was finished it was put to good use for family and for entertaining. Ed Sowers loved children and young people, and though he never fathered a child, he raised eleven orphans and a stepdaughter. His property became famous for yearly Fourth of July celebrations that attracted people from miles around. Celebrants brought food to be shared. Some brought items to sell. They talked, listened to speeches, traded, and danced into the night to music provided by local musicians. According to Daisy Catherine O'Connell, who was ninety years old when interviewed for the Irving Archives in 1977, they had little tickets that sold for five cents to allow a boy to dance with a nice girl who would accept his invitation. This helped defray the expenses of the party. She also recalled with some amusement that a double-wide swing hanging on a high tree limb was part of the entertainment. A young man would ask a young lady to swing with him and it would cause a certain amount of excitement as onlookers gathered around. The girls wore long dresses and petticoats so that a boy never saw a leg. But as the couple swung high it was often possible to catch a glimpse.

This home that Dr. D. W. Gilbert built for his family stood as a landmark for almost seventy years before the Plymouth Park Shopping Center was developed on the site. Courtesy Dr. Clay Gilbert

Mrs. O'Connell also told about the wine casks in Mr. Sowers's cellar. She said that he had two Frenchmen who made the wine for him from grapes he grew on his farm. He stored it unopened in his cellar for two or three years.

Dr. Clay Gilbert has given us information about his grandfather, Dr. Daniel Webster Gilbert, who served a broad portion of the countryside with its various communities before he bought land in the Sowers area in the early 1880s. He built a two-story, three-gable, six-bedroom home on the highest elevation of a fifteen-hundred-acre farm. It faced south near the present location of Grauwyler and Story Roads. This house was a landmark and a beloved haven for their children and grandchildren. Younger members of the family and the community often referred to the home as "The Castle."

Dr. Gilbert and his wife had one son, Taylor C. Gilbert, before she died. His second wife, whose husband had died, had one son, John Roberts. With these two children and their mutual children they raised a large family of young people who had responsibilities helping their father tend the farm, the dairy, and the peach orchard on the property. One of the sons, Dr. Franklin Monroe Gilbert, seemed quite serious when, in later years, he said that the boys were always anxious to do their chores. The peach orchard, from north of the home to what much later became Highway 183, was famous for the beauty of the blooms in the spring.

The Gilbert farm extended north of what later became Highway 183, and the dairy was near what would now be the southwest corner of Finley and Story Roads. The four-hundred-acre "Ewalt Pasture," also owned by Dr. Gilbert, extended his property from the dairy site north along the west side of what is now Country Club Drive to the site that became the old Irving Country Club and then west to Beltline Road. This pasture was used as grazing land for the large herd of dairy cows. Dr. Clay Gilbert has documentation for this information.

Dr. Gilbert initially built a small office in the corner of his yard where he saw patients. He soon built a second office in a business area near what is now the southeast corner of Pioneer Road (originally Sowers Road) and Beltline Road where he saw patients and mixed prescriptions. Hugh Lucas operated a general store, and he added a small prescription department after working with the doctor to learn how to fill his prescriptions. Dr. Gilbert took care of patients in all of the communities in the surrounding area before there was any thought of Irving. He never let bad weather or poor road conditions deter him. If his buggy could not be managed on the trails, he went on horseback. There are many reports of the special caring relationship he had with patients in all of the surrounding communities.

William Haley was a neighbor to the north toward Estelle. He arrived in 1857 with his wife Lucinda Catherine, their two children and her younger brother, Richard Ewalt, and laid a claim to one section of land. On the journey by wagon train from Missouri, they wrote letters to friends and family at home with details of the trip. After they arrived and started their lives in Texas, their reports were so glowing that several others from Missouri decided to join them, even though William wrote that their first home was a log cabin with a dirt floor and a leaking roof. He staked

The Kit Store and Post Office was a gathering place for the surrounding community and a stop for wagon trains traveling through the territory. Mail, general merchandise, entertainment, and meals with the family were available here with Uncle Ike and Aunt Nancy. She was famous for her homemade bread and plum preserves. Courtesy Naomi Ballard

a claim to a section of land and in time they had a fine farm and home filled with eight children. The older boys were growing up when Lucinda died in 1875. William buried her near their home and dedicated a one-acre site for a cemetery where many of his descendants rest. There are a number of descendants in Irving. In 1963 the plot was expanded when one of his granddaughters gave an additional two acres. This cemetery is also recognized with a Texas Historic Marker. William remarried and his second wife, Martha Jane Cates, gave him eight more children.

Tom Haley, who was three years old when his mother died, established his own farm and began a family before Irving was founded. He was destined to become very important to education and the civic life of Irving. John Haley, another son, taught as a very young man in the Sowers School. Then, after his first wife died, he enrolled in Galveston Medical School. After graduating he returned to the area and set up a practice as a pioneer physician who, like Dr. Gilbert, traveled by horse and buggy to serve people in all walks of life. A few years later his father was going blind with cataracts and refused to allow any doctor but his son to operate. Dr. John wanted to help him but lacked the knowledge and skill that was needed. He went back to medical school in New Orleans where he studied eye surgery for a year. Then he assisted an eye specialist with the operation to remove his father's cataracts. According to Dr. William Haley, a grandson, the surgery was performed on William Haley's kitchen table. We don't know what the specialist was paid, but the payment to Dr. John Haley was forty acres in the Sowers community. He built a small house there and continued his medical practice in the general area. He too was destined to become an important figure in the town of Irving.

Many of those sixteen children of William Haley married and had large families of their own. It is a major feat of genealogy to trace them, but through the years connections between many leading citizens have been remembered. This is also true of the Story, Lucas, and other large pioneer families. The young people in the area naturally intermarried and girls' surnames changed. Fortunately many of the descendants have taken an interest in preserving the histories of these interwoven families through their own or their parents' memories and research. Raymond Story, after tracing his family back to Marma Duke Story on one side and to Nicholas Farine on the other, wrote: "My mother's sisters' children called Mother Aunt Fannie and my Dad Cousin Will." Later he wrote: "The Clarks and the Storys married making my Dad's uncle, Columbus Clark, and his aunt, Mary Story, husband and wife. Am I my own grandpa? Or maybe I'm my own cousin."

The Heritage Society has worked hard to preserve the records of the contributions of pioneer families to the development, political life, and social life of Irving. The Central Library has a Genealogy Department located on the third floor where these connections can be traced. A well-established City Archives Department preserves information, photographs, and artifacts so successfully that it has outgrown the present location in the Central Library. Often it is interesting to learn that a person who has done something outstanding or who is running for public office has ancestors who were among the first to settle here.

Stories about the naming of the community of Kit have varied somewhat, but the most prominent explanation was that it was named for "Aunt" Katherine "Kit" King. Isaac Henry Story (better known as "Ike") ran a general store that was one of the first stops after crossing the West Fork of the river at Eagle Ford. It was a favorite meeting place for the community when "Uncle Ike" was the postmaster. He had petitioned the government to establish himself as postmaster in 1888. Before the Civil War, James Horton had delivered locked mail pouches to Jack Lucas's place once a week. The service was discontinued during the war. A special post office called *Gorbet* was authorized in 1889. Special post offices were not on a regular route for the delivery of mail pouches, so Ike picked up the mail at Eagle Ford and brought it to the Gorbet office for a time. In 1894, after it was put on a regular route and Isaac H. Story was commissioned as postmaster, the Post Office Department reported that the name *Gorbet* was too similar to another name in Texas and must be changed. Ike moved the office from north of the present intersection of Irving Heights and Sixth Streets to a location southwest of the same intersection and named it *Kit*. The community in the vicinity of the post office and store became known as *Kit*.

Dr. D. W. Gilbert practiced medicine first in the area known as the Grapevine Prairie before settling in the Sowers community. His practice took him to a broad area of the frontier territory and finally to an office in the new town of Irving, where he was deeply involved in the life of the community and where his descendants carried on his commitment. Courtesy Dr. Clay Gilbert

In every community the settlers soon were concerned about the education of the children. In early Kit it was Hezekiah Lucas who first took action to secure a one-room cabin where he became the teacher. Later a larger school was built which eventually offered seven grades. Netta Barcus from Dallas was a teacher there.

The other need, that was always felt, was for some form of worship service that brought neighbors together. In Kit this was described as some "pretty regular preaching" which is what they had until interdenominational meetings resulted in the building of a church near the Kit Cemetery on East Irving Boulevard and the preaching became regular. There is still a church at this location.

Uncle Ike was active in the community of Kit where he played multiple roles in the effort to make a living for his family, and he generously helped neighbors and strangers who stopped at his store. He farmed, cut wood, shaped it for various purposes, traded, hauled logs out and merchandise in. He built his own home and store where he took pleasure in entertaining. The family seldom had meals without visitors in the store who were invited to the table. One of his pleasures was to build a platform and bring in local fiddlers for community dances. Rosa Bell Walker, whose mother was Sally Story, called him grandfather and in a recorded interview, which is preserved in the Irving Archives, she made it clear that the square dances that were attended by many young people were not wild parties.

"My grandmother was sorta, well I'd say, sorta a queen and it was very well supervised. . . . If she saw some men who would come down from around Eagle Ford . . . and they would have a girl with them of questionable character, she would quietly go and ask him to take the lady and go home or not bring her there because she didn't allow it. . . . because in those days if a girl was promiscuous she wasn't accepted, back there in that day and time. Why, if people knew her reputation, she wasn't allowed to mingle with the other people." O. F. Fann, in an interview recorded by the Irving Archives, said, "All the kids were crazy about Uncle Ike and Aunt Nancy. Every Saturday night we would all go up there."

The Kit Post Office and Store viewed from the west with Aunt Nancy, Uncle Ike, Sallie Bell, and Lillie and Opal Kinney. The Star sign probably refers to the Star Mail Route. The roofline gives a clue to the additions to the structure through the years. Irving Archives

Eagle Ford had gained a reputation for having wild women, gamblers, saloons, and gunslingers. For several years the Texas and Pacific rail line, which eventually continued to Fort Worth, ended at Eagle Ford where cattle were shipped, which meant it competed with Fort Worth as cow town.

Uncle Ike wrote a series of articles for the newspaper in 1912 in which he told the story of his life as a series of ups and downs. He refers to himself as "The Old Man at Kit." It makes interesting reading both for the story and the style. He was in and out of the area several times before finally settling down for the rest of his life. This is his own account of first arriving at what would later become Kit:

On New Year's day, 1856, a poor sixteen-year-old boy, without a dollar in money and with no education (had gone to school enough to get to the dog and deer in the old blue back speller), stood away here in Texas . . . where deer, turkey, bear, and other wild game was plentiful. Well, my first job was in a brickyard north of the present beautiful Dallas County Court House. My work was off-bearing brick, at 50 cents per day. At night I would set up ten-pins for the cowboys and I soon had a little spending money. My next job was the ox whip—living at home when I had my hat on; driving oxen, hauling goods on the road, breaking prairie sod in spring and summer, camping out in the bottoms, chopping cord-wood for the flour mill companies in the winter time.

Describing one of his "downs" he wrote:

My wife and I were both in bad health, but not down and out—as we managed to get something for the little ones to eat and wear and just holding our own. The family had now increased to 5 boys and 5 girls—which wound up the little ball as to increase in the family. Then in August 1894 my wife died, which left me broken in heart and health, with my house full of little girls and *boys. . . . Although I was postmaster at Kit, there was very little money in it. I managed the best I could until the next spring. Then I got a job from Tom Bolton, assessing taxes for precinct 8. . . . The job came to $72, and Tom ran away to parts unknown and I got nothing. However, I lived over it by running the gentle plow and chopping wood for one of the boys to haul to Dallas to sell and pay for supplies for the family.*

Ike is referring to his second wife, Mary Elizabeth Tate. His first wife, Mary Duncan, had died earlier after bearing three children including Shelton Story. Mary Elizabeth had eight children. This is his account of courting Nancy King:

The old man got the notion to his head and did not have to look around much. As I was too old to go sparking among the widows, I just wrote a little note of but few words, simply business, walked over and handed it to Aunt Nancy, and passed on. In a short time I received an answer, fully as short in words, and also business. There was a match made on short order as the nights were getting long and cold; and on the 27 day of October, 1896, Uncle Ike and Aunt Nancy got in the buggy, went to Dallas, and come back man and wife. And let me say right here that every thing has gone well with us from that day till this. So if any of you young or old readers want to get married, don't put in too much time in sparking: it only wears out shoe leather, tears up buggies, and gives the other fellow a chance to beat your time. I've been there and I know.

According to a family history, researched by Betty Beaufford Bessler, Henry Eugene DeBeaufford and Catherine Eugenia Tovinia DeBeaufford, both born in France, bought a 105-acre farm in 1883—in the area that is now Highway 183, Nursery, and Grauwyler—from I. H. Story and M. E. Story. The Beauffords raised a family of four boys, and when Catherine died in 1930 there were eighteen grandchildren and two great-grandchildren. Their oldest son, Eugene, and youngest son, Henry, continued to live in Irving after they married. Eugene married Mary Anne McGuiness and in 1910 they bought land from his father that was eventually in Irving near Highway 183 and Britain and built a new home across the road from the DeHaes family home. William DeHaes was a Belgian bricklayer who built the first brick house in the Irving area. The families became close friends. Mrs. DeHaes helped deliver the four Beaufford children.

Although we hear most often about Uncle Ike Story, there were several other members of the Story family from Illinois in the area before Ike finally settled here for the third and last time in 1873. The 1900 map shows a survey of land granted to T. C. Story. He was the first son of Marma Duke Story. Several members of this family came from Illinois in 1855. We are told that they walked most of the way behind wagons that carried their belongings. Marma Duke Story had ten children. The ones we know most about are Thomas C., Jonathan, and Isaac. Charles Whitmire, a descendant still living on East Shady Grove, reminds us that on the 1900 map Thomas C. Story is the name on a survey at Kit. Raymond Story shared with us his written explanation:

The oldest son, Thomas, came and looked the area over first, some time before 1850, by family history and Dallas County history. Subsequently, he went back and persuaded the most of the family to move down here. Some of the Hunsaker family had settled in the southern portion of the county, and the Storys and the Hunsakers had intermarried in Illinois, which probably accounted for Thomas coming here.

One of the most popular stories told about the early settlers in the Gorbet/Kit area is that in 1855 Jonathan Story traded a pony worth about $40 to C. D. Peeler for his 320-acre headright and a cabin. No doubt Mr. Peeler was ready to move on as earlier settlers often did. Jonathan did not stay in Kit. He married Sophronia Hunsaker and moved farther northwest near the Finley Post Office. His first tract was east of what now would be O'Connor, and his neighbor to the west was Nicholas Farine who came from the La Reunion settlement when it broke up. The northern boundary was about where Adah Lane is and the land extended south to around

William DeHaes, who came from Belgium, built the first brick house in the Irving area. It was a gathering place for family and friends for many years. Eugene and Mary Anne Beaufford built their home across the road and it was Octavia Dumain DeHaes who helped Mary with her children. Laura DeHaes collection, Irving Archives

where Rochelle is now. To complicate things his oldest boy was also named Thomas C. Story. This Thomas Story married Helen Clark and their son, William C. Story, married Fanny Farine, daughter of Nicholas Farine and Lucinda Mills. Raymond Story was their son. These are the families that extended their holdings farther south past what became Highway 183. They farmed and cut timber on large portions of the land in this area, which later was developed and annexed to become Central and North Central Irving.

Back to the southeast Mr. Whitmire gave us information about some of the other names on the map. Harve Bowman Story and his daughters, Belle and Alice (later to become Belle Caster and Alice Moreland), lived in a house on the hill about where Edmondson Street is now. His son, Perry Hezekiah Story, with his wife, Mary Elizabeth, and their family lived nearby. Most of their six children were born after Irving was founded, and they grew up participating in the life of the town even though they continued to live on part of the H. B. Story farm, which was first bounded roughly by Sixth Street, Nursery Road, Shady Grove, and Ballywood.

An interview by Mrs. Estelle Bates with four of the daughters of Perry H. Story is in the Irving Archives. Mae Story Williams, Pearl Story Kirkpatrick, Jane Story Whitmire, and Mary Story West tell about their father working as a truck farmer and going to the Dallas market in a wagon and the house that their grandfather built where Edmondson Street is now. They remembered going to the river with several families to picnic and spend the night fishing.

The Harve Bowman Story family poses for a family photo at their home located where Edmondson Street east of Nursery Street was later established. Top row: Sue Story, Harve B. Story, and Perry Hezekiah (Kiah) Story. Second row: George and Effie Williams, Lizzie Terry holding unidentified child, Mary Elizabeth (Lizzie) Story, and Wastella and Sam Ewalt. Front row: Alex Story, Bertha Story, Katie Terry, Pearl Story, May Story, Charlie Ewalt, and Alonzo Story. Courtesy Charles Whitmire

Later their father built a house on Shady Grove Road, and when they were school age they could walk to church and to school in Irving.

Northeast of Kit, in the area later called Union Bower, William Smith bought thirty acres in 1879 and built a log cabin. He hunted, fished, and gradually cleared the land and sold cut wood for $1.50 a load. By 1888 he was able to build the house at what later became Maryland and Smith Streets. He then built the first school, which was one room with benches along the walls and a stove in the middle. There were eight children in this pioneer Smith family to be educated. Other families in the community shared Mr. Smith's concern that the children should be educated, and there were enough to fill the school with all grades in one room. Several reports declare that there were at one time over sixty students in one room and "you could hear a pin drop."

There has been some question about how the community got its name. Most versions agree that it comes from the name of a Sunday school that met there. A church brochure printed in 1976, provided to us by Reverend Linda Marcum, pastor of Oak Haven United Methodist Church, gives this answer: "In 1880 a Captain J. M. McCoy, Will Smith and his wife, affectionately known in later years as Grandma or Aunt Jenny Smith, started a Sunday school under a brush arbor on or near the site of the old church building. This Sunday school was made up of members of various denominations and was known as a Union Sunday School. Because it was held in a bower, it soon became known as the Union Bower Sunday School." Another version is that the

Kiah and Elizabeth Story. Irving Heritage Society collection

superintendent of the Sunday school was a man named Bower. People began referring to the community as Union Bower.

Estelle was the farthest northwest of the communities existing before 1900. Edgar Brown, who grew up in the community in the 1920s and 1930s, organized a very successful reunion of his peers in April 2002. He compiled a history of Estelle that is more complete than others we have reviewed. Mr. Brown circulated his history to the participants at the reunion and has given a copy to the Irving Archives. One of his sources is a letter that he received from the Harrington brothers when, as an eleven-year-old, he wrote asking how Estelle got its name. The explanation was that land granted to H. Burgoon was settled in 1881 when it was a rest stop on the route between Farmers Branch and Bird's Fort. It was just east of the line between Tarrant and Dallas Counties. The community had been called *Estell* to honor a Grapevine Prairie architect, but when a handwritten application for a post office was processed a tail on the final letter was misread and the post office location was recorded as *Estelle*. V. O. Harrington donated land for a two-story frame building constructed by masons and friends. A. J. Lucas loaned the lodge $75 to buy furnishings, and meetings began in 1884. Soon a teacher was hired and the ground floor of the building became the first school in the community. The lodge paid the teacher's salary for the first two years before a county school district was established and trustees were elected. By 1897 the school still had one teacher in one room with forty-one students.

Perry (Kiah) Story plows near the pecan tree where generations of children gathered pecans. It now stands in a yard on Chamberlain Street. Courtesy Charles Whitmire

The oldest continuously meeting church in the Irving area is now named the First Baptist Church, Las Colinas. Information furnished by Joyce Hollaway indicates that original church records date back to May 15, 1853, when nine charter members went in covenant to carry out the teachings of a Missionary Baptist Church. In 1857 the church was moved three miles east to County Line and Estelle Road and named Bear Creek Baptist Church. In 1960 the name was changed to Western Heights Baptist Church, and then in 1970 the Dallas/Fort Worth Airport displaced the church and it moved to the Las Colinas area.

The next oldest continuously meeting church in the area is the Shady Grove C.M.E. Church that celebrated its 118th anniversary on March 10, 2002, with the burning of the note marked "paid in full." According to the brochure announcing the event, the church founders in 1884 included the King, Trigg, Green, Morton, Jackson, and Crawford families. The land was donated by the Greens, and the building served for church and school. Reverend J. O. Morton, grandson of the first-known black landowner who was one of the church founders, attended school in the church and later was the pastor for seven years. In the early years families of all denominations met in the church/school to pray, sing, and socialize. Reverend Louis Simmons is the current pastor.

This 118-year-old church is located in the community which is known as Bear Creek, but it is not related to the Bear Creek Baptist Church referred to above which was in the Estelle com-

munity north of Sowers, while the Bear Creek Community is south of Sowers. What they have in common is the creek itself, which flows in a convoluted path from north to south toward the West Fork of the Trinity River. There is still another complication because the address of the Shady Grove C.M.E. Church is 3537 Gilbert Road, Grand Prairie. Annexations by Irving and Grand Prairie imposed a division of jurisdictions on the long-established community, but the realities of community still remain at the turn of the century.

When we listed communities that existed before Irving was founded, we included Bear Creek, which is not on the 1900 map. The community existed then and has an important place in the history of Irving. The devastation of the Civil War and the complicated, long, and painful period of Reconstruction were responsible for bringing many of the settlers to Texas, which was less affected by the controversy and its aftermath. The economy of the whole nation suffered. There were symptoms of general business collapse. Investment uncertainties and political unrest frightened Northern capital out of the South, which was in physical as well as economic disarray. Many of the pioneers who moved into the Irving area before, during, and after the Civil War came from Illinois. Illinois suffered more than most of us know. We think of it as

William Smith came to the area later known as the Union Bower community in 1879. In this 1902 picture of his family are Jeannie Smith, the mother holding unidentified baby, and Will Smith to her left, with boys Frank Voirin and Bert Smith between them. Standing, left to right, are L. G. Smith, Mattie Smith, Hubert Smith, Annie Voirin, Gertie Quillian, Mary Smith, Lula Smith, and Tony Smith. Irving Archives

a Union state, but in his definitive work, *The Civil War and Reconstruction*, J. G. Randall indicates that Illinois was conflicted with regard to both issues of the war and devastated by the aftermath for many years.

Many settlers came to Texas to avoid serving or being involved in any way in the war. Some brought former slaves on the trip to Texas and created different relationships with them. Freed slaves needed to have a means of providing the necessities of life for themselves, and the means were the same regardless of race or previous condition of servitude. Food and water come from the land and are accessed by labor. Different versions of tenant farming or employment were worked out. Land ownership was an option but the bottom line was the same. Everybody worked one way or the other. The community we now call Bear Creek was earlier known as Spencer Park. Families of early black settlers have kept the history and make it available to visitors in the Jackie Townsell Park. They tell us that Jim Morton, a freed slave from Tennessee, arrived about 1870 and had saved enough money to buy 170 acres. The following excerpts from material provided to visitors give some insight:

Ben and Rosa Dilworth, both former slaves from the Austin area, arrived in the 1880s. It took them six months to travel to Bear Creek with their seventeen children some of whom died along the way. . . . The Bear Creek community is recognized as the oldest African American Community in Dallas County and possibly in the state. Although there are no firm documents available, it is believed that the Holmes and Sweat families were here as well as at least three freedmen. Sam Green, Johnny King, and Uncle Spencer had settled here prior to the Civil War. . . . By 1900 there were about 30 families, both black and white, living in the area. The black landowners raised grain crops predominantly corn and milo to feed their livestock. They would then either sell the meat or drive the cattle to market. Butter and eggs were other products that were taken into Dallas on Saturday and sold. Every family had a garden with many of them planting two or three different vegetables and then trading and sharing back and forth the extra. Jim Green started a mission and school where all ages and levels were taught in one room. The children attended school and afterward would help work in the fields and care for the livestock. There was also time for hunting and fishing as well as playing.

The reaction of independent, idealistic, and well-educated individuals to years of political strife in France was to dream of an ideal community where all men became free and equal. This resulted in a venture that eventually added much to the fabric of life in Dallas and Irving. Victor Considerant, an editor of three socialist publications based on the theories of Charles Fourier, was exiled to Belgium because of his criticisms of the Napoleonic regime. He developed a plan to establish colonies in the land of the free where cultured people who loved music, art, the beauty of humanity, and freedom could live together in peace and harmony. The European American Society of Colonization was chartered in Brussels. Capital stock bearing 6 percent interest was placed on sale to the public in December 1854. Some of the buyers were investors who never intended to emigrate but many applied to make the journey to found an ideal colony. Approximately 150 members were signed on to be the first to leave for Texas. The agents who were recruiting probably exaggerated, as they had been instructed to give glowing accounts and create enthusiasm. At any rate, the recruiting and sale of stock in the company was quite successful.

A group from France, Belgium, and Switzerland loaded their tools, furniture, and personal belongings onto a two-mast boat and sailed in February 1855. Months later they arrived in Galveston thinking they would follow the Trinity River to Dallas. They did follow the river but not as they anticipated. It was necessary to place their baggage on wagons and walk to that idealized land. The land was west of Dallas and adjacent to what was later called Chalk Hill. The cliffs, formed by the outcropping of Austin stone, the trees and wild flowers reminded them of their native land. The colony was named La Reunion and incorporated by act of Santerre, LaNotte, Loupot, and Voirin. A fine village was built with a fort, cabins, community kitchen,

This home, built for W. H. Lucas in 1880 on land that later became part of the Dallas/Fort Worth Airport, is testament to his success. Members of the Lucas family became highly respected merchants in Estelle, Sowers, and Irving. The boy with the dog is Bob Lucas. W. H. Lucas and his wife, Cornelia, are seated, and standing are Mose, Doll, Cassie, Mary, and Arthur Lucas. Lucas collection, Irving Archives

and dining room. There were small gardens and a community garden. Most of the settlers were highly educated with interests and skills in the arts and letters. Eventually the beautiful experiment failed. Some settlers went back to their native countries but others remained in the area. These people made major contributions to the quality of life in Irving.

The early settlers in all of the communities that would become Irving were a diverse group from various parts of the United States and various distant countries. They were of many ethnic backgrounds. On the other hand, no matter how different they may have been, they had much in common. They were hardy and had a spirit for adventure. Each settler sought a better life, which usually meant independence, land ownership, and a way to acquire the necessities of everyday life. The way they related to their neighbors and their integrity was more important than where they came from or the accent that their native language or region of origin gave to their speech. They had endured hardships that we cannot really imagine on the journey that brought them here. They walked, drove wagons through uncharted territories, buried loved ones along the way, and foraged for food and water. There were no automobiles, buses, hotels, restaurants, rest stops, roads, phones, or rescue services. They were on their own. And when they found a place they wanted to settle, most of them built their first houses of logs they cut from the land. Once settled, they appreciated neighbors and the opportunity to give and receive help when needed and to share faith, companionship, and entertainment. Some of that spirit can still be found in Irving at the turn of another century.

Several members of the Caster family lived south of the original town of Irving in an area south and west of what is now Shady Grove and Senter. The Franklin Caster home pictured here was built in 1890 near the present intersection of Franklin and Vilbig Streets. It stood there into the 1940s. Irving Heritage Society collection

Land grants were part of the scenario that helped to lure stout-hearted adventurous people to this undeveloped area. The history of Texas land grants is a fascinating and complex one and well worth pursuing, but the complete details are beyond the scope of this story about Irving. We all know about the six flags over Texas. The Spanish government brought the concept of land ownership granted by the government to Texas, and the Mexican government sought to continue the practice for the same reasons. The settlement of this wild territory with people who derived a benefit from the government was a way to provide a buffer against the aggressive United States. These people would make the land productive, defend their homes against intruders, and form ties with the benefactors who made the land available. Spain introduced the *empresario* system, and Mexico continued to contract with agents to recruit settlers to specified tracts of land within a colony. The agent or *empresario* received land designated for a colony and could survey, record certificates of land ownership, and collect fees. Under Mexico, each settler could receive one league (4,428.4 acres) for grazing and one labor (177.1 acres) for farming. Stephen F. Austin contracted with Mexico to receive fifteen leagues of grazing land and two labors of farmland for every two hundred families he introduced, up to six hundred families. Subsequently he contracted in 1825, 1827, and 1828 and was the most successful of the agents. The land measurements and laws changed but the basic concept persisted under several flags. A package was offered to men who would settle and use the land for grazing and develop some of it in crops. More land was granted to married men than to single men.

The Republic of Texas continued the practice, altering and expanding it as circumstances changed. It was easy and relatively cheap to claim land in Texas if you were willing to work and had a spirit for adventure. Headrights were granted to heads of families and to men who served in the army for the Republic of Texas.

In 1841, the Republic of Texas authorized the Texas Emigration and Land Company, composed of twenty English and American entrepreneurs, usually referred to as the Peters Colony, to advertise, survey, and bring settlers to a thirteen-hundred-square-mile area which included Dallas and the area that later became Irving. W. S. Peters was an English musician and businessman who immigrated to the United States in 1827. He and his associates looked upon this as a business venture. Their goal was to bring six hundred families from another country to settle this land within three years. The United States was considered to be another country. The reward for the agents, or *empresarios*, was ten square miles of land for every one hundred families and five square miles for every one hundred single men who successfully settled in the colony. The land was free to the settler except that the agent could retain up to half of the settler's grant to pay for land surveys, title applications, and other services. A family had to keep 15 acres cultivated and fenced for three years to receive 640 acres from the Peters Colony. A single man would receive 320 acres. Some conflicts did arise as a result of the Peters Colony authorization. Prior land claims of Bird's Fort settlers were affected and many of them moved on. John Neely Bryan learned that he was unwittingly settled on land within the Peters Colony.

Meanwhile, Indians were still considered a threat to settlers in the general area of Texas and Sam Houston, who was then president of the Republic, met with Indian leaders at Fort Bird in 1843 and successfully negotiated the Treaty of Peace and Friendship between the Republic of Texas and nine Indian tribes. It was signed September 29, 1843. A tenth tribe later agreed to the terms which protected the Dallas/Fort Worth area from raids.

The period between the signing of the first contract with the Peters Colony group and the final expiration of the fourth contract was difficult, and though the colony helped settle North Texas, it was almost impossible to maintain control. Some settlers moved on before fulfilling the contract. Squatters infiltrated and there was a vast area to oversee. The investors and their associates were not accustomed to dealing with the type of rugged individuals who were taming this Texas frontier. The investors probably didn't profit as much as they had expected. After July 1, 1848, land within the colony was open for free laying of certificates, and new settlers could claim 640 acres from the state. This angered the settlers who had been subject to giving up part of their land to the entrepreneurs and especially those whose claims were not yet secured. Final settlement of the land titles took nearly twenty years. Later land grants were made available to encourage the establishment of colleges and other institutions deemed important to the development of the state.

In the United States, before Texas was a state, the idea of free land for homesteaders was a very early concept, but there was opposition to what became known as a free land movement. After the Republican Party, which had adopted the ideas of the Free Soil Party, was successful, Congress enacted the Homestead Law in 1862. The head of a family, twenty-one years old, or a veteran of fourteen days of active service in the U.S. armed forces, and who was a citizen or had filed a declaration of intent to become a citizen, could claim land in the public domain, not to exceed 160 acres. The claimant had to settle on or cultivate the homestead for five years. The public domain at that time did not include Texas, but our current homestead laws are based on this law with subsequent modifications.

When the railroads began to build in the United States, there was a major campaign to attract service to Texas. The need for transportation was obvious, but bringing railroad construction to Texas was a hard sell. There wasn't enough capital in the state to finance the venture, and capitalists in the rest of the world were not very interested in investing in what was perceived to be a wild frontier state. George C. Werner, in the article "Railroads" in *The Handbook of Texas Online*, informs that cities and counties issued bonds to aid construction, but in 1876 such contributions were declared to be prohibited by the Constitution. The state made land grants and loans available, and railroads borrowed from the Special School Fund at the rate of $6,000 per mile of track. The general land grant law of 1854 had offered railroads sixteen sections of land per mile of track, but then the new Constitution of 1869 prohibited land grants to the railroads. An 1876 amendment reestablished the 1854 land grant provisions but it was repealed in 1882. Mr. Werner reports that "estimates of the amount of land actually granted range from 27,000,000 acres to about 35,000,000 acres."

In 1891 James S. Hogg, the first native-born Texas governor, based his campaign on regulation of railroads and big business. The account of railroad land grants is interesting to us, and a close look at the 1900 map reveals several sections in the area that became Irving, which have the names of various railroads printed on them. None of them are in the path that the railroad eventually followed through Irving. But the railroad is of primary importance to the history of the city of Irving. Early business leaders in Dallas understood the basic importance of transportation to the development of a city, and they used every economic and political means they could muster to get railroads to come through Dallas. The Houston and Texas Central Railroad passed through Dallas County in 1872, and by 1900 the city of Dallas had become a railroad hub served by seven railroads. Towns that we now know as Dallas suburbs (Richardson, Garland, Carrollton, Farmers Branch, Grand Prairie, Duncanville, Lancaster, Mesquite, Coppell) were thriving because they were connected to a railroad. But there was no Irving. However, the birth of this town was just about to occur.

A survey crew for the railroad arrived in the territory between the Forks in 1902 by wagon train.

Chapter 2

A Town Is Born

J.O. Schulze, an engineer for the Chicago, Rock Island and Gulf Railway, had met and worked with Otis Brown, a rod man, while both young men were on a survey crew in Oklahoma. There were plans to lay out a route connecting Fort Worth and Dallas. Schulze asked to be assigned to this project and suggested that Brown join him. The plan was to go through the area between the Forks. There was already a train in operation south of the West Fork from Dallas through Eagle Ford and Grand Prairie to Fort Worth. The two men took the Texas and Pacific train from Fort Worth to Dallas, and in the words of Otis Brown, written as an autobiography for his own use and published in the *Irving News* in 1944:

We secured a spirited team and splendid rig and started out toward Record Crossing on Elm Fork to give a casual look over the ten mile division that had been assigned to Mr. Schulze. . . . Our map showed that our division started just a little east of the river near Record Crossing and continued due west nearly to the Tarrant County line. In passing out through what is now the reclaimed district of the Trinity Farm property we found that some fifteen hundred acres of this fertile river bottom land was being converted from native bottom timber land into one big farm owned and operated by M. H. Turner. Mr. Turner had leased about 75 state prisoners and these were in the charge of Mr. Underwood. . . . The farm headquarters was located on what has always been called the sand ridge and what is now Norwood. Except for Mr. Underwood's house and the necessary buildings for the prisoners and guards this was about all there was there at that time. We continued westerly feeling more enthusiastic about our new work after getting up out of the river bottom some four miles in width. Our line, we found, passed right near the home of H. W. Britain and this cozy home appealed to us in many ways, being almost exactly the halfway point of our work and almost at the edge of the right of way, besides it was only a short half-mile across the pasture to the Post Office which was called Kit and had the fine old gentleman Uncle Ike Story for Postmaster. Mr. Britain was kind enough to take us into his home to board, though we had our tent put up in his front yard for the office and sleeping quarters. . . . We had not been at the Britain home long until the fall term of school started at Kit, and . . . the Britains arranged that the young lady schoolteacher also board in their home and as usual most everybody soon became happy.

Those of us who have lived in the latter part of the century may not grasp the full import of the way these men were living happily. There were no hotels or cafes, so boarding in a home was a treat. Sleeping and having the office in a tent was good because it was in a relatively protected area. But we can hardly imagine not having electricity, telephones, running water, or indoor toilets. The people in the house didn't have these amenities either. Oil lamps, outhouses, and wells took care of these bare necessities. The Britain home was conveniently situated for water. The famous Twin Wells were near their property and there was also a well in the yard.

As travelers reached the high ground on the trail leading from Eagle Ford they found two wells, one on either side of the trail. They could rest and refresh themselves and water their working animals. Troughs had been built on the west side and a bucket was supplied for drawing

The survey crew for the new Rock Island rail line had their office and sleeping quarters on the Henry Britain home place in 1903. Irving Heritage Society collection

the water. This seems to have been a friendly community gesture typical of the way people cared for and took care of each other. Rosa Bell Walker, in a recorded interview, described the water as cool and clear and coming from an underground lake. Springs could be found in several locations in the area. Part of what made the area that became Irving attractive was the availability of water at reasonable depths.

Otis Brown continued the story of how the decision was made to found a town:

We had not been located here a month until one bright October day when driving along the road on the way to our work and enjoying the beautiful sunshine Mr. Schulze seemed to arouse suddenly and said, "Brown lets start a new town somewhere on our line." Hardly knowing what it all meant I readily agreed. It did not take us long to get all of our money together, and of course we wrote back home, solely for the one reason for a little more cash. We decided upon the location, after taking into consideration the lay of the land, the grades of the Rail Road, the distance from Dallas and the layout of the county roads. The deal was closed for 82 acres of fine land from H. W. Britain and son D. E. Britain, the price being $30 an acre. Of course many laughed at this price for raw timbered land, also at the thought of building a town, but this did not falter Mr. Schulze who had considerable experience in new town sites in western Oklahoma before I had met up with him. . . . I was glad to leave principally all of this platting, etc., to Mr. Schulze on account of his previous knowledge of this work. But a name that I had picked was gladly agreed to by him. We were several weeks in choosing the name as we had to get the approval of the Post Office Department, besides the approval of the Rock Island & Gulf Railway. . . . The naming of the streets was left entirely up to Mr. Schulze; one being named for his old state, Iowa, one for my home state, one for the street his sweetheart lived on in Iowa City and among others one was named for our good friend Mr. Britain. Main Street was laid out at right angle to the railroad, running south about three blocks and was one hundred feet.

Mr. Brown's account of the naming of the city does not prepare the reader for the arguments and outright furor that have related to this seemingly simple act. There are many stories and some very strongly held opinions on the subject. It has been postulated that Irving was the name of a local farmer, that it was the name of a man they met on the railroad job, and that the British actor Henry Irving was the honoree. When questions began to arise, Mr. Schulze, who had been a member of the Washington Irving Literary Society in college, teased with a theory that the name slipped onto Brown's list because he had been corresponding with a young lady in the West whose name was Irvine. Others enjoy this story and expand it by saying that Netta Barcus thought Otis had misspelled the name of her favorite author and corrected it. The most enduring two opinions are that the town was named for Washington Irving versus there was no particular reason and nobody or thing came to mind in the naming process except a nice name that was acceptable to the post office and the railway.

In a manuscript in the Irving Archives, Mr. Schulze related that he had been thinking about founding a town for a while. He noticed that speculators went ahead of rail construction and bought property at cheap prices where they thought towns could develop. They were able to profit from the effect of rail service on accessibility. The engineering and survey crew obviously had the advantage in this process if they would choose to get involved with front money and planning. But he wasn't thinking of multiple townships. There was a young lady waiting in Iowa to whom he was engaged, and he was ready to settle down and enjoy family life. He had started thinking about this during his last assignment in Granite City, Oklahoma, but concluded that town was not a suitable place to bring a young lady from Iowa. This new location had potable water, good soil, trees, vegetation, and a mild climate. It was located between two rival towns only thirty miles apart, and the rivalry could even be an advantage. So the decision was made that he would have a town of his own. Since he would resign from the railroad work, he needed a business. That was easy. Every new town must have food and lumber. He chose lumber, with real estate.

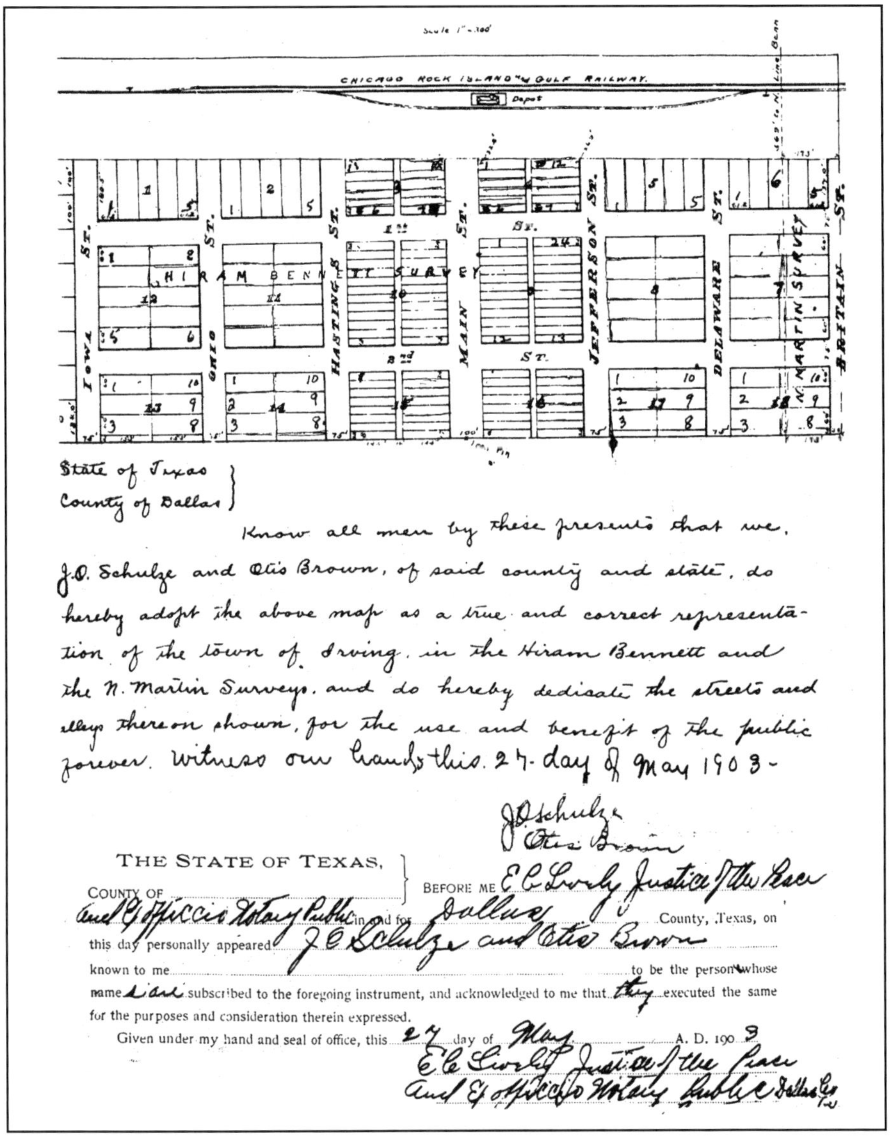
Chicago Rock Island & Gulf Railway
Depot
Iowa St.
Ohio St.
Hastings St.
Main St.
Jefferson St.
Delaware St.
Britain St.
1st St.
2nd St.
Hiram Bennett Survey
N. Martin Survey

State of Texas
County of Dallas

Know all men by these presents that we, J.O. Schulze and Otis Brown, of said county and state, do hereby adopt the above map as a true and correct representation of the town of Irving, in the Hiram Bennett and the N. Martin Surveys, and do hereby dedicate the streets and alleys thereon shown, for the use and benefit of the public forever. Witness our hands this 27 day of May 1903 -

J.O. Schulze
Otis Brown

THE STATE OF TEXAS, County of Dallas } Before me E. C. Lively Justice of the Peace and Ex officio Notary Public in and for Dallas County, Texas, on this day personally appeared J. O. Schulze and Otis Brown known to me to be the persons whose names are subscribed to the foregoing instrument, and acknowledged to me that they executed the same for the purposes and consideration therein expressed.

Given under my hand and seal of office, this 27 day of May A. D. 1903
E. C. Lively Justice of the Peace and Ex officio Notary Public Dallas Co.

The official first map of Irving was recorded May 27, 1903. Irving Archives

The plat was drawn with eighteen blocks divided into lots, streets, and alleys. The map was recorded on May 27, 1903, over the signature of E. C. Lively, justice of the peace and ex officio notary public. The work on the rail division was almost finished, and both young men took a little time out to attend to personal business. J. O. Schulze married Agnes Sueppel in Iowa City, Iowa, on June 17, and Otis Brown married Netta Barcus, the Kit schoolteacher from Dallas, on June 24. After short honeymoons they returned to tackle the job of clearing the site and advertising a sale of lots. The site was densely covered with trees, mostly post oak, except for a watermelon patch near the depot. The work was intense to get enough trees cut and stumps pulled out to make way for a business district and residential lots. In the midst of all this activity Otis Brown took time to build what he described as a modest home at First and Hastings. In late October they moved in. It was the first home in Irving. Train service started December 1, 1903.

Now it was time to sell the lots and a public auction was planned and advertised. The big day was December 19, 1903. Mrs. Brown later wrote in an article describing the event that

Otis Brown and Netta Barcus were happily "keeping company" while boarding with the Britain family. Irving Archives

Spence Dilworth cooked barbecue in a pit dug about fifty feet south of the depot. It was served with bread, pickles, and plenty of coffee. She made the coffee in a new wash boiler in the kitchen of her home. She estimated that over 150 people came for the auction. Some came on the special VIP train from Dallas, while others came in wagons, buggies, or on horseback. The weather was good. The depot was not yet finished, but a boxcar being used as a temporary office for the station master provided a place to hang the map of the lots to be sold. It had been drawn to scale on a six-by-thirteen-foot canvas wagon cloth. The auctioneer pointed out the lots with his stick as he called for bids.

Irving is probably the first and maybe the only town to be born with its own newspaper. R. M. Hudson from Dallas brought the first issue of the *Irving Index* and passed it around to the crowd. He had already circulated it in Dallas to help attract the crowd. The enthusiasm he expressed must have been infectious. We quote from this first issue:

Today the heralded public town lot sale will be cried by the famous veteran auctioneer, Capt. J. A. H. Hossack, and the attention of multitudes is focused on the Rock Island town. The Rock Island is looked upon as the giant railroad system of the Southwest and where it goes there is business. . . . Irving has a tributary area that is isolated from other trade centers. This trade area embraces nine square miles of the famous Grapevine prairie soil, and twenty-six square miles of post oak or fruit land. This fruit land is a sandy loam with a clay subsoil, and is pronounced by experts as equal in all respects to the now famed East Texas fruit lands. . . . Land around Irving can now be had for a song. Look at the map and see just where Irving lies. Eleven miles from the commercial center of Texas, with 100,000 people to feed, twenty miles from the packing and railway center of the Southwest, with 60,000 people to feed. Donna ye hear the slogan.

The ground floor people are the people who win out. The Rock Island road is a success, and the country along its line will be fully developed. Plenty of wood, plenty of water, finest fruit land, rich bottoms. Dallas and Fort Worth speculators are buying in every chunk of dirt between these two cities they can get. Don't wait till there isn't any ground floor. You name your own price in the big sale today. . . . It is one-third down and one and two years on the balance, and you name the price yourself. 'Spite of the late season boll worms and bad stands, Irving territory, raised over 6,000 bales of cotton this year and over 200,000 bushels of corn. . . . The citizenship of the Irving section is of the very best sort. Homeowners are the sort of citizens to tie to. Irving people own their homes, every homeowner is personally interested in the welfare of his community and is a worker for its weal.

Of course when Mr. Hudson referred to Irving homeowners he was reaching out to the surrounding communities since the town site of Irving had only one home on that day. What we have quoted is just a sample. The whole newspaper was filled with more of this promotional-type writing. The price of the paper was $1.00 per year.

The wagon cloth with the original plat of the town was preserved by the Brown family and finally donated to the city by Charles Brown. It is displayed on the first floor of City Hall across from the elevators. A close look reveals crosses on lots that were sold.

Schulze had preempted Lots 1 through 6 in Block 3, which provided him frontage on both First and Hastings with the railway directly north and an alleyway on the east. This was the site of the Irving lumberyard which he had already established when the lots were sold. In fact Mr. Schulze had a large advertisement in that first edition of the *Irving Index* stating:

We take pleasure in announcing to the people of Irving and of the surrounding country that we have opened up a yard with a complete stock of lumber and builders hardware. Our standard will be the best material for lowest prices. All parties needing anything in our line are cordially invited to visit us and get our prices and we believe it will be to your advantage.

All but one of the lots facing Main Street were sold. Lot 7 siding to First Street was bought by W. F. Miller and C. G. Miller. W. L. Smith bought Lot 8, B. M. Foster took Lot 10, L. Roberts got Lot 11, and Annie A. Robinson was the buyer of Lot 12 adjacent to the railway. The Millers also bought residential Lots 7, 8, and 9 in Block 14.

In Block 4 on the east side of Main Street, Lot 1, adjacent to the railway, was purchased by Jacob Sitton and W. D. Lucas. T. P. Eden chose Lot 3. Dr. John Haley bought the commercial lot which was the second lot south of First Street on the east side facing Main. In Block 5 three lots were sold. Buyers were J. W. Tate, S. T. Toler, and J. A. White. All of Block 6 sold. P. S. Smalley was the buyer of the first three lots, and I. H. and M. E. Story (Uncle Ike) bought Lots 4 and 5 which located them at First and Britain. A. B. Story bought residential Lot 7 in Block 7 facing Britain Road. When the day was over it was reported that over twenty lots had been sold. The day was declared a success, and in the next few days and weeks lots continued to sell. Obviously some lots were considered better than others and the bids varied, but the report was that the average price was $40 per lot. A record of lots sold by Schulze and Brown and of lots in later additions sold by Brown and his wife can be found in the deed records of Dallas County, Texas.

This interior of the Miller Brothers General Store shows Roy Miller, son of Fletcher Miller, on the left and Chaney G. Miller on the right. Courtesy Sue Haley Huffman

The town of Irving had been born and healthy growth began immediately. The founders had already donated a strip of right of way 150 by 2,640 feet for a depot and switching yard. In the plat of the original town, they donated all of the streets and alleys. Then they donated lots for the construction of a Church of Christ, a Catholic Church, and a Baptist Church. The congregations, which had been meeting without buildings of their own, lost no time in claiming their lots and generating activity that would lead to building as soon as possible.

Having a lumberyard in town was a great advantage over hauling lumber in for individual projects. The buildings and homes were no longer constructed of logs or rough-hewn wood, and they began to proliferate all over the original townsite. Energy was high as businesses were conceived and plans were executed. Chaney Miller had just finished his term of office as County Commissioner of District Number 2 after six years in the job and he came to Irving to live. When lots were first offered for sale, he was the successful bidder for Lot 7 in Block 3 which was the northwest corner of First and Main Streets. Then in July 1905 he and his brother, Fletcher Miller, bought Lot 8. The original buyer of the lot at auction had been W. L. Smith. The Miller brothers began operating a store on this second lot from the corner. Mabel Hill Scott, in her privately published manuscript, declares that this was the first store in Irving. Tax and deed records preserved by Sue Haley Huffman show a series of liens on the property when the Miller brothers negotiated to acquire a store and some merchandise. They sold wagons, farm equipment, general hardware, oil stoves, flour, oil, and caskets. Locating stores close to the train depot was ideal for receiving the stock. Even though a town was being created, the majority of families in the surrounding area were still engaged in farming of one kind or another.

Remembering the first year in Irving, Mr. Miller was reported in the *Irving Herald* as saying that in 1904 Irving was the "stumpiest" place he ever saw and that the citizenry had a terrible time getting rid of them. Major Robinson expressed a similar opinion in an interview reported by the *Irving Herald* in 1938. He came to Irving in 1906 and built the first brick building on the northeast corner of Main and First. He said:

There was nothing in Irving but stumps and winding, deep sand roads that looked more or less like cow paths. . . . There were only four or five business establishments in the town and they were housed in shacks. . . . The first day I was in the drug business in Irving I sold one 50-cent bottle of quinine. While I was building my brick store the old settlers would gather around me and say, are you going crazy.

Major Robinson proved that he had more business sense than they thought. While other businesses came and went or changed, his building and his business remained as an anchor. The train was an attraction not only for travel and freight, but for entertainment. People would gather to watch

Left Photo:
Miss Hicks Millinery Store was under the same roof with the Lucas and Joffre General Merchandise Store. Heritage Society collection

Right Photo:
Ike Story built this house and moved into town with the Post Office. He died in an accident and Jerry Story took over until Etta Williams was persuaded to take the job temporarily. Reprint from the *Irving Index*

it pull in to the depot, and the Robinson store became a place to sip lemonade or other refreshment while waiting to see a train and the people it brought from Dallas, Fort Worth, or Sherman. The greatest excitement was during the State Fair in Dallas when the platform would be full of friends and neighbors and the trains would be so packed that sometimes there was only standing room in the baggage car.

Although Robinson named his store "The Palace," it is still remembered as Robinsons Drug Store. It became a popular rendezvous for young people. Mable Hill Scott wrote:

It was here in the romance corner, while seated around tables, that lovers pledged their troths. Perhaps their eyes rested on a well-displayed shelf of Hofsteders Bitters and Lydia E. Pinkhams Wine of Cardia, but romance it was, for many married and are still living in Irving and we trust they are still in love.

It was not surprising that the train was popular, since going to Dallas by any other means was a long, difficult, and uncertain experience. The railroad charged one cent a mile and began selling mileage books. Robinson bought these books and kept them in the store where he sold round-trip tickets for forty cents. He made a little profit and his customers were conveniently served.

When Mr. Hudson decided to print the *Index* in Irving, he built the workshop behind his home. The home faced Jefferson and the workshop faced Fourth Street. Heritage Society collection

By 1905 the Lucas and Joffre General Merchandise Store was in business on Main Street under the same roof with Miss Hicks Millinery. Millinery was important because no lady would appear in public during daylight hours without a hat.

The Post Office moved into the new town in 1904 to Britain and First Streets where Uncle Ike had bought two lots at auction. Following Jerry Story, Miss Etta Williams served as postmistress. She was a half sister to the Lucas brothers and later married Dr. John Roberts and still later, after his death, was known as Aunt Et. Her tenure was temporary until C. P. Lively took over as postmaster and moved the Post Office to his store which was just south of the building that later became the hotel on the west side of North Main Street. One of the most popular items in his store was a snack that served as lunch. For a nickel he would cut a slice of cheese and put it in a bag with a handful of crackers. Various stories were told illustrating that Mr. Lively was a frugal man. He sold cigars, and matches were free, but to prevent customers from taking too many matches, he drove numerous nails through the bottom of a cigar box which held the matches. The sharp points discouraged greed.

Mr. Hudson moved the newspaper office to Irving just east of the lumberyard on First Street. The newspaper was printed in Dallas for several years. Later he built his home on Jefferson Street and located the workshop, where the newspaper was printed, behind his house facing Fourth Street.

Dr. D. W. Gilbert established an office in the town on First Street east of the *Index* office and west of the site belonging to Chaney and Fletcher Miller where a few years later the bank was located. He was the first physician in town and continued to serve the broader community where he had been the first and only physician for many years. He was respected, trusted, and loved for his expertise and selfless devotion to those who needed medical help. Without the services of a hospital or specialists, he treated whatever afflicted the patient. He continued to make house calls when patients were not able to visit his office. One of the most troublesome diseases that he treated was malaria. Along the creeks and river pockets of standing water, mosquitoes found their breeding ground.

In 1907, Dr. and Mrs. John Roberts were quite fashionable in their buggy. Heritage Society collection

Agnes Sueppel Schulze was afflicted with malaria, and to make matters worse she was pregnant with her first child. The intense pain, chills, and fever of the disease can be almost unbearable, but there was also concern for the survival of the baby. It should not be a surprise that by the end of 1904, J. O. and Agnes Schulze moved back to Iowa. Some accounts of the move speculate that Agnes missed the social life of her home city and did not adjust to the small frontier town for which she had an attitude of disdain. This seems an unfair assessment of the reason for leaving Irving when we consider the facts of her condition. A boy was born to J. O. and Agnes Schulze, but he did not survive.

Dr. John Haley married Anna Good in 1906 and built a new house on the corner of Ohio and Second Streets where he had bought three lots. He practiced medicine under the same primitive circumstances as his older, more experienced colleague and gained the gratitude, trust, and affection of the citizens of Irving and the surrounding territory.

The churches that had lots donated by the founders already had congregations. The history of their early meetings casts a light on the Lively Schoolhouse. The Lively ranchland was north of the railroad tracks. Lively Park gets the name from this pioneer family. An essay by Dick and Doc Lively goes back to a time when Texas steers were plentiful and the bottom land from the Elm Fork to the West Fork of the river was open grazing land and Mark C. Lively and his brother raised cattle. They reveal much about Mark Lively when they recall that once Mark shipped two carloads of steers from Eagle Ford to St. Louis and what he brought back was an organ, an accordion, and two saddles.

In 1906, Major Robinson constructed the first brick building in the new town of Irving on the northeast corner of Main and First Streets. Although it was called a drugstore, it became the most popular meeting place in town. Irving Archives

Mark married Florence Clark and they had seven children: Philip, Sallie, Fannie, Edgar, Mark, Lucy, and Richard. The need for education became clearly apparent, and while he was recovering from a broken leg, Mark studied the subjects that were needed to qualify for a teacher's certificate. Then he found a one-room store building at Eagle Ford and managed to get it moved to his land where he became the teacher. Students came from a five-mile radius to take advantage of the educational opportunity. Additions to the building were made and it became a meeting place for much more than his school.

When we received history information from the churches that were donated lots in the new town of Irving, we learned that each of them had held early meetings in the Lively School. St. Lukes Catholic Church traces its origin to 1860 when French settlers celebrated Mass in private homes. The earliest priest they remember was the Reverend Edward F. Campbell who held services in the late 1800s in the old Lively School. The family names recorded were DeHaes, Beaufford, Boinard, Bernis, Chassang, Moulard, LaNotte, Jeanette, Isidore, and Joeffree. The story is that the families brought their wagon seats into the school to use during Mass. The mission of St.

The first St. Lukes Church was located in a grove of trees on the southwest corner of Second and Delaware Streets. Irving Archives

Lukes was established in 1902 with members continuing to meet in the Lively School where the first recorded baptism was for the William DeHaes twins, Louis and Louise, on July 27, 1902.

When land was donated for a church, construction began almost immediately. Mr. Henry Moulard was the architect, and with free labor, local donations, and gifts from Dallas friends, a white frame church became reality on Second Street west of Delaware. The Most Reverend Edward J. Dunne, bishop of Dallas, blessed and dedicated St. Lukes Church on April 24, 1904. Eleanor L. Rusnak is the church historian.

The lot donated to the Church of Christ was on First Street at Delaware. The history furnished recently by the current minister, Grady D. King, confirmed that the Lively School was also the meeting place of that church as early as 1880. The first families in the record of these meetings were O. P. and Rosa Bell, C. O. and Mary (Story) Clark, Charlie and Pearl (Preston) Clark, W. D. and Mary Fulbright, Mark and Florence (Clark) Lively, Tom and Helen (Clark) Story, and Elizabeth Caster. W. F. Barcus was serving as minister when attention turned to erecting a building on the lot donated by the town founders.

Loumelia Patterson and Bucky Epperson wrote:

O. P. Bell rode horseback around the community asking for money to erect the South Delaware Church of Christ. It was constructed by O. P. Bell, C. O. Clark, and Tom Story. The congregation moved in resolving to continue in the traditions of the founders emphasizing Christian education, evangelism, and community involvement.

It was usual for each homeowner to have a well dug on his property, but people coming into town needed a source of water for themselves and for their horses, and the narrow frontage of business lots created a density that called for a shared facility. A community well was placed in the center of the intersection of First and Main Streets with a trough around the base for horses, a pump, a wooden scaffold, and a tank on top. This was the first Irving water system.

In the spring of 1904 Irving, not yet a year old, had a big party and political rally. The *Irving Index* reported that "trains from Dallas and Fort Worth brought out nearly a hundred persons to enjoy the day in the country. Buggies and wagons from the farms and adjacent neighborhoods brought in some 400 of the rural population. . . . All had baskets well filled with good things to eat and the spread was bountiful. . . . The county candidates and some of the state candidates were here . . . but there was too much merriment for a lot of campaign speaking."

The first bank in Irving was this Merchants and Planters Bank located south of First Street on the west side of Main. Irving Archives

In 1906 the little town of Irving was a busy place with businesses beginning to cluster and grow and with every type of farm, ranch, dairy, fruit, and vegetable product being marketed in Irving and in Dallas. Judge W. Riddle detected a need. He established a private bank which he named the Merchants and Planters Bank. It was housed in a frame building just south of the Ostrand store and pool hall that was on the southwest corner of First and Main Streets. Mark Wheeler was the cashier and manager. He had the opportunity to organize a bank elsewhere and turned the Irving bank over to his younger brother, Bruce, who didn't last long in the job. He was inexperienced and decided he couldn't handle the responsibility. He resigned, locked the door of the bank, and moved away in 1907. Before the closing of the bank could cause a panic. W. F. Miller came to the rescue. He made a trade with Judge Riddle and with his brother. Earnest Miller took over management of the bank in November 1907. A year later they received a charter to operate as the Irving State Bank. Judge Riddle served as president for a few years.

The Frisco Railway brought a line from Carrollton to Irving in 1907, forming the "Y" that still defines the track pattern on the north side of the Rock Island tracks in Irving. In this same year Herbert Marcus, Carrie Marcus Neiman, and Albert L. Neiman opened the Neiman Marcus store in downtown Dallas. A daring lady from Irving could ride the train to Dallas, transfer to an electric streetcar, and go right to the door of that glamorous store.

Earl Story established the first livery stable where he took care of horses for visitors to town as well as for some residents. Dr. John Haley parked his buggy there. It also served as a feed store. Heritage Society collection

J. O. Schulze persuaded his brother, C. P. Schulze, to move to Irving and manage the lumberyard. He arrived in 1905 and became known to everybody in Irving and the surrounding communities as Percy. He soon became the owner of the lumberyard and an active member of the community. J. B. Howard was already working at the lumberyard. In 1904 he had built a home at 318 Iowa (later known as O'Connor). The house is still standing at that location.

Earl Story and George Clark are the men on opposite sides of the dirt road that was First Street (Irving Boulevard) looking east from Main Street. Traffic congestion was not a problem, but sinking in deep sand or mud was a hazard. Heritage Society collection

With people coming into the little town on horseback or horse-drawn vehicles and with a major concentration of poultry and livestock in the area, Irving needed feed stores and a livery stable. A lot east of Major Robinson's drugstore was conveniently located for this purpose and that's where Earl Story opened his business. There was also plenty of work for a blacksmith. In 1906 George Clark, who had already worked as a blacksmith in Kit and in Sowers and who is said to have painted the logo with a picture of an eye on the old Kit store, bought all of the lots between First and Second Streets on Jefferson and built a house at 208 East First Street. Rural route free delivery was being extended, and in 1910 he sold the blacksmith shop and started to work for the government delivering the mail. For several years he used a horse and buggy before converting to an automobile. J. E. Witherspoon, Earl Steele, and later Tom Taylor and others also delivered mail on the rural routes. For those on the routes, this was a great convenience over going to a post office to pick up mail. However, not everyone was on such a route. Some erected mailboxes on a route and walked or sent youngsters to get their mail. Others continued going to a post office.

The town was not without a blacksmith for long. Roland Stanford Cox moved here around 1911. His grandson, C. J. Range, and granddaughter, Kathryn Pace Webb, supplied us with the information that Cox married Mabel Keeling and they had six children. He eventually owned five buildings. Four of the buildings faced First Street and one faced Jefferson Street. His blacksmith shop was east of an alley that was between his building and the one to the west that faced Main Street. As automobiles became more popular in the 1930s he gradually phased out the blacksmith

Earl Steele delivered mail in a two-wheel cart that was typical transportation for rural route carriers. Heritage Society collection

operation and began selling hardware and car parts in the front of his building while serving those who needed a blacksmith from the back. His home was on First Street on the northeast side of Jefferson. He left a building to each of his daughters who were Rellie Range, Kathryn Mae Pace, Bertie Ruth Horton, Gladys and Mildred Crawford. Through the years the buildings housed a series of businesses that mirrored the interests of Irving citizens.

The schools in each of the communities surrounding Irving that were affiliated with Dallas County were known as Dallas County Common Schools identified by numbers assigned to them. Irving citizens did not choose to create a county school. They got together in 1905 to build their first schoolhouse near the site of the Catholic Church west of Delaware on Second Street. In 1904 a tornado had blown the Kit School apart and dropped parts of it in fields as much as 3.5 miles away. The miracle was that the organ was not damaged. As soon as school started in Irving, the Kit and Lively Schools sent their students to Irving. The first fall term, most of the 125 students came from these schools. E. C. Lively had been elected to the Thirty-first Texas Legislature, and he sponsored a bill that created the Irving Independent School District. Governor Campbell signed the bill into law April 23, 1909. The school building was two stories tall with one room on each floor where all of the students in all grades were somehow taught. About an acre of the land in the school complex was donated by David Earl Britain, who inherited property west of Britain Road from his father, Henry W. Britain.

Tom Haley built a house in Irving in 1909 and moved his family to town where he thought the new School District would provide them a better education. He soon became a member of the School Board. His daughters later became legends as teachers. While he was living in town he maintained the Haley farm which was a gathering place for several generations of his extended family.

Meanwhile Otis Brown had built a new and much larger house at 321 Iowa (now O'Connor), and the little cottage at First and Hastings, which had been the first house in Irving, was sold to Chaney Miller. Deed records show two lots and a house sold November 20, 1905, for $800, with $400 cash and the balance due December 4, 1905. Miller enlarged it and added a semicircular porch with columns. Several years later, when Sarah was ill, he invited their daughter Florence, her husband W. R. Duckworth, and two grandchildren to move in. This explains why some people still argue about which store was on the west side of North Main the second door from First Street. Fletcher Miller sold his part of the business to W. R. Duckworth in 1908, and Miller Brothers Mercantile became Miller Duckworth Mercantile.

People living in the Irving area had become accustomed to the erratic behavior of the Trinity River. They knew that at any time, especially in the spring, the river could rise and cut off passage to and from Dallas for days or weeks. But in 1908 the worst flooding yet washed out the bridges to West Dallas, invaded east Irving, destroyed Oak Cliff, and caused major damage in downtown Dallas where water rose to the second floors of buildings. It was reported that four thousand people were homeless.

E. C. Lively, from Irving, was reelected to the legislature in 1908, and he is given most of the credit for the enactment of a state law providing for reclamation of lands and the formation of levee districts with powers to issue and sell bonds for improvement of arable lands. Dallas businessmen organized the Trinity River Levee and Drainage Club and sent petitions to the legislature asking that bonds be issued for improvements to the river. Civic leaders commissioned a comprehensive Dallas plan and employed George Kessler who was a nationally recognized planner.

C. W. Heppner wrote an article in the *Dallas Morning News* of November 11, 1911, urging citizens to work together and pull just one way. He predicted that another flood would cover Courthouse Square. Plans were proposed to straighten the crooks in the river and convert horseshoe bends to reservoirs. The river could be moved a half-mile west and confined between levees. The state engineers began making topographical surveys and determined that a fifteen-hundred-

Above:
Pictured is the entire Irving student body beside the two-room, two-story school house that was the only building they had until late 1913. Irving Archives

Left:
In 1911 the new brick bank building added a touch of class to the business section of Irving. It was soon a place where businessmen met to talk informally about current issues and future plans. Irving Heritage Society collection

This house on Iowa Street (now 321 O'Connor) was the second house Otis Brown built for his family. Because of the efforts of Morris and Marge Parrish, it still stands and is occupied. Finding it in poor condition, they restored and improved it and made it their home. Parrish was the third mayor to live in the house. Lynn Brown was born there. Courtesy Morris Parrish

The first automobile in Irving was this little red Hupmobile. In the car are Percy Schulze and Otis Brown, with Fred Joffre in the "mother-in-law seat." The license number was 597. Irving Heritage Society collection

foot right of way would be needed for the river and that levees on both sides should be built on a gentle slope. It was obvious that the project would not be accomplished overnight not only because there were differences of opinion on how and whether it should go forward, but because it was a huge, expensive, and complicated undertaking.

In 1911 the Irving State Bank kept the name but was physically moved to a new building on the northwest corner of First and Main. The brick building with an ornamental facade was the most impressive structure in town at the time. Later a second story was added and Dr. Gilbert moved his office there. When his stepson, Dr. John Roberts, joined him, there was another good doctor in town.

All of the pictures of North Main Street that we have found show the two-story white frame hotel at the north end of the street on the west side. Prior to 1911, Mr. W. Q. Seale had a one-story building at that location. In January of 1911 the *Irving Index* published an advertisement by the Irving Board of Trade which declared: "Irving needs an up-to-date, well-equipped hotel and needs it badly." Mr. Seale responded by expanding his building and adding a second floor to create a hotel where railroad workers, drummers, and other long- or short-term visitors could rent a room by the night or month. Earnest Vining, who had opened a general merchandise store earlier in the year moved into the new hotel in April 1911 as the manager. He bought the Irving Café, which Frank Hamm II had opened in 1909, and Mr. Hamm moved to Arroyo Seco, New Mexico.

Juanita Britain recently arranged for us to visit with Frank Hamm III who lives in Fort Worth, and he helped explain the history of the hotel that is generally referred to as Hamms Hotel, although that was never its official name. He remembers coming back to Irving when he was five years old and spoke only Spanish. In 1913 his father decided to have a hog farm in Irving. That venture was a disaster when the hogs all died of cholera within the year. Undaunted, Mr. Hamm and his wife bought the hotel building from Mr. Seale and the hotel equipment from Mr. Vining. They opened the famous Hamms Café on the ground floor and operated the Irving Hotel, which had eight rooms upstairs and family quarters downstairs. Regular boarders got reduced rates in the café, which was a popular place for "town people" to meet and eat. Several people told us that Mrs. Hamm did most of the cooking and that what she didn't cook she oversaw. There was a counter service with stools and some tables and chairs in one room and also a more formal dining room. An early advertisement in the *Irving Index* reads: "Try our famous barbecue sandwiches and plate lunches. Special chicken dinners Sundays and Wednesdays at Hamms Café."

Charles Stovall had opened Banner Mercantile in a large frame building on the southeast corner of Main and First Streets. This was a popular corner as it changed ownership through the years and people remember it in the context of their own age group. C. T. Lucas is responsible for the brick building that now houses Big State Drug. While trying to go to college in 1912, he started working in the Banner Mercantile Store. About a year later he bought the inventory and rented the building from Mr. Stovall. The next year he bought the building. He fenced the vacant lot south of the building and created a poultry farm. He sold chickens and eggs in his own store and at markets. Apparently business was good because he subsequently moved the frame building to the south and built the brick structure where he continued to operate the popular store as Banner Mercantile until the early thirties.

The automobile had been introduced, and in 1909 Percy Schulze had the first one in Irving. People in Irving still talk about that sporty little red Hupmobile with no top and one back seat on a platform called the "mother-in-law seat." It was a thing of wonder and beauty,

The water tower is in the center of the intersection of First and Main Streets in this view of the west side of Main Street, looking north, in 1912. Vic Ostrand's Grocery and Pool Hall is on the south side of First. The bank on the northwest corner does not yet have a second story. Miller Hardware is just north of the bank and the hotel can be seen as the last building on the west side of the block. The Depot is centered at the end of the street. Courtesy Sue Haley Huffman

and before long several other horseless carriages appeared on the streets of town. Streets may not be the right word because they were still dirt roads and sometimes cars had to be rescued from deep sand or mud by horses or mules. There are a number of stories about horses bolting and running wildly when an automobile approached. An interview with O. F. Fann recorded in the Irving Archives gives us a firsthand account of an incident in Dallas. His father sold his farm products at the market in downtown Dallas, and one day he took O. F. with him to market. According to Mr. Fann:

Somebody come down that street yelling, hold your horses! Here comes one of those blamed automobiles and boy everybody went out and grabbed their horses. It was there by Sanger Brothers where the market was then. They had these wooden blocks in the street paved with bois d'arc blocks set in ground just solid. You never seen such a commotion in all your life. Some of the teams got away from them. Had an awful runaway. The car came down that street, chug, chug, chug, just an old one cylinder of some kind.

It's hard to imagine growing up when there were no automobiles and riding in one for the first time. Describing his experience years later, Mr. Fann said that it didn't seem reasonable but that it was very real at the time. He had started walking home from downtown Irving when Dr. John Haley came by and offered him a ride. "Course I hesitated about getting into an automobile because, gosh, I had never been in one. Got in there and that thing started off and I looked out there and it just didn't make sense that thing moving, no mules or horses to pull it. When we got up to Union Bower and went to turn I know my eyes burst out 'cause those fenders just turned and went around the corner there. I just couldn't believe it."

Believe it or not there was an outcry around the country against the use of automobiles, which just proves again that anything new can cause an argument. Senator Joseph Bailey, speaking to the U.S. Senate in 1909, said, "If I had my way I would make it a crime to use automobiles on the public highways because no man has a right to use a vehicle on the public highway that is dangerous to the safety of other people." Those other people were riding horse-powered vehicles or bicycles.

Even Woodrow Wilson reacted negatively in 1906 when he was president of Princeton University. He considered the motorcar to be a plaything and publicly stated: "Nothing has spread socialistic feelings in this country more than the automobile. It offers us a picture of

Frank Hamm III posed for this portrait soon after his parents bought the hotel. He said he was forever being dressed up and hauled over to the picture-taking place. Courtesy Frank Hamm III

the arrogance of wealth." Those negative thoughts may have been expressed in Irving, but all we found recorded or passed down through folklore points to a love affair with the automobile. Relatively few citizens could own one at first, but many admired them.

In 1910 the magic of the telephone was introduced. A privately owned system was installed and it was popular. Service cost $1.00 a month for a party line and $1.50 for a private line. An operator at a central switchboard made the connections, and if you had a party line she wasn't the only one who could listen to your conversation.

Just a year after the telephone was introduced, another great technological advance came along when Lone Star Gas brought a line through Irving. It was the Southwest's first long-distance transmission pipeline. It came from the Petrolia field about 120 miles northwest to serve Fort Worth and Dallas. It was a big deal that right of way customers who tied into the main line had gas in Irving before Dallas customers did. By the end of 1911 the North Texas Gas Company constructed a gas distribution system in Irving and contracted with Lone Star to supply the gas. The distribution company was not able to make a profit, and they couldn't stay in business more than a year. Lone Star took over the town plant in 1912. There wasn't a great rush to get gaslights, and switching to gas stoves was even slower. The expense was one reason, but women who continued to cook on their wood or coal burning stoves said they just made better bread.

The original home of the First Baptist Church of Irving was on the site beginning at Main and Fourth Streets, where the current complex of buildings houses a large and enthusiastic congregation. Irving Archives

The Baptist Church site that was donated by the town founders was on Main and Fourth Streets. Like the other two churches that had lots donated, early services had been held in the Lively School building. With W. J. Shipman as pastor, eighteen charter members met every fourth Sunday. By 1908 they had a concrete foundation poured and were meeting in a shelter with a dirt floor on the back of their lot. With Reverend L. M. Keeling as pastor they were able to construct a frame building on the concrete foundation in 1911. The ladies of the congregation made and sold hot tamales regularly over a period of time to pay for a roof. For several years they enjoyed referring to the roof built with hot tamales.

A decision was made about 1907 to form a Methodist Church. Adolphus Clark donated a lot at the corner of Third and Ohio, and in early 1908 the finance drive began with a box supper which raised $75. A group from Sowers came in and added $300 to the construction fund. It was the same story of pooled resources, talents, and labor that turned ideas into reality in Irving. The first members on the rolls of the Methodist Episcopal Church of the South worked together to build a sanctuary while they met in the Irving School building on Second Street. The first meeting in the new sanctuary was impromptu. On a crisp November day in 1908, nobody had picked up the key to the schoolhouse. The congregation marched to their unfinished building singing all the way. Pews were made of lumber supplies and nail kegs. It was a "joyfully spirited service, inspiring to all." Several members have described the first white frame building with a steeple complete with bell tower. Children scrambled to be the ones to ring the bell, which could pull smaller ones into the air. The bell and original stained-glass window were transferred to the stone sanctuary which is still a landmark.

In 1911 Hubert Smith, from the Union Bower community, bought this "touring car." It cost $300 and he paid cash. Irving Heritage Society collection

In 1912, Major Robinson put a gasoline pump in front of his drugstore and C. P. Schulze engaged A. F. Joffre to build a fine new home at 303 Iowa (now South O'Connor). This house became a center of social activity for many years while Charles P. Schulze Jr. and his sister Mary Schulze were growing up there. This house has a basement and a well. Mr. Joffre had his office at the Schulze Lumberyard where he carefully selected the highest quality materials for the house. It stands today as a testament to his workmanship as well as to the great civic and social contributions of the family that lived there. This is now the Heritage House, which can be viewed and enjoyed by the citizens of Irving because of the generosity of Charles and Catherine Schulze.

Above:
Square dancing was always popular in Irving and the surrounding communities. Lloyd Smith was the caller in Union Bower. These musicians are Tom Owens, Earl Steele, Lillie Owens, and Tom Wright. They got together in the fall and winter because summers were too hot for dancing. Courtesy Betty Miller

Left:
The first church built in Irving by the Methodists was located at Ohio and Third Streets. The building was replaced by a stone sanctuary that is a landmark. After several stages of expansion, the church complex occupies the entire block from Second to Third Streets between Hastings and Ohio. Irving Archives

This brick building, erected in 1913, is affectionately remembered by generations of Irving citizens who were schooled there. When it was built it was the tallest building in town and considered to be a very modern schoolhouse. Courtesy Juanita Britain

While he was working on the Schulze house, Fred Joffre decided that he wanted the next lot to the south for his own. The location, soil, large oak trees, and orientation facing east appealed to him, so that he let Otis Brown know that he wanted to buy the property. Dr. Clay Gilbert told us that Joffre had asked Brown several times to sell him the lot but couldn't get an answer. He started carrying $300 in his wallet, and finally one day he saw Brown in town, began a conversation, brought up the subject of the lot and offered $300. Mr. Brown accepted the offer, and Mr. Joffre, who happened to have that amount with him, paid cash on the spot. He built his house in 1919 and became a neighbor to the Schulze family. This house still stands and is known as the Joffre-Gilbert house, recognized for historic significance not only because of A. F. Joffre, a highly respected builder, but because it later was the home of Dr. F. M. Gilbert and his family who served Irving in many capacities through the years.

By 1912 the little two-room schoolhouse was overcrowded and the School Board was making plans to build. They envisioned something bigger than anything in the little town at the time. The county schools in the surrounding communities offered only seven grades, and to continue through high school their students had to travel to a school that offered the other four grades. There wasn't room enough to house the Irving high school students, much less students from the rest of the county, so the Irving School Board bravely called for a $13,000 bond election. Tom Haley was president of the Board with members C. P. Schulze, Chaney G. Miller, William DeHaes, George Clark, and Dr. John Roberts. Although that was an enormous sum at the time, there was very little argument and the bond issue passed. Construction began on the school building, which many of the citizens of Irving still fondly remember as "Old Red." It was a three-story red brick building and was the tallest building in town in 1913.

Now a city government became the main issue. Towns in Texas operated under the laws and supervision of the County and the State. Incorporating would allow the town to have certain self-governing powers, which included making enforceable rules or laws, providing some services, and imposing limited taxes. This could be accomplished by filing a petition calling for an election and getting a favorable vote for incorporation. Leading citizens in Irving who concerned themselves with such things filed a petition April 7, 1914, and the election, presided over by the county judge, was held April 14, 1914. The motion passed twenty-seven to sixteen, and little Irving became an incorporated city. It was the beginning of independence, self-direction, and the freedom to plan and to grow as a town.

The Elm School was one of the Dallas County common schools that continued to operate long after there was an Irving Independent School District. It was near the present Metker Street, just west of what we now call O'Connor and across from what is now the Albert Farine School. For many years what is now O'Connor was known as the Elm School Road. The original school was built by five men, who each contributed $25 for materials. Most family names of children in the picture are Farine, Story, Toler, Metker, Holt, and Parker. The teacher is Mrs. Holland. Courtesy Betty Miller, Irving Heritage Society

Otis Brown, the first mayor of Irving, served from 1914 to 1917. Irving Archives

Chapter 3

Independence & Responsibility

In the newly incorporated town of Irving, Otis Brown was elected mayor by a one vote margin with Commissioners H. Moulard and George Clark. Clark was not sworn in because of a postal ruling that he could not continue his job as a mail carrier and hold elective office. He chose to continue as a government employee.

J. W. Blewett was appointed as commissioner in place of George Clark, and regular meetings were scheduled on the first Tuesday of each month. Records of the meetings are in an official minute book which is available for reading in the Irving Archives. On the first Tuesday of May 1914, the Commissioners passed eight ordinances. The first one declared: "Horses, mules, jacks, jennetts, cows, hogs, sheep, and goats will not be permitted to run at large, nor be staked or tied, so as to reach any part of a street or alley within the corporate limits."

Ordinance Number 4 on that day read: "Any and all sidewalks must be kept clear of all merchandise for display, or any obstruction of any kind except an 18-inch space for settees or seats, directly next to the business house." This exclusion allowing space for the established practice of men sitting outside stores to observe the "goings on," greet whomever passed by, exchange information or philosophy, and perhaps to argue was very important. "Sidewalks" were wood platforms sometimes referred to as porches.

In July a tax rate of "15 cents on $100 valuation of any and all properties both real and personal within the corporate limits of Irving" was set. Citizens were directed to render their properties. The Commissioners met in a special session to complete the tax rolls by placing values on properties that had not been rendered and raising values on some that were rendered. Notices were mailed to property owners. Then the Commissioners met in October as a Board of Equalization to review all valuations and hear protests.

At the July meeting the Commissioners also passed a rule requiring a license fee of $5.00 per annum from peddlers within the corporate limits. Farmers disposing of products they grew were excluded. The first license fee was collected from E. S. Womack representing the W. T. Rawleigh Medicine Company. For $5.00 they could sell all of their preparations in Irving for one year.

Only a part of the original eighty acres had been platted and sold at the auction. Sales continued, and then Otis Brown developed several additions south of the first plat. The map of the Heritage District, depicting what the Heritage Society considered to be the original town of Irving, extends the southern boundary to Sixth Street and includes three large Otis Brown additions. This was just the beginning for Brown. He continued to buy, sell, and develop land as the town and the area surrounding it grew.

While Mayor Brown was busy shaping the newly incorporated town, Netta Brown was busy on the home front. Their fifth son, Irving Lynn, was born June 19, 1914. Years later he would be the fourteenth mayor of Irving. Netta managed the household and the boys. She did a lot of cooking and sewing. The boys were often dressed alike because she made their clothes, and when she made an outfit they all got the same design in their respective sizes. The other four boys were Lloyd, born in 1905; Stanley, in 1906; Earl, in 1910; and John, in 1912.

Lynn Brown and John Brown with Charles Schulze. Parrish collection

Mrs. Lora Mae Anderson, whose husband had been killed in an accident, brought her eight children to a home on Hastings Street to be near her father, Chaney Miller. Her five boys were similar in ages to the five Brown boys. C. C. Anderson grew up to become the first full-time paid employee of the city in 1939.

The year 1914 was significant for determining the future of the Dallas area. Dallas was selected as the site for the Eleventh District of the Federal Reserve Bank. Soon large automobiles were put to use as jitneys. Mr. and Mrs. C. H. Walker, Mrs. B. J. Pierce, and others managed jitney services to Dallas. Apparently business was good even if passengers sometimes had to hang on while standing on a running board or get out and push when the car got stuck in sand or mud. In extreme cases a team of mules was used to pull a car out of trouble. The jitney offered multiple automobiles and a flexible schedule, and it never left to come home until everybody was back on board. The spring rains usually caused crossings to be impossible, and for several weeks the train with one trip in the morning and one in the evening was the only ride to Dallas. Sometimes jitneys were called on for emergency trips to hospitals in Dallas or for incidental needs. Mrs. Walker, who took calls for service, kept books, bought supplies, and arranged for repairs, said in an interview that a few times she jumped in her own car and answered an urgent call for transportation. An earlier jitney service had been operated by Shelton Story, using a mule-drawn carriage.

The announcement in 1914 that the student population had reached 500 triggered a parade to the town water well and a picture. The census count for the town of Irving in 1920 was only 357, demonstrating the fact that the school was the major business in Irving. Students from Kit and Lively came to Irving from the beginning. Now some parents in other communities sent their elementary-age children to Irving on a tuition-basis. The county schools in surrounding communities provided only seven grades, so many of their students came to Irving for high school.

Students were accustomed to leaving the campus during a lunch hour. Having no school cafeteria, they either brought lunches, went home, or walked to a store in town. Moreland's Store was a favorite. Being on time after lunch was as important as promptness in the morning. However we have several reports that everybody in town, including students, forgot time when they heard that an airplane had landed on the Shelton Story farm on the Kit Lone Star Road (Sixth Street) east of Britain. It was 1914 and hardly anybody had actually seen an airplane. Two Canadian pilots in training at Love Field had made a forced landing. They drew a crowd of curious and excited people.

Jitneys were popular around 1912 to 1915. Irving Heritage Society collection

The public well, in the middle of the intersection of Main and First, was the source of water in town. Boys were sent with buckets to bring drinking water to school. On farms and in homes it was customary to have a bucket of water with a dipper. Everybody used the one dipper. This was the practice at school until a report of disease spread by the use of community drinking vessels led to the request that students and teachers bring their own cups.

Suddenly the town that was born with a newspaper was left without one. Mr. Hudson shut down the *Irving Index* in 1913 and moved away in 1915. Irvingites were dependent on the Dallas paper, conversations around town, or the telephone party line for news. There were no radios or televisions.

In 1916, Grover Pierce came to Irving to buy the telephone company from the Earl Story family. The phone exchange was located on the second floor of the bank building. In an interview printed in the *Daily News Texan* on April 16, 1964, he gave some insight to his experience. There was still only one switchboard and one operator. One woman had to keep straight the calls of about two hundred telephones scattered over Irving, Sowers, Kit, Shady Grove, Union Bower, and Estelle. Mr. Pierce said, "You could have as many as twenty women involved in one conversation." He also said that one of the most important calls while he owned the business was the report of a fire. The volunteer fire department was alerted, but the bucket brigade was unable to stop the blaze from destroying the old Davis Cotton Gin and several homes.

Above:
This 1914 picture shows students at the public well, and the bank building with the second story added. Irving Heritage Society collection

Left:
The Shelton Story family pose in front of their home on the south side of Kit Lone Star Road (now Sixth Street) east of Britain. Front row: Evie Luna (wife), Ada, Shelton, Jonathan Russell, and Samuel J.
Back row: Annie B., Alice Luana, Isaac Benjamin, and Martin Alexander with the horse. Their farm was the site of the airplane landing in 1914. Courtesy Martha Seeber

Early phones were mounted on the wall. A good cranking alerted the operator who made connections manually.

Everybody wanted a phone, but in a period of rapid expansion the income from subscriptions at $1.00 to $1.50 per month didn't keep up with the capital costs. Mr. Pierce declared, "I just couldn't afford it." He sold the telephone business and, with Hershel Ramsey, started a grocery store where Chandler's General Store had been. When Mr. Ramsey retired, G. C. Pierce continued to provide service and hospitality until, after thirty-five years in the grocery business, he closed out and became an inspector for Tempco. He said he just wanted a job with regular hours.

The P. D. Russells, at 301 West Irving Boulevard, competed with the Grover Pierce Store from 1933 to 1941. In addition to groceries they had the first Gulf Station in Irving and sold white, regular, and ethyl gas. Because they lived in the same building with the store, customers expected them to open the store anytime including Sundays. They tried to set regular hours but seldom succeeded. They closed the store and converted it to a home where they continued to live until 1954.

In 1916 electricity had not yet come to Irving, but the use of Delco generator systems to provide lighting was catching on. An *Irving News* article reported the following on August 4: "Major Robinson has received his engines and fans and has begun wiring and making all preparations for electric lights at the Palace Drug Store. When Major can't make a deal with such companies as the Texas Power and Light Company, he goes ahead and does things up to suit himself." TP&L didn't bring service to Irving until 1925.

By April 1917 it was time for an election, and all candidates for office were instructed that they must file with the clerk at least ten days before the election and deposit $1.00 to defray the expenses of printing the ticket and holding the election. C. G. Miller got twenty-five votes and became the new mayor of Irving. There were bills to be paid. Approval was voted by the Commissioners to pay George Miller $9.70 for assessing taxes and H. O. Gunter $1.80 for two yards of gravel placed on the street at Main and Second. C. J. Range was paid $10.00 for public well service in April and May, and Miss Jewell Miller drew $1.00 for transcribing the tax rolls for 1917.

The business of the town was important but much of the activity that determined what Irving would eventually become was taking place beyond the corporate boundaries. For example, about three miles north of Irving via the Elm School Road, north of the farms of Jonathan Story and Nicholas Farine, Charles O'Connor started a dairy on twenty-five hundred acres of black land in 1917. At that time it was the latest of many large dairies in the Irving vicinity. O'Connor hired Clarence Cobb to supervise the entire operation of the farm and dairy for a salary of $20 a month plus room and board. In an interview, available in the Irving Archives, Cobb said he hadn't expected to stay long, but he worked there thirty-six years. He was in charge of crops, carpentry, repairing machinery, tending to hogs, sheep, and cattle, and seeing that the cows were milked and that the milk was processed and delivered to market. The Borden Dairy in Dallas was their largest customer.

Mr. Cobb said that he did get a raise to $1.25 a day which was his pay for most of the thirty-six years. Furthermore he pointed out that the job was not a five-day, forty-hour workweek. "Cows don't take a day off on Sunday from making milk." There were no vacations or time out for bad weather.

The concept of a forty-hour, five-day workweek was foreign to the people who lived in and around Irving. They made a living from the land. They had livestock and poultry to care for, wood to cut, crops to plant and harvest. What they didn't use immediately had to be sold or preserved in some way. Everybody was expected to help. Neighbors traded both products and work among themselves.

If we left the O'Connor Dairy and traveled south on the Elm School Road, we would roughly have the Farine farms to the west and the Story farms to the east. Nicholas Farine was

The class that graduated from Irving High School in 1916 was representative of the early settlers in the area and the founders of the town. Front row, left to right: Oston Cushenberry, Theo DeHaes, and Susie Clark. Second row: Frank Haley, Inez Moore, and Velma Duckworth. Third row: Roy Lively, Howard Duckworth, and Roy Miller. This is the entire senior class. Courtesy Sue Haley Huffman

born in Dole, France, and educated in Paris. He came to Texas with the founders of La Reunion. In Paris he was a musician and composer, but he learned to be a farmer in Texas. He brought grape cuttings with him from France and continued to cultivate them after he moved to the area that became Irving. His first 160 acres was a grant from the State of Texas signed by Governor H. R. Runnels. His daughter, Lucy Farine Bell, reported in an interview that he acquired another 232 acres by trading a yoke of oxen, a wagon, seven head of cattle, fifteen hogs, and some chickens. Then in 1861 he bought 145 acres which was a land grant to D. W. Reedy signed by Governor Sam Houston in 1860.

Jonathan Story and his son, Thomas, acquired the land parallel to and east of the Farine farms from near Northgate to the vicinity of Grauwyler on the south. Albert Farine, Nicholas'son, and Will Story, Jonathan's grandson, made their homes south of what later became Highway 183. In 1895 Will Story married Fannie Farine. Albert Farine married Rosetta Crabtree whose father, Stanton Crabtree, had a store just north of the Farine property. The descendants of these unions were blessed with rich diversity in the national origins, personalities, and talents of the extended family.

In 1917 none of the land we have just referenced was in Irving, but if we traveled that same path today, we would notice that much of the heart of what later was Irving grew in that area from Northgate to Grauwyler on what were once two large family farms. Most conspicuous are the Hospital, the Arts Center, and MacArthur High School, along with retail and residential developments.

The lunch wagon took care of workers on the Story Farm. Irving Heritage Society collection

Will Story owned a 1912 Maxwell automobile, and he was a pioneer in the use of farm machinery. He had a thirty-inch circular saw and a gasoline engine which he mounted on a steel-wheeled wagon frame. He cut timber to prepare his land for farming and hauled and sold it in Dallas. He could also take the equipment to homes and custom-cut lengths on site. He bought a big Avery tractor and a threshing machine that he used to work on large farms from the area now covered by Dallas/Fort Worth Airport to the vicinity of Singleton and Westmoreland in West

Families picked cotton on their own farms, and "hands" could be hired for a dollar a day. Tommy Evans collection, from Lurlene Evans

Dallas. But machinery did not make his workdays or weeks shorter. He just did more and the livestock still had to be cared for. The children knew exactly what their parents did because they were active participants as soon as they were big enough. Raymond Story, who gave us this information, has many interesting stories about growing up helping with his father's many ventures and walking through the woods and over the creeks to school in Irving.

South of the incorporated town the farms tended to be smaller. Vegetables, fruits, and berries were the major crops produced for the market. An abundance of poultry was also raised and marketed. The soil and the availability of water from shallow wells and springs made this section ideal for truck farming. A few cows, hogs, and sheep, rather than large herds, was the usual pattern here. Some meat and milk was sold or traded, but on most small farms these products were primarily for family use. The rule of thumb was to have necessary food for the family and some form of cash crop. Whatever was harvested or slaughtered had to be used, sold, or preserved immediately. Vegetables and fruits that were not sold fresh at market could be canned or dried. And meat could be cured in a smokehouse, but it was not unusual to see a side of beef or other type of meat on a flatbed covered with cheesecloth being peddled in town. Most truck farmers made regular trips to the Pearl Street Market in Dallas where they spent the day selling their fresh harvest. A few farmers took wagonloads to sell on selected Dallas residential streets.

Avery 25-Drawbar, 50-Belt H.P. Tractor

Will Story worked with a tractor like this but he had problems when the County started hot topping the roads. In warm weather, the tar stuck to the metal wheels and damaged the new roads. Courtesy Raymond Story

Throughout the area cotton and wheat were important crops and most farms had corn. Dallas was a major cotton market even before the Cotton Exchange Building became a nationally recognized landmark. In 1918, Dallas was recognized as the world's largest inland cotton market, leading the world in cotton gin manufacturing. The Davis and the Lively Cotton Gins were located near the Depot in Irving from which it was convenient to ship bales of cotton to market.

There were two gristmills located on the riverbanks, one at Record Crossing and one at Eagle Ford, where they could be powered by the flow of the water. They were both operating before the founding of Irving. Most often pioneers from the Irving area speak or write about the Eagle Ford mill where they took corn and wheat to be converted to meal or flour and cane to be pressed for syrup. Mr. Luck, who ran the mill, was willing to take pay "on the toll," which meant he would keep a portion of the product. All farming was labor intensive so that having a large family was an advantage. Children had chores very early in their lives and worked in the fields from the time they were big enough until they established their own farms or became self-sufficient in some other way.

Many people came into town on Saturdays to buy supplies and to meet, greet, and talk. In a recorded interview in the Irving Archives, Lorene Lucas Looper said that in those days a person going to town was going to Dallas. A trip into the town of Irving was "going up in Irving." She illustrated with the story of a boy who was asked by his teacher to go to town and get her a tablet. He answered, "No ma'am, I can't, but I'll go up in Irving and get it." Up in Irving on Saturdays people talked about farm and market conditions, weather, church events, families, neighbors, and what they had heard or read about beyond "the Forks."

Doug and Alice Lucas are behind the counter in this interior view of W. D. Lucas General Merchandise Store. Irving Heritage Society collection

Between the time that the United States was compelled by German submarine activity to enter World War I in April of 1917 and the signing of the Armistice in November 1918, much of the attention when neighbors met was related to the war. There were patriotic rallies on Main and First Streets, a Red Cross Chapter was activated, and war bonds were sold. Under the leadership of Netta Brown, who chaired the Red Cross Chapter, ladies made bandages, knitted warm garments, and wrote encouraging letters to boys in service. A memorial to Irving servicemen in all of the wars is being created as part of the one-hundred-year anniversary celebration.

In April 1919, Philip Lively became the new mayor with Walter Noah and Doug Lucas as Commissioners. A meeting on April 22 was called for the purpose of passing an ordinance setting a speed limit of twelve miles per hour and requiring closed mufflers. The penalty for violation was one to ten dollars.

By 1919, W. D. Lucas had moved his general store to a two-story brick building on the northwest corner of Main and Second which had formerly been occupied by Hudson and Davis. Lorene Lucas Looper gave this description of the way the store was run:

All of the "goods" were on shelves back of the counter. The store clerk stood back of the counter and waited on the customer. On the grocery side of the store the counter had drawers under the counter. These drawers held things like sugar, rice, beans, and dried fruits. Potatoes, onions, apples, and things like that were in boxes placed in front of the counter. Early on Saturday mornings we would weigh and sack up several pecks of potatoes, No. 5 and No. 10 bags of sugar to help us along when the Saturday rush came.

Will Story, a pioneer and innovator in use of machinery, covered a wide territory working large farms with his threshing machine, but he also worked his own smaller farm with a mule team to grow a variety of produce for his family table and for the market in Dallas. He still found time to take loving care of his livestock. Irving Heritage Society collection

She went on to explain the family involvement in the business. *Mama became Daddy's full-time partner in running the store. She took the children along and we played around the store and the back store yard. Just as soon as a child was big enough to be seen over the counter he became a part-time clerk. We all worked on Saturdays which was the big day. Closing time was when customers quit coming in. One evening all of the family, except Howard, was still at the store. He was at home making a radio from plans that had been published in the Dallas newspaper. Radios existed at the time, but nobody remembers one in Irving then. The first step to make your own radio was to wrap wire around an oatmeal box to form a coil. The tuner was a tiny wire that was touched on a crystal rock about the size of the end of the little finger. Howard called the store about 8:00, saying "hurry home, I hear music, I can hear a woman singing." They closed the store and ran home to share his excitement. They heard a woman singing right through the air. It was a miracle.*

In 1919 the Lucas brothers anchored two of the corners on Main Street. Charlie was still on the southeast corner of Main and First, and Doug was on the northwest corner of Main and Second. Both stores were social gathering places and both offered simple food like beans and biscuits. There was a potbellied stove to sit or stand around for warmth in winter. Information was exchanged, plans were made, encouragement was given, and the morals of the town were enforced because everybody knew everybody and everybody cared. Knowing you would be talked about was a great deterrent to unacceptable behavior. If somebody needed help, it was freely given either by individuals or by an organized effort. That's what neighbors were for. At

In 1915, a temporary platform and a few local fiddlers were all that was needed for dancers and spectators to have a good time. Irving Archives

Charlie Lucas's store the mood got lighter on Saturday evenings. He brought in fiddlers and his store was filled with friends who had a toe-tapping good time.

These two stores were not the only gathering places and, of course, church activities brought the community together for fun as well as enforcement of spiritual commitments. The result, with regard to children and young people, was that they were overseen by their parents, the schools, the churches, and the entire community. Nothing went unnoticed or unreported. The town and the whole area between the Forks was a community in every sense of the word.

Doug Lucas was the first to replace the wooden sidewalks outside his store with concrete and suspend his awning with cables instead of poles.
He was applauded for leading an effort to beautify Main Street. Irving Heritage Society collection

All of the people we have talked to who grew up in Irving are enthusiastic about their experiences. There was no television and no video games, but there were plenty of traditional games and made-up games that didn't require any equipment and that could be adapted to fit the number of players available. Spontaneous games were played wherever space was found. Football, basketball, and baseball games between schools or community teams were played on the school grounds, but they had to be played in daylight hours. There were no lighted fields. However a way to play basketball after dark was devised. The court was in the vacant space north of the W. D. Lucas store, with the goal on the north wall of his building. A generator was set up to power lights for nighttime playing. Doyle and Glen Spann were in charge of keeping the generator running, so they could never be in the game at the same time.

In 1964, W. C. Surratt, who lived in Irving between 1913 and 1919, wrote a letter to the *Daily News Texan*. His father worked on the Frisco section from Irving to Carrollton, and they lived in one of the railroad section houses that were near the tracks just north and west of the hotel. He said he hoed and picked cotton, stole watermelons, and sold chickens to Doug Lucas for twenty-five cents each. He described Irving as a "real boys' life town." There are many stories of how children loved to swim in Delaware Creek, but his story was different. He said that he and his friends would take off their overalls at the Rock Island Bridge, tie them on their backs, and float all the way around to where the creek crossed what now is Fritz Park. Then they would walk all the way back and do it again.

In 1919 Irving lost one of the three physicians who served the area. Dr. John Roberts died, leaving Etta Williams Roberts a young widow. She became known as Aunt Et, while her mother, Mahala Lucas Williams, was called Grandma Williams. Their large two-story house, located on the south side of First Street between Hastings and Ohio, became a boarding house. It was described as having eight rooms and one bath. It was a convenient location for teachers who, by

Above:
The first Irving High School baseball team poses for a group picture in 1914. Courtesy Sue Haley Huffman

Left:
Irving School girls who were allowed to play basketball in 1922 were well dressed. They played on the school grounds. Included here are Mae Mitchell, Exie Cunningham, Delma Crowe, Wilma Harkey, Lillian Embree, and one unidentified. Irving Heritage Society collection

contract, had to live in Irving during the week; for bachelors like Vic Ostrand, who had a store and pool hall in town; and later John Brandenburg, the much-loved banker. Mary Fields Lively lived there when she first started teaching in Irving and was not yet married. She is one of the teachers most often remembered with respect and affection by former students.

Dr. D. W. Gilbert gave up his horse and buggy for the automobile. He still traveled a broad area in and around Irving to care for homebound patients.
Courtesy Dr. Clay Gilbert

Dr. Franklin Monroe Gilbert was interning at City Hospital in New York during 1919. There he met Dorothy Bald Brandon, a nurse, and brought her back to Irving as his wife. In 1920 he began practicing medicine with his father, Dr. D. W. Gilbert. It was fourteen flights of stairs up to their offices in the bank building. His career in serving the medical needs of the area, while assuming various civic responsibilities, is legendary.

The year 1919 was in several ways a year of expansion for the town as more families moved into the corporate limits. Fred Joffre built and moved into the house on Iowa Street (now 309 South O'Connor) which he had planned in 1912 when he was building the Schulze house next door. Eugene and Mary Beaufford bought the Howard house on Iowa Street (318 South O'Connor) and brought their family into town. Betty Beaufford Bessler has an original land deed with a description of land adjacent to the house. It passed from J. B. Howard to Nicolas LaNotte through the estate of J. W. Roberts to Horace Stewart and then to the Beauffords by deed dated January 9, 1920. By this time Alice Howard, who had grown up in that house, had married Doug Lucas and they were operating the store at Main and Second. Eugene Beaufford established a successful truck farm on the land adjacent to the home in what we now know as the Heritage District. His first land extended from Third to Fifth Street along Iowa and almost to Hastings on the east. In 1926 he donated the site for the second location of St. Lukes Church on Iowa and Fifth Streets.

The very successful Althoff truck farm was already located south of what became Sixth Street. A trail parallel to what later became Senter Street went through their farm. This was not yet within the corporate limits of Irving.

Lurlene Beaufford and Mary Schulze were near the same age and they became playmates. They had a playhouse in the Schulze yard where they spent many happy hours. But other neighbors were

As a City Hospital intern and a New York City police captain, Dr. Franklin Monroe Gilbert helped man the ambulance service. After a year he returned to Irving to practice medicine with his father.
Courtesy Dr. Clay Gilbert

preparing to move from Iowa Street. The Brown boys were growing up. Irving Lynn, the youngest, was five years old when Otis Brown, founder and first mayor of Irving, decided to move out of town. He didn't go far, but still he was beyond the corporate limits of Irving. He started a dairy on seventy-five acres that he named Shadylea Farm, bounded on the south by the Rock Island Railroad tracks, west by Story Road, north by Sowers Road (Pioneer), and east by Irby Lane. His herd came from the Carnation farms of Wisconsin. They were said to be the best accredited Holstein breeding cattle south of the Mason-Dixon line. Lynn Brown often said that he and his brothers averaged milking seventy-five cows each day and some of them produced over ten gallons of milk per day. In his later years, when he was mayor of Irving, he liked to say that he still enjoyed milking a cow once in a while but only one and not every day or even every month.

Lynn was relieved of his milking duties in 1926 when Otis Brown sold his herd to A. B. Bolden and opened a nine-hole golf course. Then Lynn had other duties. He mowed with a thirty-six-inch-reel mower pulled by a horse named Mabel, picked up balls that were lost among the trees, sold tickets, and managed a concession stand. The course was open to the public for fifty cents. Many of the leading businessmen in town played regularly. According to Lynn Brown, Charles Schulze Jr. played often and lost many balls by hitting the trees. He also noted that Otis Brown, Hoot Grider, and Pat Cunningham always played the entire course with a putter.

In 1928, Otis Brown built three Tudor-style houses on Sowers Road and moved into one of them with his family. In August 2002 one of these houses at 1300 West Pioneer was facing demolition to make room for expansion of a Sonic Drive-in when the City Council authorized the use of Community Development Block Grant funds to relocate and rehabilitate it. It was moved into the Heritage District on Hastings Street between Third and Fourth Streets. One of those three Tudor-style houses is still in use on Pioneer Drive.

Eugene and Mary Beaufford, seen here in their wedding portrait, were married a year before the founding of Irving. Their first house was northeast of Irving at what is now Highway 183 and Britain Road. They moved into "town" in 1919. Courtesy Betty Bessler

Irving people were accustomed to making their own entertainment in the many ways that they interacted. In 1919, Louis DeHaes brought entertainment from the outside world in the form of movies. He set up a simple open-air structure with a facade and screen on the east side of North Main. The projector was on a post high in the air and under it was a piano where a fellow named Kelly McCrory played lively music to help dramatize the silent movies. The movies were popular on Saturday evenings. Then Mr. DeHaes had a visit from some unidentified members of the Ku Klux Klan. The Klan was enjoying a period of arrogant prejudice aimed in many directions. They were thriving on intimidation while hiding in their sheets and hoods. In this case they told DeHaes that they didn't want any Catholic movies in town. He closed his movie, although he probably would have been strongly supported by the visible community. There was suspicion that the hooded men were intruders from another area. The national "imperial wizard" was a Dallas dentist.

In 1920, Alfred Earnest Randle, who had been a frogman in World War I, came to the Irving area instead of returning to his home in England. He started working at the Stovall Dairy and was soon involved in community activities. Although Germans had recently been his enemy in the war, he courted Adina Gebert and married her. She was the daughter of Emil Gebert who had established the only German-speaking Baptist Church in the county near his home. His farm was northwest of town on either side of what later became Beltline Road with what is now Finley Road along the northern boundary. Rochelle Road now runs through what would have been about the middle of this farm. The original buildings were cleared in 1961, by Fox and Jacobs, for a residential subdivision.

Mahala Cate Lucas Williams; Henry, Doug, Charlie, and Jack Lucas; and Mary Etta Williams Roberts. Mahala was mother to the Lucas brothers and to a later Williams family, including Mary Etta who married Dr. John Roberts and was Dr. Joe Roberts' mother. This picture was in Irving after they moved from a farm, which later became part of the Dallas/Fort Worth Airport. Irving Heritage Society collection

In the period after World War I, social and economic changes were affecting the way of life in the whole country. In 1920 two amendments to the U.S. Constitution became the law of the land. The Eighteenth Amendment implemented Prohibition. and the Nineteenth Amendment granted women the right to vote. The Fourteenth Amendment, passed by Congress in 1866, had defined both citizens and voters as male. The American Equal Rights Association was founded later in the

Netta Brown poses with four of her boys about the time they moved to the dairy west of town. Parrish collection

same year. After many failed attempts, Texas women made some headway fifty years later in 1918 when they gained the right to vote in state party primary elections. Prior to that year all Texans could vote except minors, idiots, imbeciles, felons, paupers, the insane, and women.

The Texas effort to gain voting rights for women began in 1868. The prohibition campaign in Texas began in 1882 and later was joined by the National Woman's Christian Temperance Union. The WCTU was organized because of the belief that saloons dispensing liquor were destroying the family. Members learned to plan political strategy and to lobby. As women ventured into the world beyond their homes and churches, they saw child labor in factories and young boys in prisons with seasoned criminals. Their campaigns helped change these conditions, and they began to see the relationship between social reforms and the right to vote. That's why, in 1888, the state WCTU endorsed the vote for women. They thought women would vote for prohibition and other legislation favorable to families. Many women became suffragists because of their interest in prohibition.

The group of businessmen who organized the Anti-Saloon League provided the strength that finally resulted in passage of the Prohibition amendment. Saloonkeepers were perceived to have too much political power. The Anti-Saloon League was run like a business. It brought pressure on candidates to support prohibition.

In Irving the conditions that existed in big cities were not in evidence. If a man drank too much and became obnoxious in a public place, he was handled by as many men as it took to subdue and impress him. And, of course, he was branded and talked about in town. There were no taverns or saloons in Irving at that time. Many of the families in the area came from cultures that enjoyed wine and beer, and they made and stored their own supply. There were large and small vineyards and expertise in winemaking was common. A mature attitude with regard to its use was also common. Life revolved around family, church, and school.

In the churches and in the garden clubs, women in Irving talked about the positive effect that the vote for women could have on politics and legislation favorable to family and children. They conspired to persuade their husbands, sons, male relatives, and friends, but no strong campaigning can be documented. However, the performance of Texas women when legislation was passed in June of 1918 giving them the right to vote in state party primary elections is documented. They had only seventeen days to register to vote in the July primary and in those few days 386,000 women registered. They are credited with winning the Democratic nomination for William Hobby, who had helped push through the legislation. He went on to win the race for governor of Texas. Governor Ferguson, who lost the nomination, had been a strong opponent of the vote for women. Texas was the ninth state and the first in the South to ratify the Nineteenth Amendment. On August 26, 1920, final ratification gave women the right to vote in national elections.

The Eighteenth Amendment went into effect in January of 1920. It prohibited the manufacture, sale, transportation, importation, and exportation of intoxicating liquor for beverage purposes. The Volstead Act further defined the terms, provided for licensing and exemptions for medical and religious purposes, and assigned enforcement to the Commissioner of Internal Revenue. Congress never voted enough money for more than token enforcement of the Volstead Act. The Commissioner of Internal Revenue rarely had more than two thousand agents to police the entire country. They were hopelessly outnumbered by better organized and better equipped outlaws who were profiting from the liquor trade.

About this time a different kind of interest in Irving was evolving. People already living in Dallas and people moving into the area to work in offices or industrial plants began noticing the advantages of the Irving area. There was a yearning for space. A little place in the country with a relatively easy commute to jobs in the city of Dallas seemed very desirable. It also became fashionable for those who could afford it to have recreational "places" in the country. The Irving area with good location, productive soil, mature trees, and readily available water was ideal. The only drawback was the lack of good roads, but for those who worked in the cities the train offered a regular schedule for easy commuting. This trend toward smaller tract country homes or recreational second homes accounted for much of the development in Irving that began in the twenties.

R. L. and Virginia Fulton were out motoring in their Model T early in 1921. Since his return from Army service in World War I, they had lived and worked in Dallas. Now they were looking for a place in the country, although neither of them had experience in country living. They happened upon Irving, found a place that appealed to them, and bought 35 acres. This was a part of 160 acres owned by Frank LaNotte in the southwest part of the Irving area. It was on a lane, which later was named Shady Grove Road, near Rogers. LaNotte, one of the early La Reunion Colony members, was retiring from farming and was selling off his property. The R. E. Mitchells later bought part of his land west of the Fultons. These two sales were significant because of the involvement of the buyers in the way the area developed.

In an article, which was reprinted in the *Daily News Texan* on April 16, 1964, Mr. Fulton described Irving in the early 1920s: "The whole countryside was a mass of truck gardens, fruit farms, poultry farms and dairy farms. Most home sites were five or more acres. . . . Going to Dallas was not a treat." He described the road via the river bottom through part of West Dallas as "rutty" and very slick in wet weather. Repeating what others had said, he related that when the river overflowed, passage to Dallas was impossible and Irving was often waterbound for days. He

This picture, taken in 2002, shows the original Fulton house on Shady Grove Road in good condition after eighty years. The street beside it is named Fulton Drive.

wrote: "Everybody in this part of Dallas County had to work hard to make a living. But they got a heap of joy out of living."

Virginia Fulton, in an interview conducted by Estelle Bates and Mildred Eigenbrot, discussed her house on what is now Shady Grove Road and Fulton Drive. She said they borrowed twenty-five hundred dollars from a bank in Dallas and had a frame cottage built, complete with bath. They had a septic tank and a windmill which pumped water up the hill to an overhead storage tank. She said bathrooms were scarce. Most people used No. 3 washtubs brought into the kitchen for bathing and they carried buckets of water from the well outside. Word got around that the Fultons had a bathroom, which prompted people to come up to the porch where they often sat on Sunday afternoons and say "we want to see your bathroom."

The Fulton house, which was outside of the corporate limits of Irving, was not the first to have a bathroom. The C. P. Schulze and Fred Joffre houses were equipped earlier. Louise Baker, adopted daughter of Fred and Minnie Joffre, told Dr. Clay Gilbert that when friends visited the Joffre house, the first room they wanted to see was the bathroom. Water was pumped from a well next door that belonged to C. P. Schulze. Electric lights were powered by a Delco system.

Individual lighting systems and pipes from wells were becoming popular. Major Robinson had been the first to install a lighting system in a downtown store, and Philip Lively was the first to pipe water from the public well. He owned and operated the Lively Cotton Gin and he was mayor from 1919 to 1921. Mayor Lively called a meeting of the Commissioners on November 15, 1920, for the purpose of taking over the public well and waterworks system. By that time several pipes were carrying water to businesses in town and a gasoline engine powered the pump on the well. It had become obvious that the town needed an organized public waterworks and that no private company was about to ask for the job without public support. No doubt this had already been discussed among the interested parties, because the minutes of the meeting were extremely short: "The citizens of Irving agreed to give all their rights of the well and tank and also all the pipe in all of the streets to the City of Irving. This was accepted by the Commissioners. Orders issued to the Mayor to put the water works into operation." It was easier said than done. The first step was to repair and operate the pump and the tank, and the next step was to organize the effort to expand service. It didn't happen immediately, but at least the intent was publicly confirmed and planning could begin. The first four months after the takeover, the cost of parts and work on the well was $143, which doesn't seem like much unless you consider that the two-year statement of expenditures for all operations of the city totaled $648.

Pipes from the well to nearby buildings had been installed by the business owners they served. The new challenge was to create an organized water system to deliver water throughout the city. But Mayor Lively didn't have to deal with the mandate to "put the waterworks into operation." It was election time again and W. F. Miller was elected in 1921. The first report of town finances after the election showed a balance of $85 in the Irving State Bank. C. E. Range was appointed "Town Marshal, Tax Collector, and Tax Assessor." His salary for these three responsibilities was set at $5.00 per month. The question of developing a waterworks continued to be a major issue. At a called meeting of the Town Council on September 27, 1922, the minutes reveal: "An order was passed agreeing to pay the expense of C. G. Miller to visit the town of Garland to investigate the Water Works System of Garland and to ascertain any other information that would be beneficial to the Town of Irving in erecting a system of waterworks, which is now a question before the citizenship."

Fletcher Miller resigned before his term was finished. M. R. Price was appointed and then elected but he resigned before completing his term. C. G. Miller was appointed in 1924 and then was elected to two more terms. The Dallas County/Irving Fresh Water District No. 5 was established with the power to tax. Tom Pemberton was appointed to be the first water commissioner.

After much discussion and investigation he hired the engineering firm of Koch and Fowler to install a water system and fireplugs. An office building for the water district was constructed on Second Street at Jefferson in front of a new water tower. The old water well with its wooden tower was removed from the intersection of Main and First Streets when the new well and steel tower was in place.

Before the order to create a waterworks, the government in Irving had been concerned with taxes and controls like a twelve-mile-per-hour speed limit, mandatory regular cleaning of outhouses, and restrictions on animals running loose in town. The main general service had been grading and some graveling of roads. The fundamental service of fire protection did not begin with city government, and it was many years before it became a city department. R. V. Leach bought the Miller Duckworth building and business in 1921, and he hosted the organizational meeting of the Volunteer Fire Department. Our best source of information about the Fire Department is the *Irving Fire Department, Commemorative Edition* by Lieutenant Tommy Burgess and the Irving Fire Fighters Association, which can be found in the Genealogy Department of the Central Library. At the first meeting R. V. Leach was elected chief, and W. D. Hodges was hired as night fireguard for the cotton yard at fifty cents a night. He was still in high school.

Chaney Miller was mayor for a second time from 1924 to 1927.

Prior to this meeting fires were fought by neighbors who came running with whatever resources they had. It was probably the question of fire insurance that prompted the organization of volunteers. The Texas Fire Insurance Board decided Irving needed twenty volunteers for fire protection. Twenty men known as the "bucket brigade" became the first Irving Fire Association. The men elected their leaders and eventually had a constitution and bylaws. The city government did not assume responsibility for a Fire Department until the 1950s. The volunteer fire association was well organized with dedicated men who served without pay and spent time and energy raising money for equipment. According to the source referenced above: "The first fire equipment . . . was a four-wheeled pull cart on which they mounted a hand-operated pump with a 20-gallon water barrel. They also had a few buckets, brooms, gunnysacks, a small ladder, and an axe. The cart was stored in a downtown garage donated to the volunteers."

Probably the wake-up call that prompted the organization of a volunteer fire association was a fire at the primary school in February 1920. Speculation was that it was caused by a hot coal that fell on the floor from one of the coal-burning stoves. According to School Board records, the Hartford Fire Insurance Company paid a $1,500 claim, and that's likely what caused the edict from the Texas Fire Insurance Board.

In 1926 the volunteers bought their first motorized equipment. It was a 1919 Model T Ford truck. Bill Swain recently related that his father Harry Swain sold them the truck and helped convert it to a fire truck. They built a wooden bed with side steps for the men to stand on. The volunteers added a pressure pump, water barrel, hose, buckets, brooms, ladder, an axe, and a nozzle borrowed from a Dallas fireman. The truck had solid rubber tires, two gears, and a top speed of twenty-five miles per hour. They held a barbecue to pay for the truck. On its first run they ran into a pile of sand and almost everything on the bed fell off. The men threw it all back on the truck and went on to the fire.

Work on the water system was progressing and fireplugs were an important part of the system. Tom Pemberton went to Texas A&M Fire School to learn how to use the new fireplugs. Obviously fireplugs were useless without a proper fire hose. The city didn't have enough money to buy a fire hose so, Mayor Miller took a risk for the city and for his own reputation when he went to the Irving State Bank and borrowed $500 in the name of the city to buy a fire hose and other equipment. Minutes of the Commission show that the purchase of a hose, two nozzles, a hose

The Water District built offices in front of the new water well and tower. This building, on Second and Jefferson Streets, housed the Volunteer Fire Department. The firemen furnished their own uniforms, held fundraisers to buy the equipment, and elected their officers. In the world of 2003, it's hard to imagine that there was always a waiting list of men wanting to join the volunteers who were on call day and night without pay.

cart, and other necessary apparatus was approved. Naturally there were a few naysayers who pronounced that to be a very reckless thing for the mayor to propose, but most citizens recognized Miller as a man interested in progress and devoted to the welfare of the city. The first building regulations and fire zone rules were established during his term. He had served on the School Board in 1913 when a bond issue to pay for building "Old Red" was brought forward. He had established a successful business right after the founding of the town and had been the second mayor in 1917. Now he was mayor again. Considering his many accomplishments, it is interesting to note that he did not have a formal education. According to his daughter, Lora Mae Anderson, he taught himself to read, studied the dictionary at night, and worked at self-improvement throughout his life. He strongly advised his children and grandchildren to get a complete education.

Ed Caster had been supervisor of the convict camp located in the Trinity River bottoms east of Irving. He oversaw inmates building bridges in four county districts. In 1922 he became deputy sheriff for District 4, which included Irving. In a town without a police force, the sheriff was important. Ed was a native of the Irving area. He had helped his father build a log cabin on their farm near what became Shady Grove and Belt Line. In 1920 he moved his own family to a home in town at Britain and Second Streets. The site was part of the Britain family property. He served on the City Commission and the School Board and was considered to be one of the best deputy sheriffs in Dallas County history.

Another major step forward occurred in 1924 when the Commissioners passed an ordinance granting Texas Power and Light Company an electric light, heat, and power franchise. The terms were accepted in a document dated October 11, 1924, and signed by John W. Carpenter, vice president, and J. E. Van Horn, secretary-treasurer of the company. TP&L proposed to install light wires and to erect no fewer than six streetlights, which they would keep in order with no cost to the Town of Irving. The price of the electric service was to be $2.00 per light per month to be paid by the Town of Irving. Eighteen business owners on First and Main Streets entered into a contract with the city agreeing to pay each month for the lighting of their streets under the city agreement with Texas Power and Light Company. In 1925 the electric service was installed. Expansion to the residential area was inevitable. The first residential service was priced at $2.00 per month.

J. E. Van Horn, who along with John Carpenter signed the electricity agreement with the Town of Irving, bought property and made his home southeast of town where his estate was named Briardale. He raised poultry and rabbits and hosted many large picnics. He and his friends could hunt and fish in the woods and on the Elm Fork of the river east of his home. The area that was the Briardale Estate is now built up with houses but Van Horn Street at the top of the hill is a reminder of the people who lived there in the 1920s and 1930s and took part in the development and social life of Irving. Two of the three original family homes are still on the east side of Van Horn Street. His daughter's house at 718 was removed in 1997 to make way for new construction, but the huge granite birdbath which was hauled in on a TP&L truck remains in the backyard of the new house, and the J. E. Van Horn house stands at 716.

In 1928 John Carpenter bought land north of the town of Irving and established a ranch, which he named Hackberry Creek Ranch. Mrs. Carpenter, noting the rolling hills of the terrain, called it "El Ranchito de Las Colinas." The Carpenters had a house on one of those little hills and also maintained their home in Highland Park. As they bought more land to enlarge the ranch, Mr. Carpenter was engaging in many business enterprises including Lone Star Steel, Southland Life Insurance, major regional utility companies, and streetcar companies. He also operated several commercial farms and ranches. He built the Southland Center in Dallas. At the ranchito there was no hint of what Las Colinas would eventually become.

In September of 1925 an ordinance was passed "to regulate the construction, alteration, maintenance, repair and removal of buildings within the Town of Irving, Texas, and prescribing penalties for violations." It was comprehensive and covered all of the territory within the corporate limits of the city. This was the beginning of the numerous regulations adopted through the years to encourage, control, and restrict development in the city.

Through the 1920s we have to be first impressed with the community of effort that supported improvements and enhanced living conditions. As the little government took on more responsi-

At the junction of the dirt road coming up from Singleton and the road to Twin Wells and Irving, a sign points to the Twin Wells Lumber Yard. Courtesy Harwood Hinton

bilities, the old sense of every person's civic and personal responsibility did not diminish.

The Fultons thought that the one thing that was holding Irving back was the lack of good roads. What later became Shady Grove Road connected to a thirty-foot gravel road from the Singleton Boulevard Bridge through the bottom land. At the top of the hill it took a westerly direction to Meyers Road where the gravel road ended. The Fulton home was farther west. According to Mrs. Fulton, in an interview with Estelle Bates, County Commissioner Vernon Singleton told them that if they would get the right of way, he would have the road paved. The Fultons and Walter Bushear went out and asked landowners to donate right of way. They secured donations to make a sixty-foot right of way from Singleton Road to the Shady Grove community near the county line. The Commissioner kept his word, and the first thirty-foot paved road completely through Irving was named Shady Grove Road. The road is relatively straight except for "county line bend" where the owner just couldn't give up a large pecan tree in his yard. Dr. Gilbert had a farm on the other side of the dirt road and donated the needed right of way.

If you entered from the southeast in 1927, the first stop was likely to be the Hinton Twin Wells Store where general merchandise, refreshments like Coca-Cola, and gasoline were available. They sold the "New and Better Texaco Gasoline" at seventeen cents a gallon.

The Irving Poultry Association was the first successful community civic organization. It had more than a hundred members from the town of Irving and adjacent communities. The group had many community programs. Their main discussions centered around the need to improve the road to Dallas and to obtain other routes to Irving. The poultry men were prospering. Poultry shows were held often with many awards of prizes and ribbons. The average poultry farm had thousands of laying hens and fryers. Much of the demand was created by a growth of chicken gardens in Dallas where big nightly gatherings featured chicken fried dinners served with beer and liquor. These "chicken gardens" were carefully organized to circumvent the Prohibition law. While the Irving poultry farms were supplying Dallas chicken gardens with food, the Irving Poultry Association was meeting often in the homes of members. According to Robert Fulton: "Most of the members brewed their own beer or distilled their own liquor, but if they ever ran low they knew where to find the major bootleggers which abounded in both the Dallas and Tarrant County areas." The Irving area was not a moneymaking market for bootleggers since there were no saloons before Prohibition and no speakeasies during the Roaring Twenties. The action was in larger cities.

Teachers were very carefully watched. When Vera Haley, who later became Mrs. C. C. Anderson, began her career in 1927, she signed the standard contract that required teachers to use judgement and decorum in selecting companions, to reside in the district during school days and at least two weekends out of each month, and to "observe Monday through Thursday night exclusive for preparation of schoolwork. That is, to refrain from keeping company with young men and going to social functions on those nights and minimize the occasions by asking permission of the Board to make exceptions to these rules." By signing the contract, teachers also agreed "to give the board my resignation when in their opinion I become unfit to perform adequately my duties."

The Haley sisters, Vera, Bess, and Flora, were known, respected, and even loved by generations of Irving school children. Vera didn't marry C. C. Anderson until after the rule prohibiting married women from teaching had been deleted, but her older sisters, Mrs. Bess Parker and Mrs. Flora Easter had to interrupt their careers when they married. Courtesy Sue Haley Huffman

Irving citizens were always active and enthusiastic participants in politics, and it was said that no county office candidate tabulated his votes until the votes of this area were included. One of the favorite stories passed down from the 1920s is that banker A. P. Mauk announced early that there would be a candidates' speaking in front of the bank. He had a stand set up with a keg of water for the speakers. As he was about to begin, a large truck backed up on the other side of

the intersection in front of Hoosiers Drugstore. Lights flashed and an announcer shouted that a candidates' speaking was about to begin. The crowd shifted to the southwest corner where Dr. John Haley was in charge.

As the period known as the Roaring Twenties was ending, the little town of Irving still revolved mostly around family, church, and school. But young people were leaving the farm for jobs. More people were commuting to Dallas. They were dancing to jazz and ragtime music. Young women bobbed their hair and dresses were shorter.

In 1929, Lorene Lucas was working for a stockbroker in Dallas when the stock market crashed on "Black Tuesday." She said they worked almost all night.

According to Lorene Lucas Looper, this new 1929 Model A Ford was the "snazziest thing you ever saw." It was baby blue with yellow trim, and Lorene had a dress in those colors to match it. She and her brothers, Howard and Ray, are standing beside the car in front of the family home at 221 South Jefferson. Courtesy Lorene Looper

The intersection of First and Main, where the old well and tower had stood, was not congested with traffic on weekdays in 1930. Saturday was a busy day for the drugstore on the left, and the bank on the right.

Chapter 4

Testing and Building Character

The crash of the stock market took the nation by surprise. The popular belief was that the country was moving toward prosperity. Campaigning for president in 1928, Herbert Hoover declared: "We are nearer to the final triumph over poverty than ever before in the history of any land. The poorhouse is vanishing from among us. . . . We are in sight of the day when poverty will be banished from the nation." Soon after he was elected, the stock market crash and the ensuing Depression devastated most of the country. Instead of riding the wave of prosperity, his entire term in office was spent trying to deal with economic crisis and the dismal failure of Prohibition to accomplish its intended result.

This crowd, mostly composed of Beaufford and DeHaes women and perhaps out for a stroll, pauses for a snapshot on a footbridge over a creek. Agnes Beaufford is sitting on the rail on the left and Theo, Lucy, and Theresa DeHaes are on the right. Lurlene Beaufford Evans

Edgar Brown, in his excellent history of the Estelle community, recalls such sayings as "Hoover pockets" (pockets with holes) and "Hoover steaks" (rabbit). He recalls: "Jobs were scarce. Farm labor was $1.00 per day for 12 hours. Cotton pickers were paid 40 to 50 cents per 100 pounds. . . . We did not have radio or TV telling us that we were underprivileged. We accepted the times and tried to make do with what we had."

The priority for Irving mayor Dr. John Haley (1927–1932) was sanitation. The minutes of the Town Commission meeting on September 10, 1930, record "sufficient interest and apparent necessity for the installation of sewerage." The mayor was empowered to contract with engineers to supervise the project when funds were available. He was also authorized to employ an attorney to handle all legal matters pertaining to a bond election for a fee not over $40. If the bond issue failed, the attorney fee would be $20. The October election approved $20,000 in bonds to build a sewer system and disposal plant. The disposal plant was south of the town east of Delaware Creek and just north of Shady Grove Road. Many years later this was the location of the first Senior Citizens Center. Mayor Haley proposed a small increase in the city tax rate to pay the upkeep and operating costs of the system. The total city property value on the 1931 tax roll was $310,000, with a tax rate of twenty-five cents per hundred-dollar valuation.

Major Robinson owned several properties in the town when he retired from his drug business and his building became Shepherds Café. R. J. Byrd, who also owned several buildings, bought the drug business inventory and moved it to the brick building on the southwest corner of the same intersection. The drugstore on that corner was a special place for the school crowd during the 1930s and 1940s. It had a soda fountain and was the first air-conditioned store. Jerald Cannon said he worked there as a soda jerk for $20 a week. Mr. Broach, the pharmacist, and his wife Clara are remembered as favorite managers.

Delaware Creek still defined the western boundary of town in 1931 when C. P. Schulze Sr. bought almost a hundred acres west of the creek. He announced his intent to make it into the Highland Park of Irving with building restrictions for better-type residences. The addition

Robert Fulton had this map produced for the *Irving News* in 1937. The portion of Schulze Park that was developed by the City is identified. Except for the park area, Delaware Creek on the west, and Britain Road on the east still defined the city limits, but the southern boundary had been extended to Sixth Street and the northern boundary was Lively Street. Businesses in the original town are clearly depicted. The buildings on the school campus, the church buildings, and even the fireplugs are located on the map.

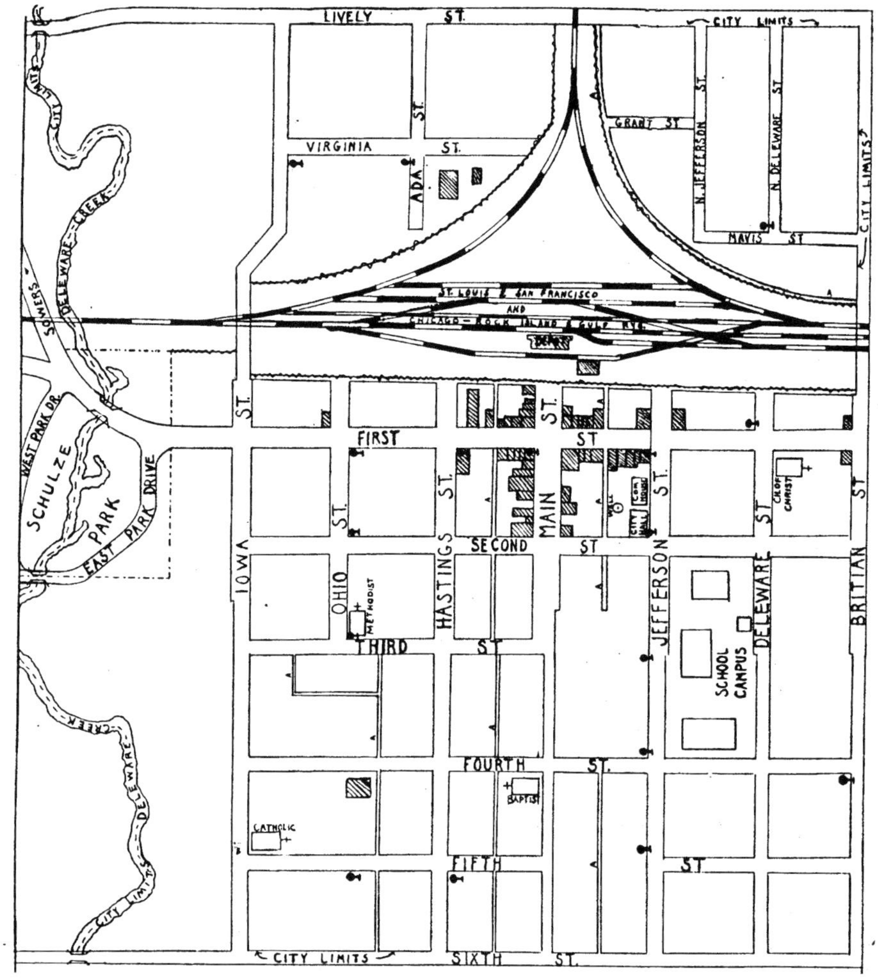

John Brandenburg came to the bank in Irving at a critical time, and gained the trust and respect of the directors and the depositors. Courtesy Eleanor Corry Bell

would have gas, water, lights, and perhaps even sewerage. This was outside the city limits, which meant that the developer would pay all costs of streets and extension of services. Utility rates would be higher for the consumer. First Street (later Irving Boulevard) ended at Delaware Creek. West of the creek the road turned north, crossed the railroad tracks, and turned again to follow a northwesterly path to the Sowers community.

In 1933, C. P. and Virginia Schulze gave the City about 6.5 acres of land along the banks of Delaware Creek from the railroad right of way to a point south of Second Street for a park to be named Schulze Park. The City agreed to develop the land and maintain it as a park. The deed to the property was to be held in escrow until December 31, 1935, when if the terms of the agreement were not met, the land would revert to the donors.

December 22, 1933, the *Irving News* reported plans for lakes, footbridges, tennis courts, a rose garden, and an athletic field. The creek would be cleaned and straightened. It was estimated that the project would need fifty men working all year and would cost $10,000. January 5, 1934, the same newspaper reported that a footbridge and ornamental rock fences were installed. The project was never completed. Several men have told us that as boys they gathered there for sleep-outs on Friday nights. If there was rain, the creek would overflow Irving Boulevard and they would offer to push stalled cars out for a quarter. Today Schulze Street, beginning west of Delaware Creek south of Second Street and turning west to cross MacArthur and end at Rogers is evidence of this attempt to create an elaborate park. As part of the 2003 centennial celebration the portion of the creek between Second and Sixth Streets is being improved and a park honoring Irving pioneers is being created. St. Lukes Church and Parochial School are located at the intersection of Schulze and MacArthur. This became the third location of St. Lukes Church when the Schulze family donated the land on what was then Perch Hill Road.

The hometown bank weathered the storm that caused bank failures nationwide. By 1933 millions of Americans had lost their life savings. Eleven thousand of the twenty-five thousand banks in the nation had failed, and panic was causing people to withdraw their money from solvent banks. In Irving, Dr. D. W. Gilbert, who had followed Judge Riddle as president of the bank, died in 1930 and was widely mourned by those who loved and admired him as their physician and as a civic leader. But confidence in the integrity of the bank continued through the services of two of his sons, attorney/banker William B. Gilbert and Dr. Franklin M. Gilbert, as president and director. John Brandenburg had joined A. P. Mauk on the staff in 1929 and quickly established ties to the community. He was a mainstay of the bank for forty-six years. The owners of the stock and the directors of the bank were townspeople. Every depositor knew and was known by the owners, directors, and staff of the bank. In Irving there was no panic-driven rush to withdraw funds and the bank remained solvent. On January 1, 1934, it became an official member of the Federal Deposit Insurance Corporation, and bank deposits up to $2,500 were guaranteed by the federal government.

Throughout the 1930s the city of Irving continued to grow and build. The "in town" population increased from 731 to 1,089. In 1930 Bowen Motor Coaches established bus service. Southwest Telephone got permission from the Town Council to raise rates. Individual service increased to $2.25 per month. A two-party line was $2.00, wall extension 50 cents, desk extension 75 cents.

In 1931 the city bought the first parkland from A. G. Senter, Robert Fulton began publishing the *Irving News*, and Dallas County Agricultural Agent A. B. Jolly reported that there were more and larger dairy herds in the Irving area than in any other part of the county. Herds in this northwest section of Dallas County were producing an average of more than fifteen thousand gallons of milk daily. The commercial dairies in Irving had their own bottle sterilizing plants and most of them had electrical cooling systems. The Dallas County Herd Improvement Association records indicated that some of the leading high-test cows were in the herds of the Irving area. One of the Gilbert Brothers Dairy cows, Queen 1st, had been a high-test cow for butter every month throughout the testing period.

In 1930, more than twenty years after the Levee District had been created, the project to move the Trinity River and contain it with levees was accomplished and ten thousand acres of bottom land was reclaimed. Through the early years the erratic river was sometimes a threat to life and property and often a barrier between Irving and Dallas, but it was also an amenity. It was a place to fish and hunt. Families and church groups gathered for fish fries and overnight camping. Churches baptized and weddings were performed on the banks of the river. Now both the Elm Fork and the West Fork were closer to Irving, and most people were excited and pleased to have the levee and a bridge connected to a road through the reclaimed bottom land and directly into downtown Dallas. The Historic Marker on the Shady Grove Road Bridge indicates that it was built in 1931 and that it was 1,778 feet long with a Parker pony truss design of the main span.

Thousands of men had been working to change the channel of the river and build levees to contain it. With the task completed, they were without jobs when the nationwide economic Depression was destroying the

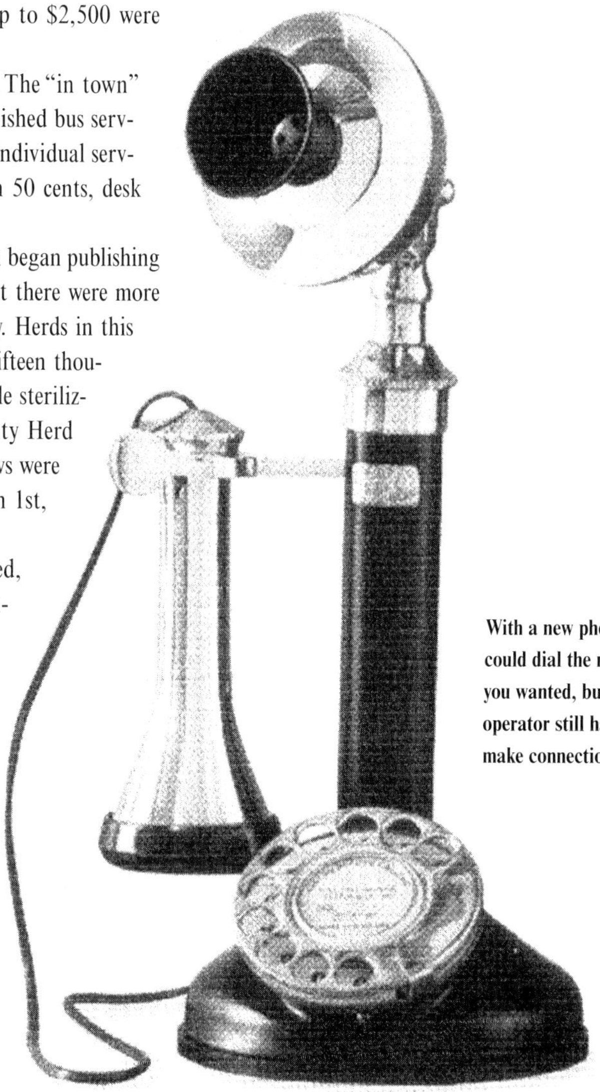

With a new phone you could dial the number you wanted, but an operator still had to make connections.

When the channel of the river was moved west, the Elm Fork was closer to Irving, and land that had been subject to flooding was protected by the levee making development of an industrial district possible. Dallas County Soil Map

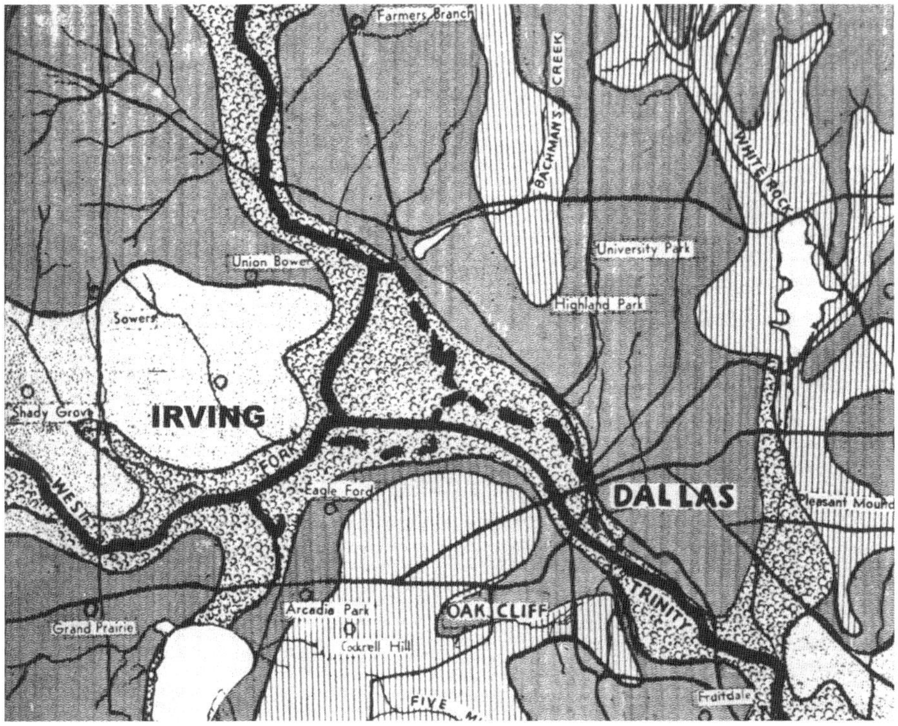

J. E. Van Horn could hunt on the river behind his home in Southeast Irving. Courtesy Valerie Weiss

job market. Some of these men with their families lived in the Irving area. They were desperately trying to survive by doing whatever they could. West Texas became the Dust Bowl, and some of the dislocated farmers migrated to the Dallas area looking for some way to survive. They were the inspiration for the popular Woody Guthrie song, "So Long, It's Been Good to Know You."

The Board of Supervisors, named to manage construction of the levees, planned to develop the reclaimed land as an industrial district to generate funds for paying off the bonds. Leslie Allison Stemmons from Dallas and E. P. Harwell from Tulsa, Oklahoma, and several other businessmen formed the Industrial Properties Corporation to accomplish the goal, but the economy caused that plan to be postponed. There were already cotton farms in the bottom lands. One had been leased for a convict camp, which the city founders had passed through on their first visit and where later Ed Caster supervised inmates who helped build bridges. Now the convict camp was gone and cotton farms were protected by the levee. Harwell owned several of the farms. The best known, called Trinity Farms, had been the convict camp, and now there were numerous small houses where workers lived. Some of them migrated with the work seasons.

In 1931, Earlie Mae Wheeler started teaching in the Norwood School, a segregated Negro school, on Trinity Farms property. She was hired by Superintendent Johnston and paid by the Irving School District, although the property was not in Irving. In an unpublished essay titled "My Life Story," written in her seventy-fifth year, Mrs. Wheeler described her experiences when as a young Earlie Mae Collins she arrived at Trinity Farms, met some parents, and found a place to live. On the first day of school, sixty-eight children and their parents came to the one-room school. The children, who were first through seventh graders, didn't know about graduation. Many didn't stay in one place long enough to graduate. In her second year they were looking forward to a seventh grade graduation. They would be the first in the history of the school to graduate from seventh grade. The adults were anxious to learn to read and write, so she taught free adult classes at night. The Red Cross donated food, and parents cooked the noon meal and brought it to the school. They were enthusiastic and grateful for the education of their children

From the time Irving was founded through the 1940s, the Forks of the river provided more pleasures than pain, even if they did sometimes rise and cut off passage to Dallas. Irving Archives

who came to school well behaved and eager to learn.

Earlie Collins married Fred Wheeler in 1938. In 1946 the farm was sold for industrial development, and the school was discontinued. She recalled her fifteen years at Trinity Farms as happy years spent with people she was able to help, and she was proud that many of the farm children earned college degrees and some became teachers. In 1949 she began teaching at Sowers No. 2 and spent summers in college improving her own education, which prepared her for the next three decades of teaching. She was the first black teacher hired by the Irving district after school segregation ended.

It should be noted that segregation laws and practices did not keep minorities from organizing. The Dallas Negro Chamber of Commerce (later the Black Chamber of Commerce) was organized in 1925. In his account of an interview with Odessa Trigg King, who grew up in the Bear Creek Community, Jon Halsey quotes her as saying: "I learned truthfulness from my grandparents and my mother taught us well how to get along with the white folks . . . 'Just respect 'em and then ignore 'em,' she'd tell us. . . ."

The quest for better roads was the initial and central reason for the formation of the Irving Northwest Dallas County Civic Organization in April 1931. There were about two hundred members from the area of Dallas County between the Elm and West Forks of the Trinity River. Dallas County was planning a road program for the next ten years, and W. B. Gilbert who was elected president of the group, said, "For the past ten years Irving and northwest Dallas County has been slighted. . . . Our roads are bad and getting worse. We believe it is time for our citizenry to bind themselves together for concerted action."

Dr. John Haley died in February 1932, and Dr. F. M. Gilbert was appointed to complete the term as mayor. He was then elected two more times and served until 1937.

By 1932 there was discussion of a Dallas/Fort Worth Master Plan. The February 19, 1932 edition of the *Irving News* reported articles in both Dallas and Fort Worth newspapers promoting the idea that the two sister cities should consider their destiny as a single great city with a unity of purpose, a single executive, and a single council of businessmen to control the entire area of the two counties. The editor asserted: "With this co-ordination of purpose and plans in the development of both great cities of North Texas, to include Irving, we are having another thing of great magnitude thrust into our lap."

Three months later, in May 1932, a group of thirty-five Irving businessmen got together and founded the Irving Chamber of Commerce to promote the specific interests of Irving. L. L. Griswold was elected president. Records in the Chamber office indicate that Claude Chambers was the main spokesman for the organization. He said, "We knew the only way to get any attention was to form our own Chamber." The intent was not to supplant but to supplement the existing Irving Northwest Dallas County Civic Organization. Two years later Mr. Chambers didn't live in Irving. He was an elected member of the City Commission, but he had to resign because he built and moved into a house at 410 Second Street that was one door east of Britain. The city limit was Britain Street.

The campaign for roads was intense with appeals to the County Commissioners, the Texas Highway Commission, and the legislature for help. Bowen Motor coaches took large delegations to Austin to plead the case for Irving. Irving promoters already had experience in organizing groups to encourage favors. They knew Irving had the best cows, and they wanted Cow Day with all of the activities and judging to be held in Irving. Cow Day had been located in Carrollton after a large delegation called on the county agent. Irving organized and went calling.

In an interview recorded in the Irving Archives, Virginia Fulton talked about the years of stock shows in Irving. She said that County Agricultural Agent A. B. Jolly would bring in judges from A& M College, and on the mornings of the shows, John Carpenter would send his two boys, John and Ben, with a stock loader to go out and bring in bulls and cows and unload them on the town lot where the show was held. At noon she would take John, Ben, and Mr. Jolly to the hotel where Mrs. Hamm served them in the dining room.

Livestock and poultry shows of all kinds continued to be popular in Irving with various types of awards. The March 31, 1939 edition of the Irving newspaper reported the Dairy Day prizes. The first premium was one quart of Soyocide Livestock Spray.

Robert "Steamboat" Fulton and his wife Virginia used the *Irving News*, which they founded in 1931, to promote numerous projects during the Depression years. The first community Christmas celebration complete with a Christmas tree was held on Main Street. The civic groups and churches joined in the preparations. Volunteers gathered donations of fruit and candy and gifts and filled little stockings for the children. Men built a platform with lumber loaned by the Irving Lumber Company. Albert Farine donated a tree, and the Texas Power and Light Company brought it in and set it up. A volunteer fireman dressed as Santa Claus rode in on a Bowen bus with his pack. An announcement was made that he was at Sowers and on his way in. Then the bus driver sounded the horn about a block away, and children ran for the corner and thronged the bus. When Santa Claus was able to get to the platform, the noisy crowd was quieted for a prayer. There was exuberant singing and firecrackers before the gifts were distributed. It was the only Christmas some people had that year.

A community Christmas tree on Main Street was a tradition for many years. The city still has a tree-lighting ceremony each year on the east side of City Hall. That first community Christmas was in the depths of the Depression. Jobs were scarce, businesses failed, prices for farm crops were low, and many farmers experienced crop failures caused by weather conditions and pest invasions.

The truck farmers in the area south of town had some advantage with the soil makeup, available water, and smaller tracts of land. They were already living according to the advice circulated by the Irving Chick Hatchery Feed Store in 1931:

The cow, the sow and the hen are the foundation upon which independence and prosperity for the farmer must be built. Even during the past year, when prices for milk, butterfat, pork, eggs and poultry have been abnormally low, it has still been possible to make a profit on products of these essential farm animals. You can't say as much for cotton or wheat or oats. And don't forget that the cow, the sow and the hen enable you to live at home, providing good food for your family and bringing you a cash income from marketing your surplus. Regardless of how much cotton you produce, if you can't sell it you can't eat it.

The Norwood School, where Earlie Mae Wheeler began her teaching career, was located in the reclaimed area east of Irving that eventually became an industrial district. Norwood Street ends at Irving Boulevard in Dallas. Irving Archives

Dallas, the first rail crossroads in Texas, was a transportation hub connected to the nation's markets. It already had John Armstrong's meat packing plant backed by Philip Armour and was a center for cotton exchange and finance before the Depression. It was at the heart of the cotton belt and strategically located in relation to the five major oil producing fields in Texas. September 8, 1930, "Dad" Joiner brought in the first producing well in the massive East Texas oil field. Banks were farsighted in making loans on cotton still in the fields and later taking proven underground oil reserves as collateral. A directory published by the Dallas Chamber of Commerce in

Mrs. Wheeler with her class at Sowers No. 2 School west of Irving. Irving Archives

This chicken house and rabbit hutches on the Van Horn estate were typical of those on many homesites in Irving during the 1930s and 1940s. Courtesy Valerie Weiss

August 1932 listed 787 companies related to the oil business. Cattle, cotton, and oil barons established homes in Dallas not only because of the business climate but because it was a cosmopolitan city with superior literary and arts institutions.

In 1921 the twenty-nine-story Magnolia Petroleum Building became the tallest building west of the Mississippi. In 1934 the largest revolving neon sign in the world was placed on top of the building in honor of the American Petroleum Institute meeting in Dallas. It depicted Pegasus, winged horse of the Muses, as a symbol of hope.

The textile industry was among those that provided jobs even during the Depression. By the late 1930s, it employed some seven hundred workers in Dallas, and more than ten million yards of fabric were produced annually. The apparel industry was growing with ready-to-wear factories where numerous women were employed. Adah Story Tillery, according to her daughter Martha Seeber, worked as a seamstress for L&L Manufacturing from 1927, when she needed to support her seven children, until she retired in 1972. While the children were growing up, they cooked, cleaned, contributed in whatever way they could, and took care of each other. During World War II, L&L made WAC uniforms. Mrs. Tillery was one of the early commuters from Irving to jobs in Dallas. The commuting trend grew as Irving transitioned from a farming to a bedroom community, and people who worked in Dallas or other cities chose to live in Irving.

Many of the jobs in Irving during the Depression years were a result of the federal programs designed to create jobs and support useful community projects. An article in the Irving newspaper on June 8, 1934, praised the Relief Cannery that was employing fifteen men and women for $3.50 per day which, according to the article, was far better pay than they could get from any commercial institution if they could get employment. The Red Cross provided pressure cookers and cans. Farmers brought in food and received half of it back in canned goods. The Red Cross distributed the other half. One newspaper writer speculated that if twenty-five persons worked, it would mean a payroll of $500 a week in the community which would be a boon to merchants and businessmen.

Several road projects were possible because of help from the WPA. Work on a community building began in November 1935 after a year of planning and promotion by the Irving Felicity Welfare Club, with Esther Hurwitz as president and Vernon Singleton representing Dallas County. The WPA had committed to the project with labor by relief men covered by a $960 federal fund. The Felicity Club had raised $883.92 through their activities and through donations from other clubs and generous citizens. Land which had been part of the Water District property was made available on Jefferson at Second Street. When completed the building had cost $1,852 and it was valued at $3,500. This should not be compared to the cost to restore it in 2003.

This building was a major contribution to the social and business life of Irving. For many years it was the choice meeting place for various groups and for luncheons and dinners. It was described as a new English-type red brick structure with French windows, a large reception room, real log fireplace, kitchen, smoker for men, powder room for women, and ceiling fans.

The Depot was still sometimes called Murphy's Mansion in the 1930s, although John Alexander Murphy, who finished building it in 1904, had been a storeowner for four years and justice of the peace for twelve years since leaving the railroad job. Lee Britain's wife, Kate, was his daughter.

The priority of the Northwest Dallas County Civic Association in 1931 was to ensure that the area got what it needed in the County road plans, including pavement from Irving to connect with Industrial Boulevard through the district created by the Trinity River Reclamation Project. Pictured in front of the water office on Second Street, that later became the first City Hall, are Tom Peters, Lewis Hancock, Dr. Francis Gilbert (small boy), Dr. F. M. Gilbert, W. B. Gilbert (president), Frank Haley (vice president), C. P. Caldwell, W. P. Gandy, T. A. Jasper, R. E. Fulton, James Poplewell, Albert Farine, J. E. Van Horn, R. J. Byrd, Bob Stewart, and C. P. Schulze Sr. This photo was first published in the *Irving News* by R. E. Fulton.

The finishing touches were put on the Community House in late February 1938, and it was dedicated on March 18, 1936, with an elaborate ceremony. W. B. Gilbert, president of Irving State Bank, was master of ceremonies. A. S. Johnston, superintendent of schools, offered the invocation. Gus Thompson presented the Clubhouse on behalf of the WPA. Esther Hurwitz spoke for the Felicity Club and County Commissioner Vernon Singleton represented the sponsor. Dr. F. M. Gilbert, mayor of Irving, accepted the building on behalf of the City.

Hard times didn't keep businesses from coming into Irving. October 10, 1931, the newspaper announced a "NEW THEATER with SOUND PICTURES." A. J. Vineyard was owner and manager. The first sound pictures were on several reels that had to be changed at intervals, and there was a large turntable because the sound was on a big phonograph record. Picture and sound were not always synchronized. The villain might grab his chest and fall in pain before the sound of a shot was heard. The theater was soon sold to W. B. Lawrence and then to E. R. Lawrence who traded up to sound on film. It was still necessary to pause for reel changes. Several people remember a man who stood outside an earlier airdome theater on Main Street on Saturday evenings with a megaphone shouting "Just commencing, just beginning. Hurry, hurry, hurry." There was no roof on that movie house, so the show couldn't start until sundown.

Charlie Lucas retired in 1932 and rented the Banner Mercantile Building to T. C. Hartin and his silent partner Mr. Bracheen. Thad Hartin was starting over after his store in Oak Cliff had failed. He didn't have enough stock for the large building, but he was creative. He put in a partition to create a stockroom, not because he needed it for excess stock but because it made a smaller space to display the stock he had. He draped some of the shelves from top to bottom and used empty boxes on others to keep the few items he had for sale from looking so frugal. His business was successful and soon he had shelves bulging with yard goods, notions, school supplies, and all sorts of dry goods. He sold housedresses for ninety-eight cents, work shirts for fifty-nine cents, and cotton sack ducking for twelve cents a yard. His wife, Ida, and daughter, Tincy Renfrow, began helping. They were the first store to decorate for Christmas and they had the first style show in Irving.

On the other side of Main Street, Mr. Moreland was still selling groceries and general dry goods, the Caldwell Insurance Agency was thriving, and the Irving Drug Company on the southwest corner of Main and First was serving refreshments as well as dispensing drugs and miscellaneous items.

The Hartins, with store hours from dawn to dark, lived in Oak Cliff, which meant they had to travel over the dirt roads through rough areas in darkness. They had reason to be concerned since there was no way to call for help, and this lonely route was near the homes and hideouts of well-known gang members. The newspapers in Dallas, Fort Worth, Denton, and towns across Texas, Oklahoma, and Louisiana reported exploits of several famous outlaws whose families lived in West Dallas. They carried guns, including machine guns, and engaged in shootouts with officers who confronted them. Floyd Hamilton was named public enemy number one, and his brother Raymond accumulated two hundred years of prison sentences.

Clyde Barrow and Bonnie Parker, who were notorious for robbing banks and stores and leading lawmen on wild chases in stolen cars, were often spotted in Irving. When Lynn Brown was a boy working for Mr. Moreland, they came in and bought a few items. After they left, Mr. Moreland told Lynn who they were. James Revier changed a tire for them and realized who they were after Clyde had overpaid him and left. Clyde Barrow was considered one of the nation's most dangerous killers and was pursued by the FBI, Texas Rangers, and sheriffs. People recognized him because of newspaper coverage and "wanted" posters. So why didn't Mr. Moreland and others in Irving call the police? Irving didn't have policemen. Ed Caster was the deputy sheriff covering Irving, but people knew that if they even seemed to recognize, they might be riddled with bullets on the spot.

In 1934 Bonnie Parker wrote a sixteen-verse poem, which is a touching insight into the situation she and Clyde backed themselves into. Four nonsequential verses tell a story:

If a policeman is killed in Dallas,
And they have no clue or guide,
If they can't find a fiend,
They just wipe their slate clean

And hang it on Bonnie and Clyde. . . .
From Irving to West Dallas viaduct
Is known as the Great Divide,
Where the women are kin,
And the men are men,
And they won't "stool" on Bonnie and Clyde. . . .

If they try to act like citizens
And rent them a nice little flat,
About the third night
They're invited to fight
By a sub-guns rat-tat-tat. . . .

They don't think they're too smart or desperate,
They know that the law always wins,
They've been shot at before,
But they do not ignore
That death is the wages of sin.

Ed Caster and Ted Hinton learned that the pair had set up a meeting and would be driving on a road that later became the route of Highway 183. Dallas County Sheriff Smoot Schmid joined the two deputies to wait at a point east of Beltline Road for the outlaws to appear. They were behind a log with rifles poised, but just as they were ready to fire, the car stopped and the gangsters jumped out and began firing machine guns. Nobody was killed but the prey got away. The Stovall Dairy was west of the scene, and Elizabeth Stovall reported that a bullet broke her window and lodged in the wall on the other side of the room. Her daughter Mary Louise, who was later Mary Louise Wadsworth, was at the table with a book propped up against a glass. The bullet took a piece out of the corner of her book.

A related story was recorded by Jerald Cannon in an interview with Helen Widener. He and his sister walked from school in Irving to their home on 360 acres about a half mile west of County Line. Periodically a really nice man and woman stopped and offered them a ride. Just before they crossed Bear Creek, the man would say "this is as far as we go," leaving them to walk on to their house. The couple camped under a big tree covered with grapevine. The children didn't know they were riding with Clyde Barrow and Bonnie Parker, who were finally ambushed and killed by a shower of bullets in Louisiana.

Many books and articles have been written about the gangsters who were like folk heroes of that era. The illusion was that they were living a carefree life of adventure, while most people were working long hard hours just to have the bare necessities. When Lynn Brown, Irving founder's son and future mayor of Irving, saw the gangsters in the Moreland Store, he was working there for $15 a week. Hours were 7 a.m. to 8 p.m. weekdays, 11 p.m. Saturdays, and Sunday morning until church time.

The statistics on unemployment, low wages, long hours at work, and the stories about wearing used clothes, being disciplined with a paddle or a switch, and getting fruit for Christmas instead of toys could make us believe that growing up during the Depression years was miserable. During preparations for celebrating the one-hundred-year birthday of Irving, the people who grew up in those lean years enjoyed getting together to talk about their experiences. Their memories are of fun, adventure, security, and camaraderie. They say they were poor but they didn't know it. They had everything they needed for a happy childhood, and they were rich in the things that mattered.

In 1934, James Revier bought the old Kit building where Ike Story established a store, post office, and home before Irving was founded. He added to what was left of the building for his station and living quarters. He used the Kit symbol on his Conoco sign. Gasoline was ten cents a gallon. Louise Henderson, who provided this picture, was born here.

There was plenty of food because they had gardens and livestock and poultry and they knew how to prepare and cook everything. Eleanor Corry Bell said that when she was ten years old she could kill a chicken, clean it, cut it up, and have it ready for her mother to fry at dinnertime. Most families had a cow for milk, but if they didn't they had a neighbor who did or they got fresh milk from one of the many dairies in town. The dairies didn't need many male calves so they sold them for $5.00 or less and a boy could raise one or more for profit or food for the family. Families preserved their own meat before Sam Hill put in refrigerated food lockers.

Eating together and talking was entertainment. Grandparents, aunts, uncles, cousins, and friends gathered on Sunday after church for dinner. Children played outside while grownups talked. There was no television. Electronic games hadn't been invented. Sometimes there was all-day preaching with dinner on the grounds, which meant that everybody brought food to share. Neighbors also shared spontaneously. If they decided to have ice cream after supper, it was a backyard affair. Someone brought the freezer, which was a wooden bucket with a metal canister in the center and a hand crank on the side. Rock salt and ice were packed around the canister which was filled with the ingredients for ice cream. A neighbor with a cow brought milk. A grocer like James Revier might bring sugar or bananas. Fresh peaches from an orchard were always welcome and regular kitchen items were supplied. Add a child to sit on top and a teenager to turn the crank and soon everybody was enjoying homemade ice cream.

Before 1936, competitive games were played on the school grounds and everybody supported the teams. Business owners left signs on the doors saying "Closed, gone to the game." Shirley

Gilbert told us that there was a time when a rope was strung around the field and it cost ten cents to get inside. Of course it was possible to see the game from outside the roped-off area.

A one-story building had been added to the school grounds in 1932, and in 1936 the gymnasium surrounded by classrooms was completed. This was the high school and the gym that was thought to be the best one in the whole county. The Dr. Pepper Basketball Tournament was held there soon after it opened. It also provided a meeting place large enough for the entire community.

In 1936, the new High School building completed the school complex bounded by Jefferson, Second, Delaware, and Fourth Streets. Old Red can be seen facing Second Street at the upper right view of the grounds. The new building faces Jefferson and sides to Fourth Street.

Music recitals and school plays were also popular and were attended and applauded by many other than parents. Piano teachers Mary Lively and Velma Haley are mentioned by so many of their former pupils that one would think that piano was a required course in early Irving. The students certainly appreciated them.

As soon as the gymnasium was opened, a place for a school stadium was found. A playing field was leveled west of Nursery Road between Irving Boulevard and the railroad tracks. A concession stand was built, and for several years noisy football fans competed with or complemented the noise of the trains.

The vacant block south of Second Street and west of Main Street was a place for carnivals, short horse races, large city picnics, traveling tent revivals, community fish fries, parking, baseball, football, or just a playground.

Lewis Hancock, in an interview by Estelle Bates, recalled the Fourth of July picnics when politicians always came out, and he said, "They did love to make a ballyhoo." But he said that the "most wonderful" occasions were the Baptist Church fish fries which were held two or three times a year. Fish were caught in the Trinity River and fried in large kettles. The good food came with some religion and some politics. He said that those meetings were so good that "other denominations sure were good Baptists on those days."

Mr. Hancock also recalled that in the 1930s the Chamber of Commerce asked Irving citizens whether they wanted Irving to be more a hometown or a business, commercial, manufacturing one. The answer was overwhelmingly for a hometown. This didn't mean that they wanted to be closed and isolated. They just liked what they had and wanted more of it. Irving was, and had been from the beginning, a cosmopolitan town. There were first- and second-generation citizens from France, Switzerland, Belgium, Germany, England, Italy, Ireland, Mexico, Spain, and Japan, as well as from many parts of the United States.

In the 1930s, the Irving area was an ideal place to enjoy the pleasures of horseback riding and to play or watch polo games. Courtesy Mary N. Weathered estate

A transition was taking place from riding horses for transportation to recreational riding. Some of those people who moved to acreage in the Irving area or had a second home in the country were interested in a fashionable type of riding. Neill English is the grandson of Roy Wadsworth, known as the father of Highway 183, who had moved from Dallas to a farm northeast of Irving. In an interview with Estelle Bates, Mr. English said his mother and her friends would gather at her father's farm on weekends to ride for pleasure. It was the custom for people to ride their horses on Saturday mornings and then meet for breakfast. Polo games were played on Sunday afternoons. Spectators had picnic lunches and sat in or on their cars to watch the games. The site was on the hill that is now just south of the Highway 183 Freeway as it passes Texas Stadium. The field extended across what is now Loop 12. The view from that hill was spectacular, with downtown Dallas as the centerpiece of a panorama. He thinks it was probably the only polo field in Dallas County in the 1930s.

The Irving Theater was the pride of the community and the center for entertainment from 1939 to the early 1950s. Irving Archives

Haley Garage was on First Street (Irving Boulevard) east of Main Street in 1933. This was the location of the Blaylock business after Haley moved. Left to right are Frank Haley, brother George McCallum (in the car), and Jack Biggs. Courtesy Sue Haley Huffman

North of town the Salvation Army had a camp complete with a swimming pool and dance pavilion. They sponsored special events and also made the facilities available for organized groups. Sometimes the Light Crust Doughboys played there. The School Administration Building on O'Connor now occupies part of the campgrounds, but there was no O'Connor Road in the 1930s. The camp was out in the country.

Back in downtown Irving the movies were getting better. Hans Smith bought the Irving Theater in 1935 and installed new seats, new sound equipment, and air conditioning. Young people who came to town could visit with friends on the street or in the drugstore and see a movie. For ten cents they could watch the movie several times and stay cool on hot afternoons.

Hans Smith wasn't satisfied just to operate that small movie house with its flat wooden floor. He had been associated with the Publix and Interstate Theaters and he envisioned a first-rate modern theater. There was a vacant lot at 136 South Main. He bought it and started the planning process in December 1938. The *Irving Herald* covered the formal opening on the evening of April 5, 1939. Some of the community leaders listed were Mayor C. P. Caldwell, Judge W. L. Thornton, Mr. and Mrs. W. B. Gilbert, Mrs. Fred Stewart and her daughters Betty and Nel Ryan, and Hans Smith. A newspaper advertisement described the elevated concrete floor with six hundred cushioned seats arranged for good sightlines from front to back, a glassed-in ticket booth, lobby with restrooms on each side, and air conditioning. It was a thing of beauty and wonder in this small town. The three features showing on opening night played for a week so everybody had a chance to see *Jesse James* with Tyrone Power and Randolph Scott, *Topper Takes a Trip* and *The Three Musketeers*.

When the new theater opened, the old one was closed and converted to a skating rink. In 1936, Fair Park in Dallas was re-created with elaborate landscaping and buildings to celebrate the one-hundredth anniversary of the Republic of Texas. Mayor F. M. Gilbert, M.D., led a large delegation from Irving to the Centennial Exposition. The Gulf Oil Corporation Building featured a national radio hookup, and Dr. Gilbert was given time to tell the nation about the many accomplishments and virtues of Irving. It was a memorable occasion.

The people around Irving were very proud of their hometown. It was growing and progressing. Between 1930 and 1940 the population within the corporate limits grew from 731 to 1,089. The city limit lines didn't really define the population, which was active in and for Irving. The expanded area that was considered Irving had a much greater population that participated in the life of the town. They just didn't pay city taxes and couldn't be elected to the City Commission.

In August 1936, Louis and Lloyd Blaylock, grandsons of former Dallas Mayor Louis Blaylock, brought a new business to First Street. They rented the Cox Building that had been the Frank Haley Garage and completely remodeled it. The front of the thirty-by-seventy-foot building was a furniture store, the back was a repair shop, and the Blaylock Finance Company was in the center. They said the decision to come to Irving was made so they could have a place to keep a cow. The Blaylock brothers were immediately immersed in the civic life of the town.

The December 12, 1938 issue of the *Irving Herald* praised R. V. Leach for presenting the community with a model mortuary and chapel which, according to the state inspector, was a model funeral home of the South and throughout the state. Mr. Leach had replaced a wood structure with the brick building, which is still in excellent condition, on the northwest corner of Second and O'Connor. Ed Smith, who was later co-owner of the business, was working for Mr. Leach in 1929.

Between 1933 and 1939, several places in and around Irving started serving beer and other alcoholic beverages. When Franklin Roosevelt ran for president in 1932, he endorsed the repeal of the Eighteenth Amendment. Like many former supporters of the Prohibition law, he did not advocate drinking but pointed out the dismal failure of the law to achieve the intended purpose. Senator Morris Sheppard, who had been cowriter of the Volstead Act, introduced an amendment to end Prohibition by voiding the Act.

R. V. Leach sold caskets at his hardware store before he built the first funeral home in Irving. In 1938, he upgraded from a small frame building to the brick complex that still serves the community in 2003 as the Chism-Smith Funeral Home, seen here.

Above:
The Rotary Club was founded in 1937 at the Trinity Hotel. Louis Blaylock was the first president with C. T. Vandergriff as vice president. In this picture, taken in front of the Community House on March 10, 1938, the only woman is Margie Andrews, the club sweetheart. Irving Archives

Left:
In 1938, the first full-time City employee was C. C. Anderson. He was brought to Irving as a child by his widowed mother to be near her father, C. G. Miller. The Anderson brothers left to right are C. C., Elbert, Emmet, Lester, Bobby, and Ray. Courtesy Sue Haley Huffman

As mayor from 1937 to 1942, C. P. Caldwell had almost no opposition at election time. He was the first mayor to hire full-time employees for the City. He established a City Hall and led the effort to improve the streets in the original town. Irving Archives

Fiorella LaGuardia of New York, in testimony before Congress, called for an official survey to let the American people know what was going on. He charged that an honest survey would reveal an organized system of liquor traffic that was costing federal, state, and county governments huge amounts of money in lost taxes, while bootleggers and public officials who accepted graft were getting rich. He said, "I will concede that the saloon was odious but now we have delicatessen stores, pool rooms, drugstores, millinery shops, private parlors, and 57 other varieties of speak-easies selling liquor and flourishing."

The Twenty-first Amendment to the U.S. Constitution was ratified December 5, 1933, and control of the liquor traffic was left to state and local governments. Texas had licensing laws and provisions for local precinct elections. In Irving, which had not had any stores or restaurants that sold liquor before Prohibition, a few places started applying for the liquor license. It is impossible to get an accurate picture of the places in Irving that served beer and liquor. No two stories are the same. Some residents hardly knew they were there, while others painted a picture of wild dens of iniquity with gambling, dancing, and other sins. The *Directory of the Forks* published by Robert Fulton in 1938 has advertisements for some of the ones that longtime residents remember. The list we compiled includes Nances' (Irving Boulevard east of Kit, J. O. Nance proprietor), Old Hickory Tavern (beer, cold drinks, sandwiches), Paradise Tavern (dine, dance, beer, short orders—Irving Boulevard east of Irving—Miss Evelyn Paradise), Dominoes (beer, Bob Cannon owner), Carl Maynerds Tavern, Rebas' (beer), Raymond Himes Grocery and Filling Station (beer), The Bloody Bucket (north of the Eagle Ford bridge—rough place). In 1938 petitions to call an election to vote dry began circulating.

The school population was growing with more people coming into town and more county school children coming into Irving. Sports activities were expanding. Superintendent A. S. Johnston, who had been a strong leader since 1926, was very busy making the system keep up with increasing demands. He had help from parents and civic-minded citizens. The Dads' Club cleaned the school grounds on Saturdays. The PTA and Rotary Club provided for extracurricular activities at no cost to the school and the teachers took their responsibilities very seriously.

The need for City services was becoming more apparent and more complicated as election 1937 approached. With the Irving history of interest and involvement in county politics, it could have been expected that at this critical time the local election would have been volatile, but there was absolutely no campaigning. C. P. Caldwell was the choice before he ran for the office of mayor and he was unanimously elected. He ran and was elected to two more terms, and in all that time he never spent a dime and he never made a political speech. He said, "If they want me they will vote for me."

Carmey Caldwell had come to Irving in 1921 to start an insurance business. He rented a corner space in a feed store and set up his office with a desk, chair, telephone, and a coat rack. He soon moved to an office on the west side of Main Street next to the drugstore where he stayed for the rest of his life.

Mayor Caldwell analyzed the status of the city and determined that the time had come to hire some employees. The first full-time employee was C. C. Anderson who became a general factotum. His title was city secretary, but his duties included whatever needed to be done administratively for the city. The next employee was George Smith, hired in 1940. He was the police chief and the only policeman.

Trouble was brewing on the other side of the world. Newspapers and radio broadcasts kept us informed about battles and bombings.

Above:
On September 2, 1939, John W. Carpenter (front row, fourth from left), president of Texas Power and Light Company, and J. E. Van Horn (standing second from left), secretary-treasurer, negotiated the deal for the Lower Colorado River Authority to purchase most of the properties of Texas Power and Light Company in seventeen counties. Courtesy Valerie Weiss

Left:
The Sanctuary of the First Methodist Church on Third Street has been a landmark since 1937. Many additions have been made to the church site, but the stone sanctuary remains in continuous use.

Mayor C. P. Caldwell (left) and Irving's first police officer, George Smith, who patrolled the streets of the town on foot, beginning in 1940. He had no car or two-way radio and he was the only policeman. C. C. Anderson collected contributions from the merchants to pay his salary. Irving Archives

Chapter 5

Influence from the Outside World

By 1940, World War II was devastating most of Europe and Asia. The United States was supportive of England and France against the alliance known as the Rome-Berlin-Tokyo Axis, but expected or wished to stay out of war.

In Irving, as in most of the country, life went on as usual. There was no television and families listened to radio programs like "The Green Hornet," "The Shadow," "The Lone Ranger," "Amos and Andy," and "The Inner Sanctum." Then Walter Winchell would come on and relate the bad news about the war on the other side of the ocean. The Lend-Lease program to help the allies was approved and Congress authorized a budget to support the effort.

Some Irving residents began commuting to jobs at defense plants in Grand Prairie, while defense plant employees coming from outside the area were looking for places to live in Irving. The influx of people who worked in downtown Dallas continued. The two-lane bridge linking Irving Boulevard to Dallas gave Irving closer and easier access to downtown than most Dallas neighborhoods enjoyed. Otis Brown had established his office in the Fidelity Building in Dallas and was actively promoting real estate in Irving. His advertisements extol the advantages of living in Irving and indicate that demand was high.

Nancy Caldwell, playing in front of her house at 215 O'Connor, watched the progress of a WPA project that brought sidewalks, curbs, and gutters.

Mayor C. P. Caldwell was intent on providing city services and good streets. Frank Pate had worked part time on a freelance basis at $1.00 for each arrest and $0.50 each for removal and disposal of carcasses. Later he cared for the fire hose and summoned the volunteer firemen with shots from the gun he was allowed to carry. Now he was the elected constable for Precinct 8, and George Smith was the first official city police chief.

Streets in the existing corporate limits were being improved through negotiated agreements with the WPA. Annexation of new subdivisions was being accomplished by petition from developers or landowners. Mayor Caldwell became a developer himself when he bought two acres of the Shelton Story Estate, created one-hundred-foot lots on Sixth Street from Britain to Lucille, extended Britain a block south of Sixth, and built some brick homes.

New lumberyards were being established to take advantage of the building trend. The closest competition with the original lumber business was the Dallas Lumber Company, which advertised better lumber for less and was just one block east of the Irving Lumber Company that J. O. Schulze had founded along with the town. This new lumberyard was built on a strip of land from Main Street to Britain Street, which was leased from the railroad. This was part of the right of way that had been donated by Schulze and Brown for the depot and switching yard. We have to wonder what the Schulze family thought about that competition.

The Water District office on Second Street at Jefferson became the first City Hall. The water tower is behind the building.

In a taped interview with Estelle Bates, Mr. Anderson said that when he started to work for the city there were about one hundred outside toilets within the city limits of Irving. Rather than force everyone to tie into the sewer system, they just didn't allow any new construction without sanitary sewer connections. This included additions to existing structures. He also said that the tax rolls were handwritten and it was hard to tell what was paid and what needed to be pursued. It took several years to get rolls typewritten and clearly documented. As tax assessor and collector it was his responsibility.

The Irving Fresh Water District was like a separate government with the power to construct and manage the water system and collect fees. The Commissioners decided to consolidate services by taking over the Water District. They voted to transfer the properties of the Water District and its bonded indebtedness to the City. The building at Second and Jefferson became City Hall, where all functions of City government were centralized. The building was gradually expanded along with the growth of services. The water and sewer system was the key to expansion for the city. Water lines could be extended beyond the city limits at the expense of the developer. The water rate was one and a half times higher for customers outside the city, but they didn't pay City taxes. Although developers could petition to have their platted land annexed, the city was limited by the capacity to furnish services. C. C. Anderson cited the 1949 bond program as a major turning point in the history of Irving. By providing funds to construct a new sewage plant farther southeast of Irving, it increased the capacity to serve larger areas and therefore enabled the City to annex more land. "This program opened the gate for the rapid growth the city of Irving enjoyed from that time on." That growth is progressively reflected in the size and location of post offices.

But just getting the downtown streets paved, even with help from the County and WPA, presented an unexpected problem. "Jack" Johnson remembered a time when, as a Commissioner, he and Mayor Caldwell had to meet with some very unhappy merchants every day. Asphalt for paving was piled in the middle of Main Street and on First Street from Hastings to Jefferson when it rained for more than two weeks. The only way to get to the "downtown" stores was from an alley.

The Leach Byrd Funeral Home began providing ambulance service to Dallas hospitals for

This Normandy-style house was built by Doctors Charles and James Martin in 1940. The site had been part of a thirty-acre farm belonging to Dan C. Wingren. It had a good woodbine well and a twelve-hundred-foot Paluxsey well to supply all uses. The brick was salvaged from old buildings to give an antique appearance and timbers from old bridges, hewn down with an ax, were used for beams and arches in the living room. Courtesy Morris Parrish

$3.00 one way or $5.00 round trip. They also offered insurance policies for free service anywhere in Dallas County while the policy was in force.

Way up north where there were no roads, just paths, the Salvation Army Fresh Air Camp on Savage Lake was still a very special recreation area. Swimming, dancing, campouts, games, and various kinds of performances were enjoyed there in a secluded area, which later became Lively Park south of the National Guard Armory. Delaware Creek followed a somewhat convoluted course through the campsite, and Lenora Muense described the path or road from the north as running between what was later developed as Limetree and Broadmour. She also remembered a cable across the lake and a tower to allow swimmers to climb up, swing out on the cable, and drop into the water. Eventually the lake was filled in and a concrete swimming pool was installed.

The vast area north of the little town was mostly in large farms, but there were some interesting estates where farming was not the main occupation. One example was a house built in 1940 by the "Doctors Martin." The architecture was unusual and the owners were seldom seen, which created an aura of mystery that led to all sorts of speculation about what might be going on there. The home was referred to as "the castle" or "the mansion." Dr. Charles Martin and his father, Dr. James Martin, who had the Martin X-Ray and Radium Clinic on Gaston Avenue in Dallas, built the place so that their families could live together in the country. According to a letter to Walter Rogers, of First Federal Savings and Loan, written by Dr. Charles Martin in 1960, they moved away in the 1950s because they became the victims of progress. "Huge cheap housing developments surrounded us and it became evident that we would soon be within the city limits of Irving with high taxes to pay and must give up the place into which we had put so much effort."

The house on a three-acre site, bounded by Wingren, Rochelle, and Warren Circle, was transferred to the Episcopal Diocese of Dallas in 1960 by Rolfe and Lorraine Carlisle and, according to a summary by Veronica Giesecke of the history written by founding member O. L. McClister, the first vicar lived on the second floor and church services were held in the large living room, with a balcony for the choir and a wide staircase for brides to descend in weddings. Sunday school was held in other rooms and in the two-story coach house. They had goats to keep the lawn mowed, and the pool was used for swimming lessons. By 1963, the church needed more space and a new sanctuary was completed in 1964. In 1982, the old "castle" had to be demolished and now the site is fully developed with facilities that suit the programs of the Episcopal Church of the Redeemer.

In 1940, the town of Irving was not yet anywhere near that remote location. Highway 183 had been conceived and enough right of way had been acquired to designate a dirt road as

The Post Office that had been in the little stone building at Main and Second moved out when the government contract for which it was built expired. Porter's Shoe Shop moved in and the building is still a shoe shop in 2003.

The Post Office moved to West First Street across from the Irving Lumber Company. The building has housed several businesses since the end of the 1940s when the Post Office was moved again.

The Martin house had a private swimming pool before such amenities were popular. The coach house had a complete machine shop on the first floor and a motion picture projection room on the second floor. Courtesy Morris Parrish

This landmark hotel at the north end of Main Street became the Deel family home, with a few rooms to rent. The famous Hamms Café was converted to a washateria. The balcony was enclosed to add two more rooms, which made eight bedrooms and one bath upstairs.

In 1945, Highway 183 was still a narrow dirt road, but it was going to connect Dallas and Fort Worth and open the area north of town to development. This 1945 picture of Etta McKinney and Betty Tyndall was published in a 1964 edition of the *Daily News Texan* celebrating the Golden Anniversary of Irving.

Clara Gibbs, English and drama teacher, was the sponsor of the first Student Council in Irving schools. This organization planned the first homecoming, inaugurated Book Week to add books to the Irving Library, and took a leading role in all school activities. From *The Lair*

Highway 15. Will Story, Albert Farine, Dr. D. W. Gilbert, and Elizabeth Stovall had each given twelve acres or more for the project. When Tilla Lindsay and Thelma Coleman moved to the area in 1940, they rented a hundred-acre tract at Britain Road and Highway 15 (later Highway 183) for $25 per month. Their father raised cattle. When they bought a home on South Britain at Seventh Street in 1945, they were still outside the city and did not have a telephone or sewerage. But they were close and were very soon annexed.

George Henry Deel brought his family to Irving in 1939, and by 1941 they were living in the famous hotel at the north end of Main Street which he had bought and remodeled. Five of his children—Louise, Burnis, Burnise, James, and Guy—were in the Irving school system during the 1940s. George, the oldest, had already graduated. Through the years these people have contributed in many ways to the life of the city. Guy, who was only six years old when they moved here, has achieved nationwide fame as a professional artist and has been called back to Irving to produce a painting for the Centennial Celebration.

The seniors who graduated in 1941 were rightly proud of their accomplishments. Among other things they published the first school paper, the *Tiger Rag*, and produced the first annual which they named *The Lair*.

On Sunday, December 7, 1941, radio announcers broke into regular programs to report that Japanese planes had bombed U.S. ships in Pearl Harbor. Teachers called around and agreed to take radios to school the next day, so that everyone could hear President Roosevelt speak to Congress

Left:
These 1941 senior class officers were pictured in *The Lair*: Marthajohn Cannon, reporter; C. J. Range, vice president; Mildred Green, secretary; Edwin Tiffin, president. Their clothes are typical of school dress in 1941.

Below:
Irving girls played good competitive basketball in 1940, while Dallas girls were not allowed to play any contact sports. Front row: Dortha Brown, Jean Haggard, Forestine Collins, Genevieve Smith, Martha Mathis, and Annie Hatfield. Second row: Mary Etheridge, Juanita Kirkpatrick, —— Evans, Earlene Anderson, Eva Mills, Betty Page, Eva Thompson, and Jerry Lucas. Back row: Coach Atkins, Jean Thomas, Doris Hatfield, Lucy Davis, Martha Trate, Mamie Gallini, Dorothy Dorety, Frances Ronning, and Coach Kelsey. Courtesy Genevieve Smith

This house, at 221 South Jefferson, pictured in 2002, was built by W. D. and Alice Lucas in 1928 across the street from the school complex, during the time that they were operating the general store on Main Street at Second. After Doug Lucas died in 1931, Alice rented rooms, and in the 1940s she cooked noon meals for teachers and for some business people in town. Some of her "regulars" were the Hartins, the Harkeys, and the Gibbs.

The Tiger Den was the next door north of the Lucas home. It was a favorite place for students to get hot dogs, peanuts, ice cream bars, and a little socializing. Irving Archives

and the nation. Students and teachers heard those now famous words: "a day that will live in infamy." Each person, in his own way, began to face the reality that the United States was at war.

Carolyn Jeter Cooper described, in a taped interview, how her mother reacted to the news. She immediately began to agonize over the thought that Joe, her only son, would have to go to war. Ruby Jeter got her china out and broke every piece that was made in Japan. Imagine her reaction later, when Joe announced that he had joined the Navy Air Force and would leave in three days. Movie stars made the service seem glamorous and some Irving boys were going to exotic places. He thought he would be sent to training in California. But he was wrong. They shipped him to a training camp in northern Oklahoma. Burnis Deel related a similar experience. He was drafted and expected to go to San Diego, but he was put on a bus and sent to boot camp in Corpus Christi, where he had the pleasure of living in the enlisted men's barracks. Douglas LePori joined the Air Force to fly fighter planes and, two days later, was transferred to the Infantry to be a communications specialist.

When, as a teenager, Lorene Lucas had her first job, she bought this lot at 521 South Delaware, with a three-room house for $750. When she married Arthur Looper, they built this house. In the 1940s, their children fished for crawdads, using meat on a bent pin, in a pond across Sixth Street, which was a gravel road. That crawdad hole was on the site where the First Christian Church now sits.

Irving boys were being drafted as soon as they graduated and some were enlisting when they turned eighteen, even if they hadn't graduated. Some women also enlisted. Nel Stewart Decker served four years in the Navy. Soon, not many young men were left in Irving. Lynn Brown was in the Navy CBs, Claude Chambers was in the Air Force Strategic Command, Arthur Casey was a Marine fighter pilot, LeRoy Toler was in the Army Air Corps. Hardly a family was untouched. The newspapers published stories about the men in service. People met in the little ice cream parlor, between the shoe shop and the Irving Theater, to exchange information and share letters.

Unemployment was no longer a problem, with defense plants growing and employing thousands of people. Both Clay and Ruby Jeter worked the graveyard shift in a Grand Prairie defense plant. The sign that this was not unusual was the availability of childcare to accommodate that schedule. There was a facility across the street from the school where children could be brought before 3 a.m. They slept on cots the rest of the night. In the morning they had breakfast, dressed, and walked across the street to school.

Many women who had never had jobs joined the work force. Younger people, and older people had to fill in to handle jobs and duties.

Dan Matkin came to Irving from Fort Worth in 1945 and entered Irving High School. As he sat in class, a siren sounded and two of his classmates crawled out the window and ran across the grounds. The siren was on top of the water tower and the boys were officially designated to help the volunteer firemen. The volunteers still had a very strong organization, but the geographic dispersal of jobs affected the timing for leaving the workplace to rush to a fire. The school was across the street from the City Hall where the fire truck was housed. One blast of the siren meant a fire in town, two blasts meant a fire in the country, and three blasts meant a major fire where everybody was needed. The fire truck pulled out with the first men who arrived at the station. The location of the fire was on the blackboard, to route those who arrived after the truck left. In 1940, the firemen bought a one-ton Chevrolet truck with a 250-gallon water tank. Then, after the end of the war, they bought a war-surplus tanker truck with two water tanks and a gasoline-powered pump. It is noteworthy to remember that these men furnished their own gear, had sirens on their personal cars, and raised money to buy and equip the trucks. Their yearly barbecue, picnic, and play day was the most popular fundraising event. Fish fries were also popular. The first pay they got from the City was in the form of credit on their water bill.

C. J. Range and Joyce Palmer both graduated from Irving High. They married and she went with him to Arizona where he was a pilot instructor. In a recorded interview, he said that all he ever did was fly airplanes and haul gasoline. He got a commercial drivers license when he was thirteen years old so he could haul gas and kerosene for the business run by his dad and uncle. Irving Archives

The volunteer spirit was always strong in Irving. In 1942, Uncle George Smith got some help. The Irving Police Auxiliary was formed. It was the beginning of the police reserves which became a tradition. In January 1942, volunteer enrollment cards had been distributed with work opportunities. At the top of the list was civilian defense work as firemen and policemen. A newspaper article on January 2 concluded: "The call is being made for all to do their bit. If you have had experience or have not, it makes no difference. You are needed. We are all needed."

People who had grown up in Irving during the Depression years were uniquely prepared for home-front life between 1942 and 1945. Civilians nationwide were urged to plant Victory gardens. Truck gardens had been the major business in early Irving and most families still had what they called "kitchen gardens" for their own uses. Rationing and limited production brought back the "save it, fix it, make it do" mentality. Everybody in the nation, including children, was periodically issued a book of stamps, which had to be presented to buy rationed items like sugar, gasoline, and tires. Even shoes were limited, so the shoe-repair business prospered. No automobiles were even manufactured between the 1942 and 1946 models. Clay Jeter was in the right business: selling auto parts and employing a mechanic. He and Ruby Jeter had the contract for the Continental Bus Station.

William and Art Lee Trigg answered the call to service and experienced worlds far beyond the Irving community. Odessa Trigg King provided this picture of her brothers to the Irving Archives.

The 1940s have been called the golden age of train travel. The Zephyr and the Rocket were luxury trains with leather seats, dining cars, sleeping compartments, and smokers. The Rock Island Railroad, so important in Irving history, had been in receivership with aging rolling stock, deferred maintenance, and decreased ridership, but a number of factors contributed to the revival of the railroads during the war years. Troops were moved by train, more people were traveling long distances or commuting to jobs in employment centers.

With so much focus on the war and war-related work, there was still plenty of attention to

Harry and Patsy Spencer were married in April 1942, and five months later he entered active duty in the Army Air Corps. In November of the same year he was copilot of a B-17 transport bomber that crashed onto the Greenland Ice Cap where crevasses covered by frozen snow caused unsuspecting men to fall one hundred or more feet and some were lost. The crew was isolated without food or other provisions in severe arctic weather. After eighty-nine days of failed rescue attempts, some of them, including Spencer, were flown to safety. He received the Legion of Merit for his performance during the ordeal. The fascinating story of this adventure is available in the Irving Archives.

Joe Ponce and two of his brothers played football for Irving High and each of them went to war as soon as they graduated. Louis joined the Army and received a Purple Heart after he was severely wounded in France. Manuel was a Marine. Joe came back from service in the Navy and continued his education. He was principal of a school in Dallas when, as a reserve officer, he was called back to duty. During the Korean War, he was in Austin as head of the draft board for the southwestern area of the United States.

local civic programs, ongoing controversies, and school problems and triumphs. In 1941, when Esther Hurwitz wanted to start a library in Irving, she went around town asking merchants to donate space. One store owner said: "What in the world would anyone want with a library?" But Louis Blaylock agreed to give her a seven-by-twelve-foot corner in his store and that was the beginning of public libraries in Irving. Donations of books and use of the library grew quickly. In less than a year a vacant building across the street was available for $20 a month and the library moved. With donated lumber and labor the building was renovated and bookshelves were built. A partition created a "friendship room" for meetings and programs. Volunteers became librarians.

The year 1942 was one of victory for citizens who wanted to prohibit the sale of alcoholic beverages in Irving. A mass meeting of prohibition forces was held at the First Baptist Church on June 12. Petitions calling for a local option election were circulated and in July Irving was voted dry.

Those who considered dancing to be sinful were not so successful. There was no provision for a referendum to outlaw the activity, which was so much a tradition of the life between the Forks. There was, however, a strong effort to keep dancing out of the high school. The large gymnasium seemed an ideal place for a school dance, but enough pressure was applied to prevent that use for several years. Students had grown up in the town that had dances on Main Street, at picnics, in homes, and some church gatherings. It was hard to understand that some of the prominent preachers condemned it from the pulpit and used their influence to keep it out of the school. Obviously, in a town with such cultural diversity, everybody didn't agree and students found places to dance. Cora Caster let students dance at her house on the northwest corner of Second and Britain but they always pulled down the shades. She was talked about anyway.

When the School Board did allow school dances, Mary Louise Stovall Wadsworth was one of the teachers who sponsored them. She said that she was reprimanded on Sunday morning. A teen

Right:
Esther Hurwitz was involved in numerous projects and organizations in Irving and in the county, but she is best remembered as the "library lady." She and her husband lived on fifty acres of good grazing land off what is now Irving Heights Drive. He operated a dairy there. They were not living within the city limits of Irving when she was promoting the town, organizing groups, and seeking help to establish a library.

Below:
In 1942, the library was in a converted feed store at 113 East First Street, and was a popular place for both children and adults. There were no school libraries. A partition created a meeting room for various groups, which Mrs. Hurwitz called the "Friendship room." The first Girl Scout Troop met there. Irving Archives

During the war years, train travel increased everywhere. The Irving Depot was busy with more people living in Irving and working in the Dallas business district. Even if they had automobiles, they needed to conserve gasoline, tires, and the vehicles that couldn't be replaced.

Dr. Joe Roberts postponed starting his private medical practice to serve as an Army medic in North Africa and in Italy. As a reserve officer, he was called up in 1941 and returned to civilian life in 1947.

canteen became a regular Saturday night event. For twenty-five cents, students could play games, socialize, and dance. But for the class that was in high school during the war, when dancing to Big Band music was an art form, the school dances were not enough. They initiated bridge dancing. A bridge over Delaware Creek that was going to connect to Second Street was popular for one group before that western extension was constructed. They called it "Do Drop Inn." The larger bridge over the railroad tracks where Route 12 was planned was completed before the roadway was built. Using a dirt path from the south it was possible to get onto the bridge. Radios were tuned to the same station for music. The enthusiastic accounts of former students who danced on bridges back then make it seem like more fun than going to the Adolphus or the Plantation Ballrooms and it was a lot cheaper.

Boys had enjoyed watching Clem Joyce, who was the telegraph operator at the depot. The job became unpleasant when the wire brought bad news about young men who were wounded or killed in the war. A boy on a bicycle sometimes delivered telegrams, but the Western Union man in a car delivered the bad news. Families were frightened every time they saw that car on their street. Then, late in 1945, the war ended and families rushed to meet the trains that brought their boys-turned-men home. But thirty-three of them didn't come home. The first project of the Lions Club, which was organized in 1945, was a permanent memorial to those young men.

When George Smith retired in 1947, Joe Reynolds was hired and the city bought the first police car, but there was no police radio until 1953. A red light on top of the water tower signaled him to contact the switchboard operator. As he drove around town a porch light alerted him that help was needed. Sometimes he was asked to arrange transportation to a hospital in Dallas or get a doctor or settle a domestic dispute. When Joe Reynolds caught mischievous children or teens violating the laws, he sat down and talked to them in a way that made them understand. The result was not only better behavior, but also an army of young people who respected and loved the one-man police force.

Left:
Eliodoro Reyes (left) was writing home from Alaska. He married Helen Alonzo and they raised their family in Irving. Courtesy Helen Reyes

Below:
The boys in the Hi-Y Club were working to earn their "spending money," but they had time and energy to serve the community and to have fun. Most of them would soon be old enough for military service. The club sponsors, standing on either side of the back row, are F. N. Wilson and Opal Duckworth. Students who could be identified are Charles Briscoe, George Crump, Shorty Johnson, Dick Wadsworth, Tommy Rose, Billy Smith, Vaughn Massey, F. M. Gilbert Jr., Garfield Andrew, James Carmean, Bob Lee, Bobby Haley, George DeShazo, Dusty Rhodes, and John Mitchell.

Above:
The Lions Club was organized in 1945, and their first project was a monument memorializing Irving boys who lost their lives in World War II. It stood on a pedestal on the south side of the intersection of Irving Boulevard and Main Street until it was moved, without the pedestal, to Heritage Park.

Right:
The names of those boys are still prominently displayed at the entrance to the park.

In the late 1940s there were twenty-one airports in Dallas County and two of them were in Irving. The Jap Lee Airport came first. In 1942, T. J. Lee, who was an American Airlines pilot, paid $3,000 for forty-eight acres with a house and a barn west of what later became MacArthur Boulevard. The barn soon had a windsock on top and the pasture became a landing strip for Mr. Lee's personal plane. It attracted boys who wanted to learn to fly and men returning from military service who had airplanes. This was a busy little airport until Lee died in 1959 and his widow sold the property. The school district bought a site on Carlisle for the T. J. Lee Elementary School. Ben Carpenter began building houses east of the school site.

The larger airport was south of Highway 183 and east of Story Road. A control tower and four Quonset-hut hangars supported enthusiastic owners of small private aircraft when the old home of Dr. D. W. Gilbert was still standing on the other side of Story Road.

It was North American Aviation that brought Jackie Townsell to Irving when she was ten-year-old Jackie Mae Howard. Her mother and aunts worked at the Grand Prairie plant and became acquainted with the Bear Creek Community to the north. Mrs. Howard liked the spirit of the community and wanted to bring her children up in that atmosphere. There was a spirit of caring and sharing the good and the bad, a strong sense of decency enforced by families, and the positive outlook that kept the fun in life regardless of circumstances. That was reason enough to move from West Dallas to Bear Creek. Some old-timers still question the name Bear Creek, saying that the area is really Spencer Park.

But everything was not peaceful in the community. Parents were concerned that the county school that still served their children was lagging years behind in housing and equipment. Other county schools were being closed and annexed to independent school districts in the cities.

The Irving Independent School District was progressing, but it was in deep trouble. The number of grades had increased from eleven to twelve in 1941. Students from the County common schools were bused in for high school, some elementary students were coming in by choice, and the general population had grown rapidly. More schools and more teachers were needed, and financial resources simply weren't keeping up with demands. A. S. Johnston, who had been the superintendent since 1926, retired at the end of the 1946 school year and B. E. Dunagan replaced him. Johnston had established an overdraft arrangement with the bank, asked for and received $2,000 from the County to help pay teachers, and proposed a bond election to meet the financial needs of the schools.

Following the untimely death of Mayor Caldwell in 1942, Commissioner E. J. Johnson was appointed to complete the term as mayor. He was then elected twice to serve until 1947.

Hans Smith, who had been bringing movies to Irving for more than a decade and was called Uncle Bud by the children and young people, was elected mayor in 1947 and served until 1951, when the town was growing much faster than City services could be provided and it had no credit rating. By the time his term was over, the city was four times bigger than when he was elected and bond brokers were looking favorably on the potential of Irving.

The students at the Sowers Colored School in 1946 were blessed with good teachers who insisted that they behave well and excel academically, but their facility and equipment lagged behind the Irving schools, where other county schools were being absorbed. Courtesy Dixie Caraway

Superintendent A. S. Johnston had faced many problems in the twenty years he guided and nurtured the Irving school system. It was hard to imagine the school without him when he retired in 1946.

The situation was aggravated when, near the end of the 1947–1948 school year, students came to school one morning and learned that both the elementary and high school principals were to be released. An agitated body of students from all grade levels met in the gymnasium and decided they had to take some type of action because they loved and respected both Mr. Drummond and Mr. Copeland. Some were saying, "Let's strike!" Others didn't know what that meant, but agreed not to go to class. They planned to attend the School Board meeting to express their opinions and to ask for an explanation. Parents sent their children back to school the next day, but they attended the Board meeting with them and voiced their concerns. More than eight hundred citizens met in the gymnasium. Dick Hatfield was the chair and Charles Whitmire was the designated speaker for the students. Eleanor Bowles and Martha Jo Lucas were also active in the discussion, but the meeting ended with questions unresolved.

The situation only got worse when in May the Dallas County School Board decided to dissolve most of the common schools in the county and send the students to established independent school districts. The Estelle School had already closed in 1944. More than half of the Elm School children had already been attending Irving schools on a tuition basis. With this move all children would have the same privileges. Mr. Dunagan tried to explain that the Irving Board needed time to consider the annexation proposal saying: "The buses are loaded to capacity now." There was really no need for the Irving Board to act because state law said that if a school could not accommodate a child in the curriculum, the child had the privilege of entering the nearest school.

By July, one principal and the superintendent had resigned and, on July 23, all seven members of the School Board resigned. In August 1948, a new Board was elected. With Paul Keyes as president, they hired John Beard as superintendent. The problem of meeting the needs of this growing school system intensified, but the community settled into a temporary calm with regard to the schools.

For a week beginning September 13, 1948, parents picketed the Sowers Colored School. The signs said they wanted some of the bond money and they wanted representation on the Board of Trustees. Basically they wanted materials and books equivalent to what the white students had. The event was well covered by Dallas newspapers. This community was still in county territory outside the corporate limits of Irving.

The gymnasium in the center of the high school at Jefferson and Fourth was the place for large community meetings as well as school plays, sports, and many other activities. It was the pride of the community. Even after half a century, many longtime residents declare that it was the best gym Irving has ever had.

After the students met and decided to strike, many of them made signs from whatever they could find, and picketed the school on foot or on bicycles.

When the school at Estelle had closed, the Bear Creek Missionary Baptist Church, organized in 1853, was still located in the Estelle community with no prescience of the future airport that would displace it. Edgar Brown described it as a "typical 'prairie type' one-room wooden building with hand fans furnished by a funeral home." There were still outhouses in the 1940s.

In 1945, C. P. Schulze persuaded Charles Schulze Jr. to return to Irving and help with the lumber business. He built a new house at Third and O'Connor across from his parents' home.

In 1947, the Irving State Bank moved east, across Main Street, to a new modern building. They were growing along with the town. Courtesy Eleanor Corry Bell

Above:
On opening day, the bank employees were at their stations ready to greet customers.

Left:
John Brandenburg welcomed Albert Farine to the bank opening. Mr. Farine came into town to visit every Saturday.

Dr. Franklin M. Gilbert was living in the house that Fred Joffre built for himself in 1919. The Joffres gave the house to their adopted daughter, Louise Baker, who sold it to William B. Gilbert in 1936. Dr. Gilbert bought it in 1939, after which there were few private moments in this house. People who needed medical help or advice felt free to drop by anytime. Courtesy Dr. Clay Gilbert

In 1949, Dr. Franklin Gilbert and Dr. Joe Roberts opened the Gilbert Roberts Clinic at Irving Boulevard and O'Connor. This was the first clinic and therefore an important milestone in medical services for Irving. With what was the most modern equipment at the time, professional services were improved and expanded. Interns and licensed doctors were brought in to create a balanced staff. Many of the well-known Irving doctors of the next thirty years were "incubated" in this clinic before they moved on to form clinics or to private practice. Long John Silvers now occupies the site. Courtesy Dr. Clay Gilbert

Above:
In the late 1940s, Hans Smith closed the skating rink and turned the old Quonset hut back into a movie house called the Rio. It had a new façade similar to the Irving Theater. Double features, western movies, and serials were very popular at both theaters on Saturdays. Tuesday night special was ten cents. Weekend price was thirty cents. Irving Archives

Left:
Southwest of Irving, the church was important in shaping the lives of future leaders. The young people on the front row were active in their church and grew up to be positive contributors to Irving, even though their schools were segregated in the 1940s. The young people, left to right, are Delmus Morton, Dixie Morton, Ben Briggs, Elmer Sweat, and T. J. Green. Courtesy Dixie Caraway

Throughout the1950s, Dr. Franklin Gilbert made house calls with his little black bag, just as his father had done. Patients were treated at home or diagnosed and sent to a Dallas hospital. There was no hospital in Irving. New doctors moving into Irving also made house calls. Courtesy Dr. Clay Gilbert

Chapter 6

Growing Pains

The struggle to keep up with growth had been constant from the time Irving was incorporated. A review of the census figures, beginning in 1920, shows that the population more than doubled with each decade. The numbers went from 1,089 in 1940 to 2,615 on the 1950 report. But then a real growth spurt occurred and the 1960 census reported 45,895 residents within the Irving city limits. At the end of this decade Irving was officially recognized as the fastest growing city in Texas. During the 1950s there was no rest for the small city government or the independent school system with demands always ahead of resources.

Under these circumstances one has to wonder why they wanted the ability to annex more territory. But one of the issues discussed while Hans Smith was still mayor was the need for a Home Rule Charter that would empower the Commissioners to annex adjoining property without a petition or even consent of owners. This issue was pursued by C. B. Hardee when he was elected mayor in 1951.

The building, at 217 Main Street, that housed the Irving Library from 1952 to 1962 was busy with activities including book review clubs. The Library moved, but the building is well preserved and still used in various ways by the community in 2003. Phil Baker is part of a group of musicians who meet there to enjoy making music for the fun of it. Irving Archives

The little Irving Library Association already had a State Charter, obtained by J. E. Van Horn, W. E. Harrington, and Esther Hurwitz, and they had a rather prestigious Board that had helped raise some funds. By the end of 1943, they had bought six lots on the corner of Main and Third Streets for a total of $2,100. Mrs. Hurwitz, who was active in starting the Dallas County Library in the Records Building, persuaded the Commissioners to send County crews to fix the drainage problems on the lots by filling in the low places. In 1950 the land was ready but there wasn't enough money to build the two-story brick structure she envisioned. The County had acquired a five-room house in a row settlement which they thought was worth $6,000, but Mrs. Hurwitz offered $1,000 which was the entire Library Fund and they took it. With donated materials and labor the house was renovated, and in 1952 it became the Irving Public Library although it was not City owned or funded. The little library was another attraction to Main Street that was still the focal point for shopping, entertainment, banking, and socializing. Big State Drug had replaced the dry goods store in 1948 and was a favorite gathering place for the high school crowd. In addition to the soda fountain, banana splits, and chocolate sundaes, they had a juke box and air conditioning.

Some people were still attracted to the outskirts of Irving because they wanted a place large enough to have a horse, a cow, or a garden but many just wanted a house. Irving needed developers and a means to direct and control development. A Home Rule Charter could give the local government zoning powers and it could provide for hiring a city manager. In order to adopt a charter a city needed five thousand residents living within the corporate limits. It was the right time for C. B. Hardee to be mayor. He was an energetic young developer who had lived in Irving less than a year when he was elected. His three terms in office, in the middle of the first hundred years of Irving history, were years of dramatic growth and change in both the city and the schools.

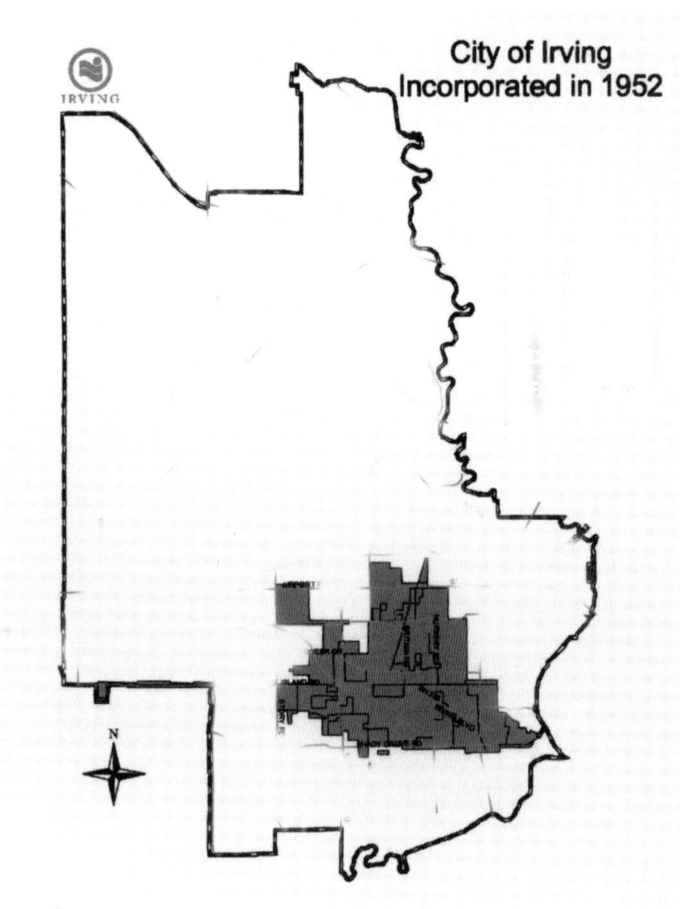

The Hardee-Pipkin Company and Mayflower Investment Company, headed by Carr P. Collins, were building homes west of Delaware Creek and annexing them to the city. Collins started building between Rock Island and Sixth Street with streets named Wanda, Leslie, and Collins. Hardee developed Sandra, Charles, and Larry between Schulze Drive and Sixth Street. Then Collins moved northwest to the Sowers area and developed the Plymouth addition while Hardee continued building on the south side. He had a 208-home project south of Senter Park, had started the Riverview fourplex community and was planning 146 brick homes west of Senter Road and south of Shady Grove Road. Many other developers were building and annexing smaller additions.

The first shopping center outside of the original town opened in 1951 on property that had been part of the Henry Britain place, where the founders had camped in 1902. The Irvingate Shopping Center, on the quadrants of East Irving Boulevard and Nursery Road, brought chain stores for the first time along with more owner-operated stores, a bank, a storefront savings and loan, and a movie theater. It served a growing complement of homes and apartments on the expanding east side of Irving, including the new high school between Lucille and Nursery on Sixth Street.

But with all of this growth the official population of Irving had not reached the five thousand mark necessary to vote its own Home Rule Charter. The young mayor appointed a fifteen-member Commission to work toward the goal. Charles Schulze remembered that he and a number of other men walked door to door asking residents to sign petitions to be annexed. The Chamber of Commerce had a Charter Committee that worked three years to push the idea and to instigate annexations. Attorney Balford Morrison drew up a charter based on Commission members agreements as to the type of government Irving should have. On October 25, 1952, with population well over what was needed, the Charter was submitted and approved by a 377 to 96 vote. It stipulated a six-member Council and a city manager–council form of government.

Above:
By 1952, annexations had expanded the city limits far beyond that little rectangle that was Irving. Population exceeded the five thousand needed to adopt a Home Rule Charter. The outline represents 2003 boundaries. Ron Ruthven, city planner, provided information and Tim Williams, GIS technician, created the map.

John Stiff, a civil engineer graduate from A&M, was hired as the first city manager. C. C. Anderson became tax administrator and Mary Gilliland was hired as city secretary. The Council was creating ordinances to regulate everything allowable under the Charter. Most important to the way the city would grow were the requirements for developers. Zoning regulations determined uses of land for residential, commercial, or industrial purposes. Developers were required to install streets, sidewalks, and water and sewer lines to city standards. It may be surprising that, as a prolific developer himself, Mayor Hardee strongly advocated this course. He said that developing was free enterprise and government should not financially support private enterprise.

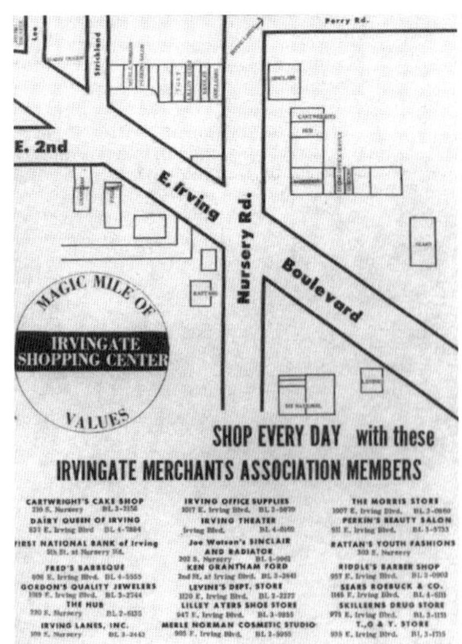

Right:
The Irvingate Shopping Center was a response to the growing population. The remarkable thing was that it was all planned, built, and opened in such a short time and brought large chain stores like A&P grocery, Skillerns, Levines, and Sears. Irving was accustomed to owner-operated stores.

The new High School faced Sixth Street. A new Junior High faced Edmondson, leaving space for practice fields between them. Tiger Stadium was built east of the High School.

There was plenty of room for the pep squad, cheerleaders, and band to practice.

Right:
Students raised funds to buy a live tiger from the Marsalis Zoo for a mascot. When that was disallowed, they used the money to buy a bell and mounted it in front of the school. It rang most wildly when the football team won.

Below:
In 1950, the Junior-Senior Banquet at the Melrose Hotel in Dallas was a gala affair. Irving didn't have a facility to provide the space or the service for such a function. Courtesy Eleanor Corry Bell

In a recorded interview, Ray Lowery said that developers thought John Stiff was the "meanest man in the world." They not only had to install and pay for water and sewer lines and paving, they had to follow strict guidelines like houses so many feet from the sandbag and certain size backyards. In spite of the competition among builders they thought they should band together and get rid of him. Later they realized that all these regulations had added to the value of their projects so that the loan companies were willing to give them more money. Mr. Lowery said, "It wound up we thought a lot of old John. He was bringing us prosperity all the time we were cussing."

All these new buildings were assigned street numbers. Until 1948, there had been no numbers and no mail delivery except to route or post office boxes. Postmaster Carl Range had kept a promise to provide home delivery of mail when numbers were assigned.

Until 1953, Joe Reynolds was the police chief. He had recruited A. R. "Pinky" Delay to patrol from 6 p.m. to 2 a.m. and they got a two-way radio. The frequency was shared by all of the policemen in Dallas County, which made it one big party line and sometimes caused confusion. Deputy Sheriff Lumie Lewis was their backup, and later he and Delay operated the D&L Security Service.

The word around town was that known criminals, sometimes referred to as the Southwest Mafia, were living in Irving, but newcomers were assured that the town was safe because they did business in Dallas and protected the town where they lived. This theory was confirmed by Delay in an interview recorded in July 2001. He said sometimes gang members would come around and ask if he had any problems. They assured him that nobody would come to Irving to pull "jobs" because "we live out here. We'll kill them." Among the known criminals he named were Jeddy Bass, Nick Tassio, Olin Ray Tyler, and the Callahans.

W. J. Cooper became police chief in 1953. Pictured, left to right, front row: Louis Spears, R. W. Henderson, Pinky Delay, and Chester Copeland. Standing: Cy Courtney, Glen Blythe, Harvey Derrick, Cleo Pruitt, Councilman Harry Spencer, City Manager John Stiff, S. P. McDonald, Mayor C. B. Hardee, Councilman Boots Roberts, Police Chief W. J. Cooper, and Councilman A. H. Trotter.

In 1953, Irving celebrated the fiftieth anniversary of the founding of the town. In September, there was a pageant of homes featuring the first home built in Irving at 101 South Hastings and fourteen new model homes in ten subdivisions. An old-timers reunion, with hoedown music and dancing, was attended by all ages. The final celebration was a ceremony at the depot where the original lots were sold.

By 1953, both the Police and Fire Departments were growing with City support. Bill Dorety was the first full-time paid fireman and James "Pistol" Mitchell was the fire marshal. The Fire Station was enlarged to accommodate four pieces of equipment including a new Mack fire truck. Four more firemen were hired and they got radio equipment. Fire alarms came through the police dispatcher on that shared frequency. The story of the Fire and Police Departments from that time on was growth, expanding service, and improvement. By 1959, the Police Department had thirty employees, including twenty-two patrolmen, and there were twenty-five police reserves. The Fire Department first hired from the volunteers. By 1959 they had twenty-eight paid employees and their own radio frequency.

The first manufacturer in town was Sam Hill who made ice and then his own line of ice cream. By 1948, he had six hundred frozen food lockers and in 1951 he began to process meat. Fry Roofing was the next manufacturer and then Dixie Chrome opened the largest, most modern

The house at 101 South Hastings, built by the first mayor, Otis Brown, and enlarged by the second mayor, Chaney Miller, was featured in the fiftieth anniversary pageant of homes. Mrs. W. R. Duckworth was assisted in receiving visitors by American Airlines stewardesses. Courtesy Sue Haley Huffman

In 1953, the City enlarged the Firehouse to accommodate four pieces of equipment. There were five full-time firemen assisted by volunteers.

chrome furniture manufacturing plant in the Southwest. In 1952, they reorganized and became Southern Consolidated Manufacturing Company producing a complete line of machine parts.

A much larger industrial development, destined to have a long-term effect on the development of the city, came in 1954. Hal Darr, who was a founder of Frontier Airlines, bought the Caterpillar equipment franchise for sixty-nine counties and he needed to locate a site for the operation. Major Bill Long, who was involved in founding Love Field, owned property in Irving, including the polo field had been popular in the 1930s. They made a deal for twenty-five acres. The Darr headquarters that for Caterpillar equipment was located north of Grauwyler and accessed by Darr Street. A portion of the property at the top of the hill, fronting on what would eventually become the 183 Freeway, was made available for other development. Later the Baxter house and a Howard Johnson's located there and attracted many of the social and civic gatherings for the next twenty years. Arnold and Alice Martin, who came to Irving with Darr Equipment, have been deeply involved in the community in numerous positive ways since he came as vice president of the company.

The Fire Department grew rapidly and a second story was added for firemen. Raised lettering was added above a new entrance to City Hall.

It was the Elm Fork of the Trinity River that ensured that the company would be in Irving. Hal Darr, W. F. Long, and Ted Hinton joined with a group of about seventy-five Union Bower residents who had petitioned for annexation to Dallas. March 29, 1954, the Dallas Council passed an ordinance annexing three square miles near Union Bower which included the Darr property. But Irving had already annexed forty-nine acres of the area. C. B. Hardee and John Stiff met with Dallas Councilmen. Hal Darr told them: "I don't want to be in either city but if I have to be in a city then I want to be in Dallas." However the Dallas Council decided that they had made a big mistake. Roderic Thomas said: "I am going to recommend that we rescind the action and get out of there. If it were up to Dallas to serve the area with sewers, I do not know how many years it would take."

In contrast to all of the growth and activity there was a tranquil recreation area just south of town with an entrance at Oakdale and Bolden Road. David O. Hale, whose family lived there from 1953 through 1965, provided information in a letter to archivist Jan Hart. Money willed to the Dallas National Guard Association was used to buy the Spring Lake property for an "R&R" center. The spring-fed lake was stocked with fish by the State, and the grounds developed for recreation uses. The white stucco house with a red tile roof was used as a clubhouse. Mr. Hale's family lived free of charge in another house on the property in exchange for the management services of his stepfather who was also post engineer for the National Guard.

The Spring Lake National Guard recreation center on Bolden Road had a clubhouse, lighted sport fields, picnic tables, brick grills, restrooms, and fish in the lake. The Bolden Dairy was west of the complex. Courtesy David O. Hale

Before this land was used by the National Guard, it was home and playground to some of the boys who became very important to the life of Irving. Arthur Casey, whose family moved onto ten acres there in 1931, and Harold "Shorty" Watkins fished and played in the lake and the gravel pits while they were attending school in Irving. Of course duties like taking care of chickens, hogs, and the garden had to be completed before any playtime was allowed. Arthur Casey was principal of several schools before becoming assistant superintendent for instruction, and Dr. Watkins was appreciated not only for his profession, but for numerous contributions to improving life in Irving.

In 1954, Irving received much local and some national publicity for a remarkable project that started in Mrs. Ruth Compton's high school sociology class. It might be called an example of successful progressive education. The topic for a discussion in the class was the growing problem of juvenile delinquency. After exploring what the students thought were the basic causes, the class sent surveys to students in all of the schools asking questions about how they spent their leisure time and what they would like to do. The class made an inventory of recreational facilities and asked what would benefit everybody. They decided that Irving needed a community and youth center. Members of the sociology class were invigorated and they didn't stop until the job was done. The class elected a committee to lead the project. David Reese was chairman with committee members Donna Cottrell, Ruth Ebert, Ellen Monser, Jack Rockett, and Louise Shelby. They presented the idea to PTAs, Dads' Clubs, and civic and church groups. Lonnie Shelby drew floor plans which included all the things the committee agreed were needed. There was even space for adding air conditioning later. Enthusiasm grew among students, teachers, and civic and social organizations until the City Council approved a project and John Stiff was in charge of carrying out a building plan. The sixteen-acre site was parkland that had been acquired earlier from Senator A. G. Senter and was where Carl Althoff and his friends had enjoying playing and swimming in the creek.

High school seniors Marvin Randle and Dale Cain delivered new furniture to the Community Youth Center, which was being equipped by contributions from the community.

The Junior Garden Club chairman, Mrs. Pierce Shannon, asked that the club be allowed to plan a dedication ceremony in December. They sent invitations, made decorations, and met in the evenings with their husbands to plan promotions. The men urged help from the business and professional community, which resulted in donations of furniture, juke boxes, records, radios, equipment, magazine subscriptions, and money.

City Manager John Stiff supervised construction of the $75,000 Community Youth Center and the first municipal swimming pool.

When an enthusiastic crowd turned out on December 10, 1954, the two-story building with an outdoor swimming pool was wrapped as a Christmas present to the community and decorated with hundreds of handmade angels.

The committee met to lead the planning process and reported to the class, which provided input and then worked to carry out plans.

An editorial in the *Irving News* said there were too many backs to pat because it seemed that everybody in Irving was involved in some way. On CBS radio news it was called "a recreation center *for* and a tribute *to* Irving young people." The project was widely praised as "community leadership backed by community spirit." The pattern was repeated many times in future years as citizens worked together to create a better life in their city.

National publicity of a different kind came in 1955. A controversy over school administration deteriorated into what was termed "the civil war of Irving." For four months newspapers in Irving, Dallas, and Fort Worth and even some in other states carried front-page stories covering the antics of the school personnel, the Board, and the war between opposing factions in the community. People who had never heard of Irving, Texas, formed opinions about the city. Almost fifty years later there is little objectivity on the subject except from those who say: "I guess I was involved, but I never really understood what was going on."

Labor unions were gaining strength and were considered to be Communist infiltrated. Joseph McCarthy had been conducting his famous Communist witch hunt which was applauded by some and condemned by others. Cities and schools were struggling to keep up with overwhelming demands related to growth while the war between conservatives and liberals was raging and minorities were demanding equality.

Many Irving teachers were members of the National Education Association and some were also interested in John Dewey's theories, which were being translated into suggestions for curriculum and teaching methods called progressive education. To make matters worse, they attended summer precinct conventions. Many teachers supported Ralph Yarborough over Allan Shivers for governor. Superintendent John Beard was warned that influential people were displeased and that

he should control his teachers. He thought they should have the same rights as anybody else.

On February 14, the Board asked Beard to resign. The next day he refused, saying the Board had not given cause for dismissing him. The following day the Board chose Mr. Lasater for superintendent, but he refused the honor and joined seven other principals to ask that Beard be reinstated. On the seventeenth the Citizens Committee was formed and began to ask for an explanation of the Board's actions. The answer was that they were fulfilling their obligations as elected representatives. The answer to an appeal for a public hearing was that Dr. Beard would have to appeal to the courts or to the State Board of Education. Then they would present and defend their actions in a legal arena. The issue at that time was simply to have some reason for suddenly firing the superintendent. The Board fired Balford Morrison who was their attorney.

Having collected two thousand signatures, the committee still could not get answers from the Board and on February 28 teachers met and decided to walk out. Teachers, principals, bus drivers, cafeteria workers, and some office employees didn't go to work. One hundred and seventeen teachers stayed away, leaving only forty-nine on the job. The Board fired the principals and ordered all other employees back to work. When they didn't obey the next day there was a mass firing and applications for replacements were solicited. Meantime parents and other volunteers moved in and kept the schools open.

Disagreements sometimes became physical. Two prominent citizens who resorted to a fist fight were brought before young Jim Widener who was the Corporation Court judge. He fined each of them $25 and warned them that the fine would double if they were brought in again.

To the charge that Dr. Beard ordered teachers to strike, the teachers and principals responded that they had minds of their own and that their reasons related to intolerable working conditions. It was possible that their previous involvement in politics and Dr. Beard's failure to control them was at the root of the problem. A report in the *Texas Observer* on March 14, 1955, quoted one teacher as saying that teachers in Irving worked in "confusion and insecurity. We knew that certain school people had been questioned on their voting in a precinct election. . . . How did we know that we wouldn't be the next ones to be picked off one by one?"

As soon as it opened, the Center became a second home to Irving young people, and a full-time director was hired by the City. Programs for children and adults were added, but the teens had first choice on reservations for Friday and Saturday nights.

It was a sad sight for many former students and teachers when the High School "with the best gym in the world" was demolished to make way for a shopping strip. The other school buildings were already gone.

April 7, 1954, the *Dallas Times-Herald* ran a story about the razing of an Irving landmark. The Irving State Bank had bought the old hotel at the north end of Main Street and planned a drive-through facility.

Two other issues were mixed into the confusing controversy. The schools had accepted federal and state aid for school lunches and to help fund the building program. Some citizens were adamantly opposed to any federal or state aid. The other was the failure to require Latin, and the inclusion of some vocational education courses. One Board member was quoted in the *Texas Observer* as saying that "people who work with their hands ought not to go to high school."

March 7, the Citizens Committee filed a petition with Judge Sterrett to call an election to abolish the Irving Independent School District. The purpose was to depose the Board without waiting for the next scheduled election. While all of this was going on the community was being polarized. Speakers were brought in to lecture on the dangers of Communism that was infiltrating and attempting to take over our government and institutions. The Save Our Schools Committee and the Citizens Committee each produced and distributed masses of flyers, special newspapers, and letters. They were distributed door to door, by mail and some leaflets were even dropped from an airplane. Just before the election a newspaper named *The Irving Truth* was distributed to every house. Some of the literature got pretty radical. A parable about seven monkeys and a big baboon is amusing to an outsider but it was probably a bombshell at the time. It is obvious that the members of the School Board are the monkeys being led and used by the baboon. The Citizens Committee was accusing the SOS Committee and the Board of being pressured by or being part of a political clique that intended to control the city and the schools.

Finally, on March 26, almost 90 percent of the qualified voters turned out and the majority voted to abolish the school district. A date for a second election was requested and the County School Board appointed a three-man Board to oversee the Irving schools, which had become county schools until the next election which would recreate the IISD.

A "Watchdog Committee" called a public meeting to investigate "sinister outside influences directed toward establishment of pinko and leftist ideologies." Speakers were brought in to describe how the NEA and other groups with socialistic and collectivist views tried to take over in school controversies elsewhere. But after all of the warnings and investigations and protests the election, which reestablished the school district and elected a new Board, resulted in a Board made up of four Citizens Committee members and three Save Our Schools members. For all of that trouble they were only going to serve twenty days until the next regular election on May 7. When all seven members of the Board elected were from the Citizens Committee, Dr. Beard and

Responding to citizens' requests during the strike, Mayor Hardee made unannounced visits to the schools. He reported that they were being run in an orderly and efficient manner. He could see no reason to keep children out of school. This teacher is Mrs. Mary Herndon. From *The Irving Truth*

Flyers warning of sinister forces bringing Communist ideas into Irving schools were sent to every home in Irving.

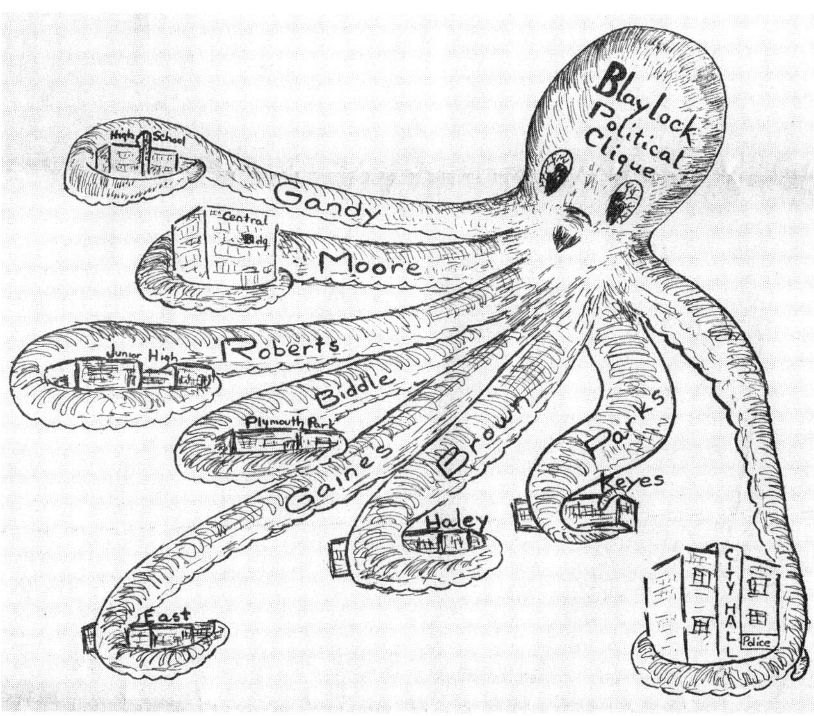

Flyers sent to every home illustrated the belief that a political clique was seeking control of City Hall and the school system. Each Board member is depicted with one of the schools.

On February 21, 1955, Irving Savings and Loan Association, which had originally been in the Irvingate Shopping Center, opened in a new location at 101 North Main at Irving Boulevard. The historic bank building had been remodeled and air-conditioned. R. J. Whitmire managed staff members Melba Johnson and Dovie Huckabay. Financing new homes was a booming business.

most of the former staff were rehired. When he was fired, Dr. Beard was just two years into a five-year contract and his salary was paid to the temporary replacement.

Hearings and protests and court cases continued and the community was torn for several years, but school continued and began to settle into a normal mode. Dr. Beard retired a year later and accepted a job teaching at Howard Payne College. School Board policies were gradually developed, recorded, and codified.

During the height of the school controversy, the city elections occurred and Mayor Hardee was running for reelection. He ran as an independent not claiming support from any group and he certainly wanted to stay out of the school business. Melba Johnson remembers that he came into the Savings and Loan office on Main Street with tape over his mouth making it clear that he didn't want to talk about the schools. In spite of having three opponents, he was elected to a third term.

While it seemed that all of the attention was on the school controversy the city government had its own challenges in the same time frame. After getting approval to build five hundred three-bedroom brick houses, Carr Collins had come back to expand the subdivision to twelve hundred houses. Then he requested commercial zoning on thirty-five acres that had been the Gilbert homestead, when he already had commercial zoning on thirteen adjacent acres. He was proposing a shopping center that would be occupied in a short time.

There were spirited discussions around town about the merits of the case, and Zoning Board members disagreed about granting the zoning. On the one hand the downtown merchants were already not getting enough boost from the growing population. On the other hand, if Irving didn't provide goods and services, business could go out of the city and revenues would be lost. The growing population created a need for a shopping center on the west side. There was also the concern that so much commercial property should not be in the hands of one man. And furthermore, all that had been developed on the thirteen acres already zoned commercial was a service station and a drive-in grocery.

In 1954, the Plymouth Addition was a dramatic change from the orchards and pastures and owner-built homes that had been northwest of Irving. Many citizens deplored this invasion of the countryside.

This was the first segment of the Plymouth Park Shopping Center. It expanded rapidly along with the numerous subdivisions that soon surrounded it.

When the Zoning Board met in the high school gymnasium, all of the chairs and most of the bleachers were filled. After lengthy argument, a compromise reduced the 35 acres to 26.2 acres and back-zoned the 14 acres to residential. The Mayflower Company was storing building materials in two of the hangers on the old airport property. Jackie Townsell's father, Jack Howard, was a carpenter for the company.

On October 13 through 22, 1955, the grand opening of the Plymouth Park Shopping Center was a mammoth ten-day celebration. There were carnival rides, balloons, prizes, and fireworks. Several musical groups, including the Lightcrust Doughboys, played multiple times each day. Fifteen businesses were already open, including six major chain stores, a large cafeteria, and a new bank chartered by Carr Collins. The bank was soon moved to a new freestanding building and sold to local investors. Southwest Bank was viewed as competition with Irving State Bank, but it also brought new customers from the growing surrounding area. Businesses continued to move in until the center expanded across Story Road on one side and across Irving Boulevard on the other. The huge parking lot surrounded by buildings became a favorite place for celebrations, which reminded some older residents of the Fourth of July parties at Sowers before Irving existed. The Sowers School, represented by Board President Harry Field, requested annexation by the Irving School District and probably the successful growth in this area influenced the Irving system to assume their bond debt and annex the schools.

Irving is privileged to have a major university that has for the past forty-seven years quietly contributed to the quality of life as the city grew in size and resources, The University of Dallas started in 1952 with the shared hopes of the Sisters of St. Mary who had operated Our Lady of Victory College in Fort Worth since 1930. They needed more space and wanted to be closer to the center of the diocese. Bishop Thomas Gorman gave permission to campaign for funds and search for land, Eugene Constantin and Edward Maher, whose children had been taught by the sisters agreed to spearhead the effort. A Board made up of businessmen, including Charles Schulze from Irving, soon had larger visions of a major university and set an initial goal of $2,000,000, which they raised in just six months.

After looking at twenty-four sites they favored a thousand acres of land on a hill northeast of Irving. Ben Carpenter offered to give them 150 acres and sell more at his original cost. Adjoining property was available from the Cleghorn and McCune families and Mayor C. B. Hardee assured them that the City of Irving could serve their utility needs. He lost no time getting the property annexed to Irving, although the businessmen were leaning toward becoming

The Cistercian Monks built their Monastery northwest of the main University of Dallas campus. Nine Cistercians were on the faculty when the University opened.

part of Dallas. The Dallas Council already had realized they couldn't carry utilities across the Elm Fork. Irving was overloaded with expansion projects, but they began surveying to determine how they could serve the area. It was inevitable that surrounding properties would be developed. Mr. Carpenter was already planning University Hills.

In just over a year, six buildings were erected on the hill and the name University of Dallas was confirmed. The charter of the original University of Dallas had been dormant since 1928. A reminder of earlier history is known to many Boy Scouts in Irving, who can locate Turkey Knob on the property. It was a campsite for Indians and a landmark for early travelers. California Crossing is about a mile north.

Dr. Kenneth Braested, president, hired Dr. Eugene Curtsinger to teach literature and act as academic dean and with the Sisters of St. Mary they began academic and administrative planning. Cistercian Monks, who had left Hungary because of Communist oppression, were welcomed to the diocese in 1953 and became a part of the planning for an intellectually rich curriculum. The Dominican Fathers came later in 1958. When the Sisters of St. Mary moved to their quarters west of the campus the University had three resident teaching orders forming the core faculty and a lay faculty of diverse faiths was added. In September 1956, instruction began with a ninety-six-member freshman class and the story has been one of growth in size and quality for a world-recognized university.

Also in 1956, Ben Carpenter bought the two-thousand-acre O'Connor Dairy and started planning some major developments.

Large delegations of Irving and Dallas County officials and Irving Chamber of Commerce representatives were making repeated trips to Austin seeking Highway Commission support for desperately needed road projects. State Highway 356 from Westmoreland to the bridge needed to be four lanes, The two-lane bridge was a bottleneck and the two-lane road from Britain past Irvingate Shopping Center was totally inadequate.

The Highway Commission wanted to turn Highway 15 into a freeway because Highway 80 between Dallas and Fort Worth was overloaded. The people wrestling with roadway problems had little time to devote to a school controversy or to worry about Communism. The old bridge where Irving Boulevard and Shady Grove converged was left in place and a new bridge was constructed about a quarter mile north, with a new and straighter leg of Highway 356 from Irving Heights.

Turning two-lane Highway 15 into the Highway 183 Expressway involved some "horse trading" which was covered in newspapers as far away as New York. The tiny city of Irving loaned big Dallas County $300,000 to buy right of way that wasn't even in the Irving city limits. The State had agreed to pay 90 percent of the cost and the County was obligated to furnish 10 percent, which it didn't have. The part of the deal that wasn't publicized was that the County repaid Irving with over a million dollars worth of work on road and bridge construction in the city. Mayor Hardee thought it proved to be a good trade.

When the Expressway was completed, Britain Road, which had been the only link between original Irving and the territory north of Highway 15, was divided and the drive-in movie was at the end of the south section. Ponce Road, intersecting Britain Road about halfway between 183 and Grauwyler, is a reminder of a family that came to Irving in 1914 and made many contributions to the good life in the city.

The idea of navigating the Trinity River became a hot topic again along with other issues related to the river. In 1955 the legislature established the Trinity River Authority of Texas, which included seventeen counties in the Trinity watershed, and a master plan for the basin with four major projects including a regional sewage collection and treatment system for the cities of Irving, Farmers Branch, Carrollton, Grand Prairie, and Dallas. Although the legislation was not aimed toward navigation, it spurred a renewal of interest in that possibility.

Some of the earliest settlers "between the forks" had been artists and musicians and craftsmen. Their talents had contributed greatly to the pleasure and enrichment of early Irving, but until the mid-1950s the closest thing to an arts organization was the garden clubs. When Barbara Turrentine and Lil Cartright, whose father was a well-known portrait painter in

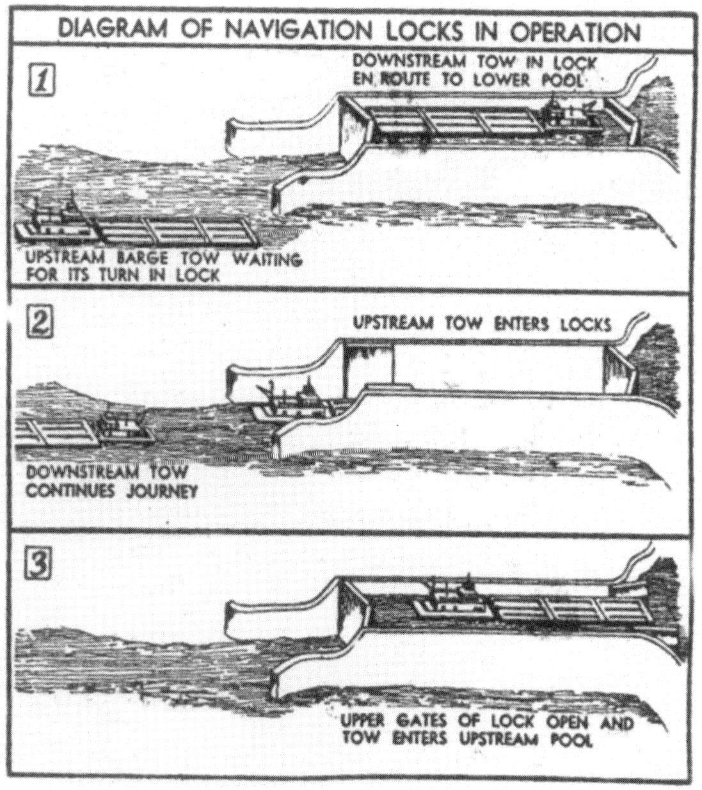

In 1955, boosters of navigation on the Trinity River claimed that the watershed could handle barges transporting 6 million tons a year and boost the economy along its path. A plan for locks and gates was developed and widely publicized to generate support for the project.

The Berean Christian Academy opened in 1954 at 1012 East Sixth Street. In 1956 a gymnasium was added and dedicated by Governor Price Daniel. There were seven private schools in the 1950s that offered first and second grades, but only Berean and St. Lukes offered a complete elementary school curriculum.

Dr. Paul Laird started his tenure as mayor with six new Commission members. He served from 1957 to 1959.

England, discovered their mutual passion for the visual arts they soon gathered friends who enjoyed painting together and formed the Irving Art Association. As they painted in members' homes they discussed the need for an art museum in Irving and the possibility of exhibits. In the summer of 1956, they hired a teacher from Dallas for a children's art class at the Salvation Army Campgrounds. According to Barbara, the future O'Connor was a dusty lane with chains across either end at Lively and Grauwyler. They held three annual sidewalk shows at the Plymouth Park Shopping Center where over one hundred artists rented booths.

Professional artists came to meetings to demonstrate in various media. When attendance outgrew the homes, the Association had meetings in the TP&L Building on Irving Heights, the First Federal Savings and Loan Building, and the Garden and Arts Center on Senter Road. They were looking for a permanent location for meetings, classes, and exhibits while actively promoting art in Irving.

Some of the organizers of the Irving Community Concert Association in 1958 had been acquainted with the national organization through the Dallas group that brought the concerts to McFarlin Auditorium on the SMU campus. The national Community Concerts Association engages a variety of professional musicians and performers each year. The local organizations meet with a representative and choose a season. They handle promotion and sell season tickets. The volunteers who worked with Community Concerts were enthusiastically and energetically devoted to enjoying and sharing some of the world's top entertainers with Irving citizens. The Irving High School auditorium was not always completely adequate for the performances. The quest for a performing arts center started in the 1950s and escalated as the number of performing arts organizations increased.

Two of the fundamental necessities for a city to survive are transportation and communication. Irving had a newspaper the day it was founded beside the railroad track. By the 1950s there were radios and a few televisions and Irving had the *Irving News Record* and the *Irving Daily News*. The biggest challenge for government was providing streets, roads, and drainage.

When Mayor Hardee decided not to run for a fourth term in 1957, he had served with twenty-one different Council members. It was a difficult and time-consuming job.

Dr. Paul Laird had come to Irving in 1953 after serving in the Korean War and completing a residency in surgery. He and his wife, Naomi, wanted to settle in a small town near Dallas. They chose Irving and immediately became active in the church and service clubs. In a very short time, he was president of the Rotary Club and a director of the Chamber of Commerce and involved in transportation issues. When Hardee announced he would not run again, some community leaders suggested Dr. Laird should run for mayor as an independent candidate. He was elected in 1957 along with an entirely new Commission. Within three months, City Manager John Stiff resigned and C. C. Anderson manned the post until C. A. Scrimshire was hired in November. Drainage was a problem especially in the original part of town. C. C. Anderson warned that the streets could not serve traffic and drainage. Water standing in the streets would destroy the surfaces. The floods in 1958, after six years of drought, alerted the staff and the Commission to the potential for disaster if attention was not directed to planning future building.

Dr. Laird and the Commissioners worked on ways to make everything the city did more "businesslike." Ordinances required open bids that were competitive, mandated clearing properties of trash and weeds, and the securing of right of way before letting contracts on roads and bridges. They didn't want to repeat the dilemma experienced by a former Commission when a bridge was out in a pasture with no roads to it. They adopted the Standard Plumbing Code and the Southern Standard Building Code and instituted air pollution control. They appointed the first Park Board, established a Health Department, and named Dr. James May as the first health director. They put in several thousand feet of new water lines, installed a five-million-gallon reservoir, and proposed two overhead storage tanks. They heard 140 zoning cases.

The City and the Irving School District bought the Salvation Army Camp. A new High School was planned on one side of the lane that would be O'Connor and the first Administration Building was started on the other side. In a recorded interview with Estelle Bates, Dr. Laird said that the city had grown so fast that an Armory had been built and a School Administration Building and High School were emerging with no road to them. "We had to immediately give right of way and build O'Connor Road, which ran from Pioneer to Grauwyler."

A step forward in the long-term planning process was initiated when Dr. Hugo Leipziger was engaged to update the master plan for the City. He was a professor at the University of Texas who was known throughout Europe for his work in planning and executing major projects. The plan that was developed was a reference for development for many years.

It was no secret that Irving needed a hospital. The increasing population and number of doctors in the city created a burden on Dallas hospitals. The distance was both an inconvenience and a danger. In 1954, the Hamilton Report revealed that Dallas County was below the minimum safety standard of 4.5 hospital beds per one thousand residents. In 1955, Russell Stephens, president of the Chamber of Commerce, requested that Irving physicians meet and make plans for a hospital in Irving. Dr. Laird remembered that when the physicians first met, Dr. Joe Roberts said, "Well, we're going to have air conditioning." Most of the doctors used Methodist Hospital at the time and it was not air conditioned.

In February of 1959, the Irving Commission appointed a fourteen-member Advisory Committee to analyze the feasibility of a local hospital. They had "started the ball rolling."

In 1958, road and bridge work didn't move fast enough to suit Bob Nelson. He demonstrated the poor condition of the Story/Rock Island Bridge by sticking his head through one of the cracks. Courtesy Bob Nelson

The story of the career of the brilliant young city attorney who wrote that ordinance is amazing and tragic. He was a study in contradiction. Corporation Court Judge Jim Widener and City Attorney Balford Morrison had both resigned to give more time to private practice, leaving vacancies. Joe Henry Hodges was hired in a little over an hour at a called meeting of the Commission. His credentials were so good and his personality so engaging that no background check was needed. An investigation would have revealed that compulsive gambling had resulted in problems that forced him to leave Beaumont, Texas, his hometown, and that he had been arrested in Zanesville, Ohio; Midland, Texas; and Roswell, New Mexico.

Dr. Paul Laird was the first mayor to present a "State of the City" speech. The Planning Council of the Chamber of Commerce sponsored the event for the general public at the new National Guard Armory. They expected three hundred people, but almost three thousand attended. Irving people were really interested in their city.

He performed well as city attorney. He was well versed in law, was a financial whiz, and energetic in his work. For two years he rebuilt his life. He taught Sunday school, sang in the choir, and was respected in his relationships with a broad spectrum of business leaders and local citizens. He had given up gambling. But one day a well-known Irving businessman asked Joe if he shot craps and invited him to a game that was going on in a van parked on a construction site. The compulsion took over and soon he had bookies taking bets on ball games, was participating in every type of gambling going in the city, and was flying off to Las Vegas. He made thousands of dollars only to lose and borrow to pay his gambling debts, then lose what he borrowed to gambling. The story of living on the edge, including the inside story of behind the scenes gambling in Irving, is revealed in the book *Compulsion* by Robin Moore. It reads like a suspense novel, but it is the true story of Joe Hodges with a psychiatric analysis at the end by Dr. Robert Custer, a specialist in addictive disease.

In general, the outlook for Irving as a city was good because of the complete involvement of the citizens in whatever they each thought was important. Interests and talents varied, but almost everybody was doing something to enhance life in Irving.

The new Post Office built on a 125-by-145-foot lot facing Third at Hastings was the first government-owned Post Office in Irving. It was finished just as the lease on the two-story building on the northwest corner of Main and Second expired.

Chapter 7

Coming of Age

In 1960 the U.S. Census Bureau named Irving "the fastest growing city in Texas." Population had grown from 2,615 in 1950 to 45,895 in 1960. After Home Rule Charter status had been established the city continued to annex land in all directions. From 1952 to 1959 the city limits grew from one to twenty-eight square miles and another twenty miles were under first reading. Irving was still a residential city with state and county roads leading to employment centers in surrounding areas. Improvements to State Highway 356 (Irving Boulevard) from the eastern city limits to Iowa Street were in progress. Loop 12 was being constructed to Highway 183 and planned to extend farther north. It was not yet a freeway.

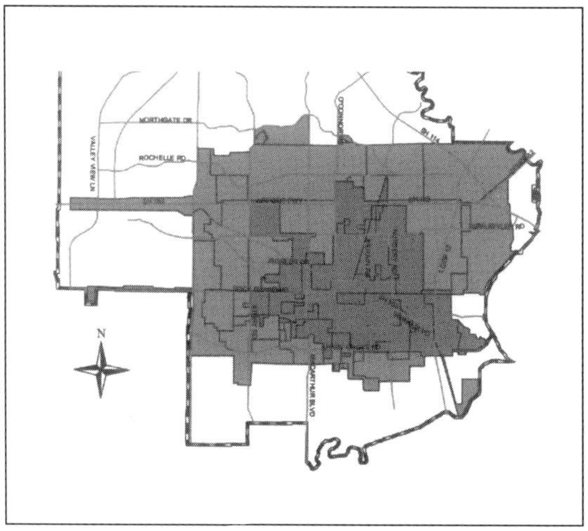

By 1960, the twenty-eight-square-mile footprint of the city looked like this, and more expansion was already planned.

The year 1960 began with 187 city employees and C. C. Anderson acting as interim city manager after C. A. Scrimshire had resigned. In April 1960, Morris Howard was hired as full-time city manager. Within the city limits there were now more than 175 miles of city streets to be maintained. The Police Department had thirty employees, twenty-two of whom were patrolmen with a salary from $300 to $360 per month. The volunteer Police Reserves had twenty-five men. The Fire Department employed twenty-eight men, including the chief, a fire marshal, two captains, four lieutenants, and twenty firemen. Another twenty volunteer firemen helped as needed. New Fire Stations at 1306 North Story Road and on East Grauwyler supplemented the original station.

The increase in responsibility for all City services had been rapid, but citizens were united in the effort to not only keep up but to constantly improve living conditions in their city. There was a strong sense of ownership. A long-term planning process was initiated when Dr. Hugo Leipziger was engaged to develop a Master Plan for the City. He was a professor at the University of Texas who was known throughout Europe for his work in planning and executing major projects. Reports on the phases of the Master Plan were published at intervals and a summary of the completed work was published in July 1960. It was intended to be a flexible tool for guiding City officials and potential developers as the city continued to grow. Alert citizens read it and discussed it with mixed reactions. Proposals for effecting a central business district generated some controversy between visionaries and longtime property owners in the original townsite. The report stated: "No matter how much outward growth a city experiences it must have a central Core, a tightly knit entity with a full range of retail, administrative, financial, service, and entertainment facilities. The District must be compact with minimum distances between components, for it is the pedestrian who uses it and for whom it must work. . . . The present CBD of Irving grew out of the original concentration of commerce at the intersection of Main Street and Irving Boulevard. The City has long since outgrown Main Street. Instead of the more desirable core there is now strip development of Irving Boulevard."

Lynn Brown, was mayor from 1959 to 1967.

Mayor Lynn Brown was actively interested in the possibilities of expansion. Only two of the annexations he pursued were not completed as planned. City Planner Irwin Harris discovered that there had never been a reading on property between the Trinity River levees. Irving took first reading all the way to the Commerce Street Bridge. Of course, Dallas was not pleased and took the matter to court. The judge was Dallas Blankenship. Mayor Brown said: "The law was on our side but the judge was not. . . . It was a good try."

The other "good try" ended more amicably. The City annexed territory to the north that had been acquired by the Carpenter family, including the original Hackberry Ranch. A lawsuit followed. When he lost the lawsuit, Ben Carpenter went to the Council and pointed out the fact that there was no way the City could extend services to all of that area. He suggested that they annex sections as they were developed and that the ranch land should remain under agricultural zoning as long as that definition applied. The Council agreed.

A shopping strip, anchored by a Buddies Supermarket, soon occupied the original school site between Second and Fourth Streets. Duke and Ayres, which had been the only chain store on old Main Street, moved to this new location. Young adults working or shopping there remembered their school days in the buildings that had disappeared from the site.

The schools were still the biggest business in Irving. The school system covered forty-three square miles, but eleven of the thirteen schools were within the twenty-eight-square-mile city limits. The segregated Ledbetter and Bear Creek Schools for which the IISD was responsible were outside Irving city limits. The County schools serving other surrounding communities had closed

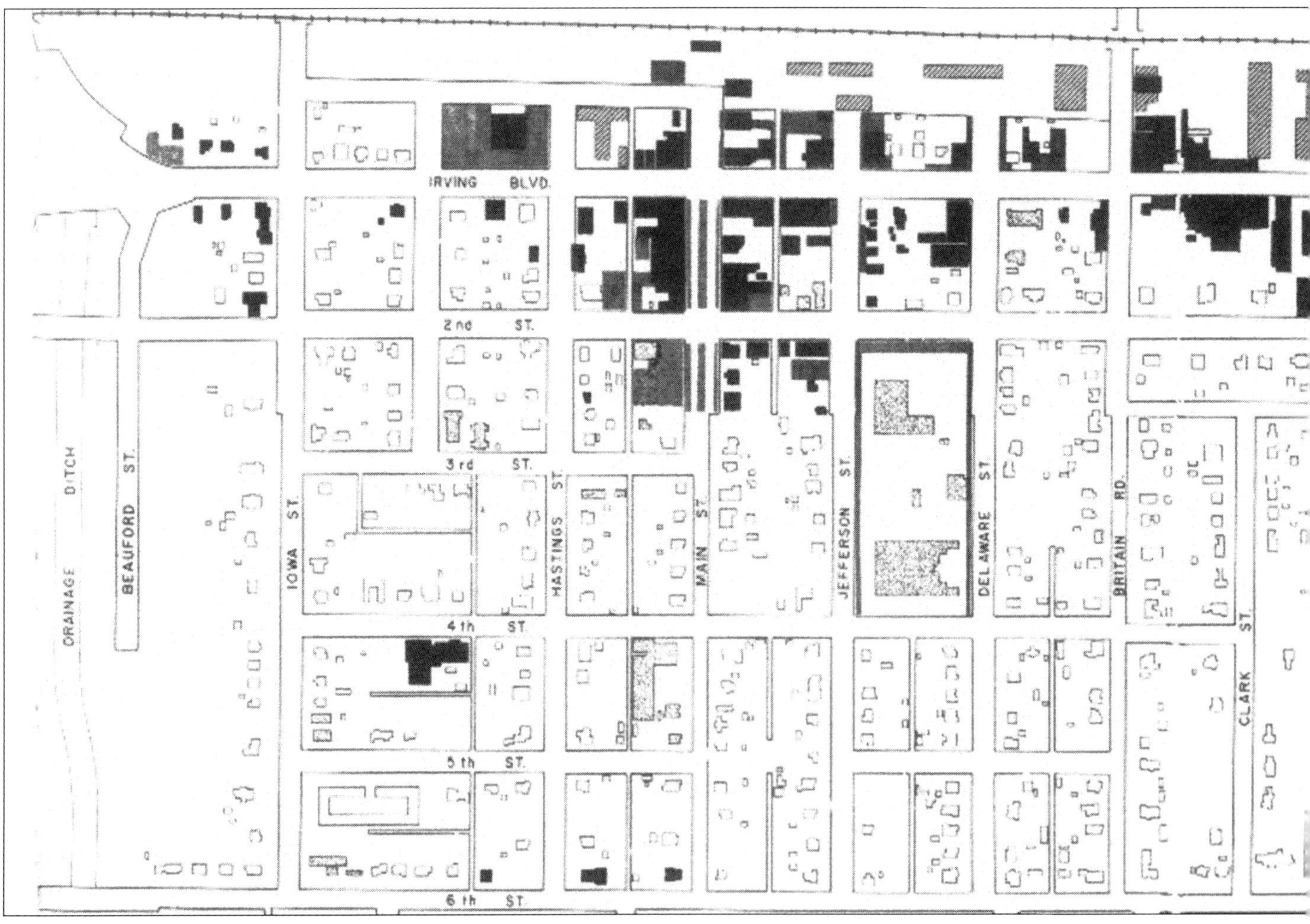

Left:
The new City Hall at 845 West Irving Boulevard was the beginning of the large complex of government buildings that eventually occupied the tract just west of Delaware Creek. Irving Boulevard continued to extend west with commercial development.

Below:
The Leipziger Plan identified the strip of largely commercial development along Irving Boulevard from South Iowa Street to Loop 12 as the Irving CBD. It was noted that Irving Boulevard and Second Street were one way in opposite directions between their west and east points of intersection.

Within the pictured "strip business district" researchers found nearly all of the lawyers in Irving, half of the doctors, half of the apparel stores, three-fifths of the insurance agents, a third of the realtors, a third of the restaurants, and a fifth of the churches.

Irving High School was the pride of the community, providing a large auditorium for meetings and performances of all kinds. Support for school activities was strong. The time had passed when everybody knew everybody in Irving and they came to Main Street on Saturday to visit. But newcomers were likely to meet established residents in the halls, meeting rooms, cafeteria, and auditorium of Irving High. The football team was still enthusiastically supported by what seemed like everybody in Irving.

The J. O. Davis School was named to honor Miss Josye O. Davis, the first teacher in the Sowers School No. 2. She taught grades one through seven in one room. She was also one of the founders of the Ben Washington Baptist Church. Courtesy Dixie Caraway

and their students came into Irving even though many of them still lived outside the city limits. The IISD built a new brick school in the Bear Creek community. Residents there chose to name the new building J. O. Davis to honor one of the first teachers in the community who had taught grades one through seven in the one-room Sowers No. 2 School. "Miss Josye" was also a leader in the community and in the church. Use of the new modern building was phased in starting with grades one through seven. Finally, in 1960, J. O Davis offered grades one through twelve. This segregated school was the focal point and the pride of the community. Students excelled in sports, music, and essay writing and achieved statewide recognition. The outstanding performance of their band and drill team in the Irving Golden Anniversary parade was so impressive that it still lives in memories of many who witnessed it.

When Irving High School moved to the new building on O'Connor, the Junior High that faced Edmondson became Central Elementary School and Bowie Junior High students moved into the former High School building on Sixth street. The Junior High had been named Bowie when Crockett Junior High opened in 1957. Central Elementary later became Lee Britain, honoring a longtime School Board member and descendent of the Britain family that originally owned the property on which the city was founded. The growth in the school system from 1954 to 1960 had been frantic, and it continued unabated through the 1960s. Superintendent W. T. Hanes was working hard for his $15,000 annual salary. The city manager salary was $12,500 and he had to post a $15,000 bond. School administrators were struggling to deal with the constant need to build and equip more schools and hire more teachers. MacArthur High School was built in 1963 and Nimitz High School was built in 1968. The citizens of Irving were actively involved in the evolving programs and activities of their schools.

Peck's Office Supply, that had started in an Irvingate Shopping Center storefront, moved to their freestanding building on West Irving Boulevard, where Etta Williams Roberts' boarding house had stood just west of the first house in Irving, sometimes referred to as the Brown/Miller house. Parents lined up to buy school supplies packaged from lists supplied by teachers. In keeping with the tradition of the stores in "old downtown Irving," it was a mom-and-pop store and the Peck children helped when they were big enough.

Bill Stevens became manager of the Chamber of Commerce in October 1960. He found energetic leaders with a real need for a manager. During the 1950s, the Chamber had been briefly in six different locations before finding a home upstairs over Christy's Furniture Store in 1962. They were $2,500 in debt, but their members were actively involved in the development issues of the city. The story of the Chamber of Commerce is success from that point on. In 1962, City Secretary Mary Gilliland was the first president of the Women's Division of the Chamber. They provided and served refreshments at Chamber functions. The Division president was an ex-officio member of the Chamber. Women did not serve on the Board. By 1964, the Chamber of Commerce was out of debt and had a $2,800 surplus and they had become a force in the growth and politics of Irving.

There were dozens of social, civic, service, professional, and special interest clubs and organizations where citizens interacted regularly. The Jaycees emerged as one of the most active organizations in civic affairs. Most of their members were also active in one or more of the service clubs including Kiwanis, Optimist, Rotary, Civitan, or Lions. When the Masons built a new structure on their land at Second and Jefferson the Jaycees took over the second floor of the old building on the southwest corner of Main and Irving Boulevard.

The League of Women Voters had researched, published, and distributed five thousand copies of a handbook titled *Know Your City—Irving*, which was a requirement for having a certified local League. The printing of the handbook was financed by twenty Irving businessmen. The

Above:
In 1962, when the season's thus far undefeated Irving Tigers met the Wichita Falls Coyotes, who had a seven-year record of wins in the district and had won two state championships in the four straight years they had played in the state finals, excitement ran high. The Toy Tigers Drill Team, which Lucille Casey had founded in 1959, was on one of the seventeen train cars that carried Irving fans to Wichita Falls. They were singing: "Irving will shine tonight. Irving will shine. . . ." And they did shine. Irving won. Casey collection, Irving Archives

Left:
The Tigers were playing the Arlington Colts, and the Grand Prairie Gophers were playing the Wichita Falls Coyotes on the same night. The Colts, with only a loss to the Coyotes, could get into a playoff if they won over the Tigers, while the Coyotes defeated the Gophers. They were ahead 9–7 in the final minute of the game with a 4 and 1 on their own twenty-yard line. The plan was to punt when the coaches yelled "Gophers won." The quarterback thought the instruction from the sideline was "go for one" so instead of punting he ran the ball to try to get one yard needed for a first down.

The Tigers stopped the play and scored the winning touchdown on a pass from Freddy Akin to Kenny Johnson. Players in the picture are Kenny Johnson catching the ball and Richard Bridges. The Tigers' win that year was described as one of the biggest upsets in high school football history. Courtesy Kenny Johnson

The Masons built this new hall on property they owned at Jefferson and Second Streets. They used the side entrance just as they had done in the building at Main and Irving Boulevard. For many years Lone Star Gas Company occupied the lower floor with a front entrance.

basic mission of the League, dating from the time women got the right to vote, was to be informed on issues and to encourage informed voting. The Irving members advocated election code reform that would abolish the poll tax and provide for ongoing registration, but they nevertheless promoted the payment of the poll tax as long as it was a requirement to vote. They were deputized and set up tables in supermarkets and public buildings to register voters who paid the required $1.75 during the yearly window of opportunity before elections. They even visited offices to register voters. They published profiles of elected officials at all levels of government and "Voters Guides" which featured facts on both sides of issues and candidates' answers to questions about their qualifications and positions on current issues. The first programs that presented the mayoral and City Council candidates to answer questions at public forums were named "Face the Public" and arranged in partnership with the Optimist Club. Having studied the Leipziger Plan that had been commissioned by the Council they strongly advocated the employment of a full-time qualified planner and implementation of suggestions in the plan. They were especially concerned with the preservation of open space in the design of the city. A joint planning group was appointed with representatives from the Chamber of Commerce, the Jaycees, and the League of Women Voters. In 1964, the Irving League began participating in the production of a weekly half-hour TV show called "Voters Digest" on Channel 11. Subjects were discussed by experts in various fields and by persons involved in controversial issues.

The City left all of the responsibility for planning, funding, and construction of the Irving Community Hospital to the Board, which the Council appointed. Seated: Robert Nelson, Mrs. John Hunter, Clinton Howard, Mrs. Karl Hudgins, Wre Sutherland. Standing: Dr. Tom Murphy, Dr. Joe Roberts, Joe Glover, Jerry Scheen, James Ratteree, and Judge Lloyd Russell. Don Peck is missing.

There were only two medical clinics in Irving. The South Delaware Clinic founded by Drs. Richard Bates, Joe Kugler, and Sam Huggins was located in the first block south of Irving Boulevard across from the South Delaware Church of Christ. The Gilbert Roberts Clinic at 101 South Iowa was still bringing new physicians into Irving. Funeral homes were providing some ambulance service to Dallas hospitals and the police escorted automobiles on emergency trips. In 1966, the Leach Funeral Home at 129 South O'Connor was sold. Edward Smith had worked for Mr. Leach in the store on Main Street and in the funeral parlor. He and Harrell Chism became partners and changed the name of the parlor to Chism-Smith.

By January 1960, the Hospital Authority, that had been appointed by the City Commission to develop a plan to finance and construct a hospital, was having difficulty agreeing on a course of action. There was stiff opposition in town to applying for Federal Hill-Burton funds. They rejected contracting with an outside organization to construct and manage a hospital on a profit-sharing basis. Lenders were not interested because there was little industry or business in the city. Brokers weren't interested in hospital bonds when school bonds backed by tax money were safer. Wre Sutherland suggested they try a community-wide fund drive and offered to ask the Chamber of Commerce to create a hospital foundation. According to Board minutes the ball started rolling by June 1960. The community got involved. Businessmen and physicians started fundraising. An Auxiliary and a Junior Auxiliary were formed.

The Irving Community Hospital was the only hospital in Texas that had an Auxiliary before it was built. Even more unique was the Junior Auxiliary, organized by Mrs. John Hunter in 1963. They were called the Active Angels. These teenage girls pledged their time, efforts, and talents to the Irving Community Hospital.

Above:
By August 1964, Irving had a Hospital and a good parking lot. The road left much to be desired.

Right:
At the groundbreaking for the Hospital, the National Guard set up a field kitchen and iced down cold drinks for an old-timers picnic after the ceremony. The Active Angels served the honored guests.

Ninety women from sixteen churches and twenty-two civic groups were planning to raise money.

Hans Smith offered ten acres on Rochelle Road. Dr. Prosser offered ten acres on Greenview and Esters Road. Ben Carpenter and his sister, Carolyn Williams, offered ten acres on Carpenter Road and Highway 183. Of course there was some disagreement in the community about which site was best, but the Carpenter Road site was chosen. This land was part of the Albert Farine farm, which had been bought by the Carpenter family in 1950. Lucy Farine Bell, who grew up on that farm, had been involved in the transaction. Carpenter Road, which provided access south from Highway 183, was just two lanes. It was later widened and became MacArthur Boulevard.

By December 1963, construction was well underway. Carpenter Road, which would later be widened and become MacArthur Boulevard, is lower left. The surrounding area is relatively undeveloped.

As the need for funds intensified, the objection to federal funds dissipated enough that application was made and Senator George Parkhouse became a strong partner as he guided representatives from Irving on several trips to Austin, and championed the allocation of Hill-Burton funds for the Irving hospital project.

A community fundraising goal was set at $750,000. Money was contributed in large and small amounts. The Hoblitzelle Foundation gave $10,000, Irving physicians pledged contributions, and Eugene Kahn Sanger urged Dallas County residents to support the drive. He referred to the shortage of hospital beds in Dallas County and wrote: "The fact that the energetic citizens of Irving are rising to meet this need is as important to Dallas as it is to Irving."

The division of the drive headed by Dr. Eleanor Reckery got a lot of attention, generated enthusiasm, and exceeded its goal by a large margin. The newspapers ran announcements that on Sunday June 24, between 1:00 and 3:00 p.m. Irving women would ring bells for the hospital. Dr. Reckery was quoted: "We feel that every family in Irving will want truthfully to say that they had a part in building the hospital. We intend to see that they get that opportunity." At the

The Irving High School Band gave a rousing performance at the Hospital dedication

In 1962 the first Irving Municipal Library opened in a new 2,100-square-foot building at 915 North O'Connor Road. The private Association dissolved and donated most of their holdings to the new library. Verna Dornbluth was the first public librarian.

appointed time, five hundred women fanned out, going door to door, to visit every home within the city limits.

Albert Scheidt, who was administrator at Parkland Hospital, was not one of the forty-five applicants for the job of administrator of the new hospital that was being planned, but while he was serving as the consulting administrator he expressed an interest in the job. The Authority was pleased to formally offer him the position. On May 15, 1963, he personally carried hospital plans to the State Health Department and met with officials for review and approval.

Construction began in August 1963 and opening ceremonies were November 8, 1964. The citizens of Irving felt a very real sense of ownership in Irving Community Hospital.

While so much attention and energy was being invested in getting a hospital, the citizens of Irving were promoting other means of enhancing life in the city. A municipal Library was basic, and that little house on Main Street had become totally inadequate to meet the expectations of the city Irving had become. With some persuasion, the Council was convinced that the project was urgent. A Library Board was appointed from among the activists urging City involvement in the creation of a more adequate Library. The first municipal Library opened February 24, 1962.

Music had always been a part of life in Irving. The first settlers brought various forms of classic and folk music with them and spontaneous "homemade" music occurred at most gatherings. The High School had an outstanding band and choral group and the churches were rich with choral and instrumental music. The only thing Irving didn't have was a symphony. Peggy Peterson is credited with bringing nine musicians from Irving and Father George Ferenczy from the University of Dallas Music Department together to form a string ensemble. As the group grew into a symphony orchestra she became the manager and Father George was the director. He was a highly educated refugee from Hungary who was familiar with twenty languages. The first small concert was free to the public at Lynch Hall on the University of Dallas campus. The small group was billed as a Symphonette. Other concerts followed at Lynch Hall, and at the old Irving Country Club, which was in the area where Country Club Road joins Las Brisas in northwest Irving. The nine music lovers who formed the nucleus of what became the Irving Symphony Orchestra were from various backgrounds. Violinists were attorney Mike Grisham, Church of Christ minister J. B. Taylor and his teenage daughter Sheryl, mathematician Franz Selig, music teacher Ray Brisbone, and Beth Smith. Librarian Betty McDonald and Mrs. M. K. Abdo played viola, and Kathy Grace played cello parts on the bassoon.

By 1965 the Library was too small to meet the demands for services. An addition increased the size to 9,800 square feet, which included a small auditorium with a stage for Library-sponsored programs. The Friends of the Library helped with funding and promotion of services.

The ladies who founded the Art Association were sponsoring art exhibits, classes, and art sales wherever they could find a place. Their long-range plan was to have a fine art museum in Irving. They opened a savings account labeled "Museum Building Fund" where they deposited any money they raised. Courtesy Barbara Turrentine Fryrear

On the evening of December 19, 1962, twenty-three volunteer musicians presented the first Irving Symphony performance, financed by more than a hundred citizens who had responded to the invitation to be sponsors. The Irving High School A Cappella Choir, directed by Neil Davidson, made the program even more exciting. The eighteen-hundred-seat auditorium at Irving High School seemed almost full. The conductor told the extremely enthusiastic audience: "Your reaction shows that Irving definitely wants and can maintain its own symphony."

Called upon to speak, Mayor Brown said that business chooses to come to cities which have good all-around community life and the cultural advantages are high on their list. There was already a complement of small visual and performing arts groups with their supporters searching for spaces to meet, work, perform, and exhibit.

In November 1963, all of Dallas County was excited to hear that President John F. Kennedy was coming to Dallas. Irving citizens lined the streets in Dallas to greet the motorcade, while many Irving city leaders waited at the Trade Center where the president was to join them for lunch. Those who were near Dealey Plaza witnessed the impact when the president was shot. Turmoil followed the announcement at the Trade Center. The sense that it just couldn't be true was intensified in Irving when it was learned that the assassin had taken his rifle, wrapped in a blanket, from Ruth Paine's garage on West Fifth Street in Irving on the morning of the assault. His wife, who spoke only Russian, and two children were staying with Mrs. Paine and some Oswald household items were stored in her garage. A new book by Thomas Mallon, titled *Mrs. Paine's Garage*, relates the entire story of the experience of the devout Quaker woman who befriended Marina Oswald and her children in a time of need.

People in Irving knew Ruth Paine as a sincere and generous person. Among other activities, she encouraged the West Irving Improvement Association (WIIA) that sought better schools and living conditions for the Bear Creek community. A Montessori School for preschool children was housed in one of the war surplus buildings that had been brought in for classrooms after fire destroyed the Sowers No. 2 County School.

The WIIA held meetings in another of these buildings that had become available after Irving built a brick school next door. Kenneth Hearn helped to launch the Association and generate the support needed to establish a community ball field. The Jaycees were involved in that project and they supported the request from Bear Creek residents that they be permitted to use Irving City facilities such as the Library. Access was granted by ordinance in 1965. It was unusual for any city to allow persons who were not citizens of the city to check out library books. The Dallas County Library was open to all county citizens who did not live in a city.

Mrs. Kathryn Manning was the library director from 1966 to 1973. She worked with a very active Library Board that always wanted more and better services.

A stage complete with scenery was built on Tiger Field for the "Golden Year Pageant," which featured eleven spectacular performances including a skit based on the story of Irving. The theme was "how times have changed." It ran three nights. On the first night an estimated eight hundred people braved wind, lightning, and the threat of rain. The next two nights attendance was even better.

Residents of Bear Creek wanted better streets, water and sewer connections, and police and fire protection, but many of them resisted annexation to Irving. They feared high taxes on their land and the possibility that the city would mandate that substandard homes be renovated or demolished. They treasured their heritage as the first black community in Dallas County and one of the first in Texas. Their concern was intensified by the experience with school integration. Irving schools began integrating two years ahead of the federally mandated deadline without any of the protests or riots that were experienced in some districts, but Bear Creek had paid a price. Their successful and beloved J. O. Davis School was closed and students transferred to schools in Irving. The Ledbetter School in West Dallas was also closed to achieve integration, and its students were absorbed by J. O. Schulze Elementary School in 1965.

The desire for services in Bear Creek won over negative concerns and about two and a half square miles of Bear Creek was annexed in 1968. Police and fire protection and garbage pickup were immediate, and work on water and sewer lines started. The Park Department began building a Recreation Center. Although Irving wanted to annex the entire community, the precinct line had been drawn many years earlier and Grand Prairie successfully argued that annexation should follow that line. The result was that the community was divided between Irving and Grand Prairie. Some community leaders felt that integration of the schools and annexations had done them a disservice. Kenneth Hearn said: "It robbed us of ourselves. We lost our identity." Some residents sold out and moved away but others stayed and insisted on preserving their heritage and way of life. Much of the land surrounding the community had been zoned industrial, but developers began building upscale single-family homes and multifamily dwellings. Residents new to Irving were impressed by the convenient location and the beauty of the landscape.

Four square dance clubs, the Swingin' Squares, Hix and Chix, Circle I, and Wagon Wheels, staged a big dance at the National Guard Armory to celebrate the Golden Anniversary. Charlie Ahlfinger was the caller.

Meanwhile Irving citizens celebrated the Golden Anniversary of their incorporation in a wholehearted way. There were parades and dances and picnics and performances. An editorial in the *Daily News Texan* on April 18, 1964, recognized Leo Jackson as the guiding force of the celebration and praised Robert Nelson, president of First Federal Savings and Loan, who donated Jackson's full-time services to making the celebration successful.

While all of Irving was celebrating the Golden Anniversary, Ben Carpenter opened the Las Colinas Country Club, complete with an eighteen-hole golf course, tennis courts, and a large luxurious clubhouse with dining rooms, large meeting rooms, a ballroom, and a complete staff for services. Special letters of invitation were sent to prospective members. Some who were invited thought that the club would not succeed. It was up there in a relatively undeveloped area, and most people who wanted to belong to a country club already belonged to an established one. Others thought the cost was too high or that people in Irving would not like the idea of an exclusive club that voted on applicants. Although it was a private club, it immediately became popular for business meetings, luncheons, dinners, and all types and sizes of social functions and fundraisers. Irving always seemed to have

James Ratteree opened a modern lumberyard on Rogers Road adjoining the railroad track. He also provided retail sales and services.

Charles Schulze marked the Golden Year by opening Handy House at 129 West Irving Boulevard, the site of the original lumberyard. It was a retail store where individuals could shop for an array of building supplies and tools. He later said it was the forerunner of stores like Home Depot. Mayor Brown sawed a two-by-four instead of cutting a ribbon at the opening.

a full calendar of fun-type social events many of which were fundraisers for special projects. The Art Association and the Symphony League were among the first groups to schedule their fundraising functions there.

The first Center for the Arts was a project of the Jaycees in 1966. The Irving Art Association was not the only group that wanted a place for exhibits and art-related activities, but it was the "young men of action" who ultimately made the first building a reality on the south side of Highway 183, east of Story Road. The Parks and Recreation Board was brought into the mix, and plans were recommended to the City Council. The existing park with a creek, a ball field, playground equipment, and gardens was to remain. The Jaycees would coordinate the construction of a building for the arts. It would be paid for with Jaycee funds and other donations. All of the work was volunteered at no cost. George Edwin was architect, Granville Bruce did the architectural renderings, and Frank Maykus was the official contractor. Muscle and materials were donated. The Art Association gave the museum funds they had been saving and then raised more funds. They enlisted some Dallas Cowboys to help by painting on a huge canvas, which was raffled off at the Las Colinas Country Club. The City provided the land, utilities, an inlet road, and a parking lot, and agreed to maintain the center along with the rest of the park.

The suggestion that Dallas and Fort Worth should have a joint airport dates back to 1927, but it fell on deaf ears. By 1928, Fort Worth was building Meacham Field and Dallas was converting Love Field with its old Army buildings into a municipal airport. When Dallas and Fort Worth both sought federal funding in 1940, the Civil Aeronautics Administration suggested they establish a joint airport and $1.9 million was earmarked for a project. The Army wanted a centrally located airport. American and Braniff Airlines wanted one centrally located airport so badly that they offered to buy the land for the project. They tried to work with Arlington to make Midway Airport fill the need. In fairly rapid succession, Fort Worth acquired the airport, named it Greater Fort Worth International Airport–Amon Carter, and then in 1953 enlarged it and renamed it Southwest International Airport. It was at the county line just south of Highway

It was still 1964 when James Widener opened the Central Park Shopping Center on Irving Boulevard and Pioneer Drive. This was considered to be the geographic center of Irving. He engaged his sister, Gloria Cardwell, and brother, Richard Widener, as manager and leasing agent. A small private hospital, medical offices, and a pharmacy developed on the other side of Irving Boulevard.

Dallas Cowboys, Dan Reeves and Craig Boynham, got some pointers from Elizabeth Shannon before painting a canvas that was auctioned during the Arts Benefit Dance at Las Colinas Country Club. Courtesy Barbara Fryrear

The Shady Grove Ramblers have gained state and national recognition, but they belong to Irving. Many of their hometown fans think it's not a celebration without the Ramblers. In 1967, Tom Uhr, a teacher and football coach; Eddie Green, a science teacher; Loyd Hinch; and Bobby Emberton got together in a garage to enjoy "pickin" together. They all lived around Shady Grove and Glenwick, so when they began appearing on stages, radio, and TV they took the name that became famous. Pictured at work in the early years: Buddy King, Loyd Hinch, and Tom Uhr. Courtesy Tom Uhr

183, but it was in Tarrant County and the terminal faced west. Dallas passed a major bond program to expand Love Field with new runways and a new terminal. By 1961, the Civil Aeronautics Board (CAB) was insistent on a joint airport and Federal Aviation Administration (FAA) executive Najeeb Halaby declared that the FAA would not "put another nickel" into either independent airport. Hearings were ordered.

Finally in 1964, after the hearings closed, the CAB ruled that neither Greater Southwest nor Love Field could meet the future needs of the region and began preparing to find a new site, if the two major cities couldn't do it within 180 days. Faced with that ultimatum, the cities were able to identify a site that straddled the county line and was exactly seventeen miles from the central business district of each city. It was in the center of a vast expanse of undeveloped or sparsely developed land.

Meeting in 1966 as an Interim Airport Board, chaired by Dallas Mayor Erik Jonsson, the cities bought the first 175 acres of what would eventually be a 17,000-acre airport for the North Texas region. When the creation of a Regional Airport Authority was balloted in 1967, the proposal passed by a narrow margin, but there was not a clear mandate from the region. Even the voters in Dallas County rejected the proposal. The vote in Irving was positive. The two major cities knew what they had to do. In 1968, the Dallas/Fort Worth Regional Airport Board was formally created with Dallas Mayor Erik Jonsson as the first chairman.

The Irving City Council, Chamber of Commerce, individual businessmen, developers, and real estate professionals followed the process with mounting interest. Landowners north of Irving were especially interested.

During that same time period, community leaders were engaged with another destiny-changing plan. Clint Murchison Jr., owner of the Dallas Cowboys, could not get the Dallas City Council to agree to make any improvements in the Cotton Bowl, which his winning team had outgrown. He made several proposals, including a new stadium in downtown Dallas, but in 1966 the Council was preoccupied with issues that seemed more important than a football stadium. A public rally might have focused attention on the need for a new stadium, but even to some avid cowboy fans the

In 1967, the ten-story Irving Bank tower was the first "skyscraper" in Irving and was as close as the original town ever came to creating the kind of central business district that was advocated in the Comprehensive Development Plan. The concentration of offices and the large meeting room brought more life back into the aging commercial area that had always been centered around Main Street and Irving Boulevard. Business, political, and social meetings were held in the room on the east side of the top floor where a glass wall framed a view of the Dallas skyline.

A number of buildings were removed and Jefferson Street was closed to make way for the extensive parking garage. There was ample room for occupants and visitors to the building. Parking was free and open to anyone who wanted to use it.

Cotton Bowl was sacred. After surveying the metropolitan area, Mr. Murchison chose a site in Irving that he thought was the best location in Dallas County for a stadium. It was on Highway 183 where the future extension of Loop 12 and completion of Highway 114 would eventually form a triangle surrounding approximately one hundred acres.

In a taped interview conducted by Estelle Bates in 1986, Robert Power reviewed how Irving got involved in owning a stadium. As a member of the Irving City Council, he was contacted and asked why the Irving Council had refused to discuss with Mr. Murchison the possibility of a stadium in Irving. Apparently the mayor, without informing the entire Council, had told Mr. Murchison that Irving was not interested. As requested, Mr. Power called together a group from the Council, Chamber of Commerce, and various city leaders to meet at the old Dallas Gun Club with Mr. Murchison. They were told about the site in Irving where, if he couldn't negotiate improvements to the Cotton Bowl, he wanted to build a new stadium. The Irving group in that meeting was excited about the possibility, but they knew that the City did not have the financial capacity to make a commitment even if a majority of the Council favored it. In response, Murchison assured them that he would front the money and would quietly buy the land using other names. There were about fifteen different owners of land in that triangle. Then, if the project went forward, he would convey the land to the City for just what he paid. There was agreement but no official action. Everyone left knowing that Mr. Murchison would still attempt to

Above:
Robert Power, mayor from 1967 to 1971, was a key player in the negotiations that made Irving the home of the Dallas Cowboys.

Right:
The Braniff Tower on the high elevation of the University of Dallas Campus can be seen for miles. A $7.5 million gift from the Blakley-Braniff Foundation funded the tower and the Braniff Graduate Center. Several major gifts from the University family supported the physical expansion of the University as the academic scope broadened during the 1960s. The standard of scholarly excellence that characterized the University was never compromised. Without becoming embroiled in the politics of the city, the University was open as a resource for Irving.

deal with the possibility of improving the Cotton Bowl while also acquiring the land in Irving. Obviously they didn't want any publicity.

A few months later, Bill Stevens, manager of the Chamber of Commerce, was overcome by enthusiasm while speaking at a function in Farmers Branch and said: "We're probably going to build a new stadium in Irving for the Dallas Cowboys."The next morning the *Dallas Times-Herald* headlines announced a new stadium for the Cowboys in Irving. Murchison, who was in New York on business, called Robert Power and requested he hold a press conference that afternoon. From that point on the media was alive with accounts of the reactions to the possibility of the Cowboys leaving the Cotton Bowl. Mr. Murchison was vilified. Dallas leaders were irate and Dallas newspapers were vicious in their comments about both Murchison and the City of Irving. There was no place to go but up.

Robert Power ran and was elected mayor in 1967. The premise on which discussions continued was that if a stadium was built in Irving, it would have to be at no cost to the taxpayers. In the midst of controversy and with nothing in writing, planning continued to design a stadium and complete the roadways that had already been projected. In his interview with Mrs. Bates, Mr. Power recalled headlines in the Dallas newspapers that said: "State engineer says Irving building a death trap." He assumed that the Highway Department had been under political pressure when the State Engineer wrote a letter to Mayor Power, but sent it to the Dallas newspapers before sending it to him. After going through several lawsuits and the refusal of the State Attorney General to approve bonds, the method for financing a stadium was announced to the public. Season tickets to Cowboy games would be available only by buying a seat option bond. Seats between the thirty-yard lines cost $1,000. Others cost $250 for the bond. Bondholders still had to buy their tickets each year. These were forty-year bonds that would pay back $300 on a $250 bond at the end of the period. They were secured by revenue from the operation of Texas Stadium and the real estate. In spite of the fact that they were not very good bonds, there were orders for about $8 million in a very short time. Mr. Murchison agreed to buy bonds that were not sold up to the $15 million needed to start the project. The bonds were at the Attorney Generals' office for approval when an Irving citizen filed a lawsuit, which prevented approval.

The campaign for Texas Stadium was hard fought with intense feelings on both sides. The Chateau Theater in the Plymouth Park Shopping Center was a good place for a sign.

The plot got so thick that the only solution was to call a special election in Irving to decide whether the City would proceed or drop the stadium plans. The city was alive with activity on both sides of the question. It seemed that everyone in Irving was involved in campaigning. No City funds could be used, so the Chamber of Commerce raised money, and many hours of volunteer time were invested. The vote was favorable by about 65 percent, and the next day the Council approved the bonds. Robert Power, Dan Matkin, and Mary Gilliland signed for them and hastened to get the bonds registered before another lawsuit could be filed. More people started buying bonds and, although questions and attacks continued, building started in April of 1969.

Every city planning document, the "Goals for Irving" essays, and the Council of Governments projections during the 1960s mentioned that some form of mass transit would be needed to solve congestion problems and meet mobility needs that could already be foreseen. Ironically, in 1969 passenger rail service on the Rock Island was discontinued.

It had been a very busy and eventful decade, which was pivotal to the way Irving would develop both physically and culturally.

True to Irving tradition, square-dance clubs staged an exhibition inside the mall soon after it opened.

Chapter 8

Coping and Celebrating

The 1970 census reported Irving population was 97,457. An airport that had been identified as critical to the future growth of North Texas was being built on the west side of Irving, and Dorris Borah had sold what was believed to be the oldest dairy in the area to the airport. A stadium for the Dallas Cowboys was being built on the east side of town.

The proposal to adjust the route of State Highway 114 and upgrade it to freeway standards had prompted the formation of an Irving citizens committee to obtain the needed right of way. Ben Carpenter accepted chairmanship of that committee and began by donating several miles of his property. Other landowners were influenced to donate, until eventually 90 percent of the right of way for the Highway 114 Freeway leading from Dallas to the north entrance of the airport was free of any cost to taxpayers.

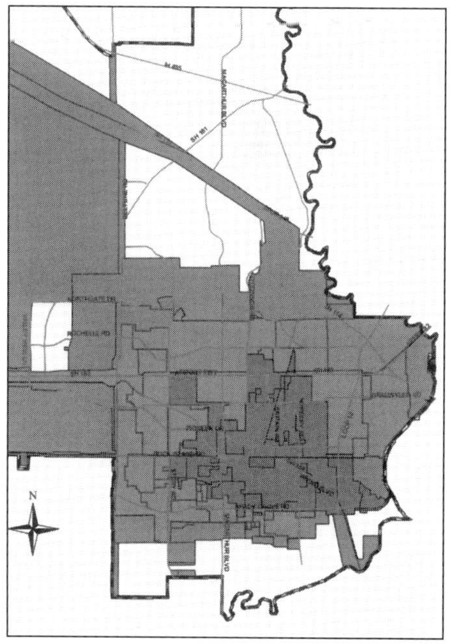

By 1970 annexations had made Irving an odd shape. Landowners had donated the arm reaching to the north end of the proposed airport, the right of way for Highway 114, expecting to be annexed to Irving when they developed their land. Annexation west of Beltline to the county line was a protective measure for the City and landowners. A new zoning category, industrial airport-related, was adopted.

The City Council and staff had already been struggling to catch up with roadways and other infrastructure; now they were faced with predictions of greatly increased traffic to serve the airport, the stadium, and job-generating developments in neighboring cities. Texas Highway Department engineers and airport staff worked together to design a road network that could funnel thousands of cars daily to the regional airport. Planners were warning that shopping centers, apartments, and other traffic-generating developments should not be permitted along these roadways. That included Highway 183, which had been a longtime Irving project.

The 850,000-square-foot Irving Mall at Beltline and Highway 183 was already planned to serve Irving and the surrounding area. With seventy-seven stores, it was one of the first enclosed shopping malls. In 1973 it was the only center in the Dallas/Fort Worth area that was 100 percent occupied.

R. T. Gregory of the Texas Transportation Institute was one of many who suggested that other forms of transportation would be needed to serve the airport, such as air taxis, monorails, or high-speed surface trains.

In 1970, Dr. John Townley followed W. T. Hanes as superintendent of schools, inheriting twenty-two schools, an administration building, a school stadium, and a raging battle over the length of boys' hair and girls' skirts. He appointed a committee to study the student controversy and community reactions to arrive at a solution that his administration and the School Board could live with. A dress code was adopted that limited the length of boys' hair, forbade facial hair, and specified a minimum length for girls' skirts. If girls' skirts, measured from the kneecap, were too short, the girls were sent home to change; however, when a boy was expelled over hair length, lawsuits followed. Eventually, three hundred students filed a class-action suit affirming the right of boys and parents to choose hair styles without threats of being suspended or expelled from school. During and after this highly publicized battle, the school population kept

Dr. John F. Townley led the IISD through difficult times with constant demands for physical and curriculum expansion and controversial adjustments to changing social and political mores. He worked effectively with a broad spectrum of community leadership.

growing, more facilities were built, and teachers hired.

The Leipziger Plan was still being discussed but only with regard to the ongoing need to preserve open space as more land was developed. The report had explained the need for a core downtown to qualify as a city, and had outlined a plan, on page 89, for service tunnels to develop the original town site into a core downtown for Irving: "At Stage II the superblock, bounded by Second, Iowa, Fifth and Britain Streets, would have service tunnels under the present Hastings and Jefferson Streets. At Stage III the second superblock, bounded by Second, Britain, Fifth Streets, Nursery Road and Irving Boulevard, would have such tunnels under the present Lucille Street and Falcon Drive. Separation of goods and passenger vehicles would have a tonic effect..." The tunnel plan got very little attention. The only evidence that the idea of concentrating offices and retail development in the original downtown was seriously pursued is the ten-story office tower that was built in conjunction with the Irving Bank expansion. Suburban sprawl—scattered office developments and shopping centers—continued. In fact, the pattern was beginning in the larger cities, including Dallas.

In 1970, the Park Department, directed by Bill Enlow, published a "Master Plan for Parks and Recreation." Irving was attending to the open-space requirements with a combination of municipal, school, and private properties. The same year, the Department of Community Development, directed by Earl Ayles, began a process that involved the resources of the city staff, business, landowners, civic organizations, and the general public in a series of studies, open

This 1950s map gives a clear picture of the path of Delaware Creek before heavy development closed in on it: from near Beltline Road on the northwest to the West Fork of the Trinity River on the southeast corner of Irving.

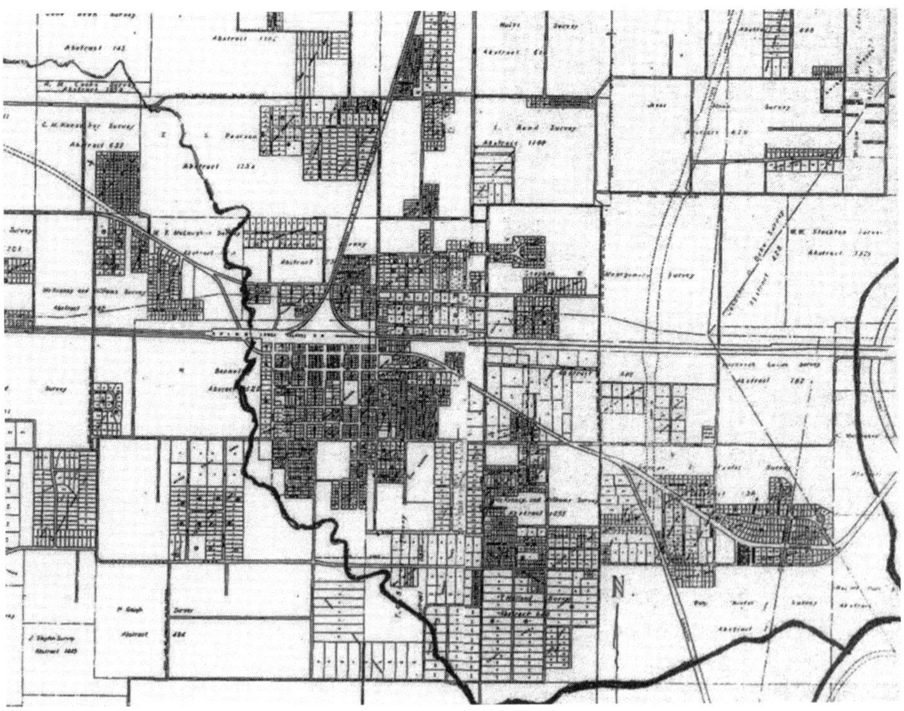

forums, and town meetings. The Jaycees, Chamber of Commerce, and local League of Women Voters were heavily involved in organizing those opportunities for public involvement. One of the league's best-attended annual "informa days" was on the subject of urban design. The city was divided into eight study areas that were each addressed over a five-year period. The result was a working document with a "buy-in" from city leaders.

Dan Matkin, who was elected mayor in 1971 after being involved with the Jaycees, the Planning and Zoning Commission, and four years on the City Council, was a known factor. Numerous citizens appreciated his support of libraries and the arts, and the business community appreciated his approach to fiscal responsibility. In a 1986 recorded interview, he said, "I believed you ought to try like everything to pass a bond election and then work hard to not sell the bonds, to do as much as you could for cash and not wind up having a heavy bonded indebtedness."

The two most controversial issues in planning were apartments and Delaware Creek. Some residents opposed any apartments being built, especially near their neighborhood. A multifamily zoning case always brought protesters to City Hall. But the crowd filled the council chamber and spilled onto the parking lot after Delaware Creek rose and invaded homes, becoming a recurring menace. The building boom of the fifties and sixties had resulted in less natural absorption. More runoff was being directed to storm sewers, creeks, and drainage ditches. New homes had been built right on the banks of Delaware Creek and drainage ditches that fed it. When Lewis Patrick was employed as public works director, he found the city without an ordinance requiring developers to make necessary drainage improvements and wrote the first ordinance.

With the help of consulting engineers, a master plan was developed that allowed developers to see what they would have to do to handle drainage if land upstream was developed. The U.S. Corps of Engineers created detailed flood maps for all the creeks and floodplains. In 1970 the Corps was working on a plan for Delaware Creek that captured the attention of community

Dan Matkin, mayor from 1971 to 1977, worked to solve roadway problems and enhance citizens' quality of life. He led the city in funding numerous projects while limiting bonded debt.

In November 1971, Councilman Joe Bailey and architect Jim Scoggins discussed the flooding on Delaware Creek on "Voters Digest," which aired on both Channels 11 and 13. Scoggins advocated a long-range plan to create a series of parks with lakes and land linkages winding through the city. Bailey said it was too late: with land along the creek already about 90 percent developed, eliminating flooding should be the priority. He said money being spent on the Corps of Engineers study should be diverted to correct the problems already known to exist by straightening and concrete lining. "We can't wait these many years to make this creek beautiful."

Above:
The First Presbyterian Church completed an educational building in 1955 and a new sanctuary in 1967. In the seventies, it shared its first little church, built in 1935 on the corner of Second and Lucille Streets, with the community. The historic building became a home to the Irving Community Theater, which staged several productions there before a fire destroyed it.

Right:
The Police Building, west of City Hall at 845 West Irving Boulevard, was constructed with the anticipation of a second story, which was added in 1972. It housed the growing department and provided a locker room.

leaders and caused heated discussions. After criticism, Pilar Pena, in charge of the Corps project, said, "If they want a solution, they will have to get involved. Volunteers will be sought to staff six workshops on proposed alternatives to the flood problem."

The Hospital, needing to grow, began a building program to add another one hundred beds and expand services. By March 1971 there was a new surgical wing, and a new nursery, labor, and delivery area. Land west of the existing structure was bought for $17 per acre. By August the fourth floor was completed, and the third floor was shelled in. LPN classes were being graduated from the hospital, and teaching programs in conjunction with El Centro College were in place.

Another expansion plan was being discussed to increase bed capacity to four hundred when Morris Parrish became the administrator on April 11, 1973. Revenue bonds were sold to complete the third floor by July 9, 1973. With quiet and courteous determination, Mr. Parrish tackled the ever-present challenges to expand the facility, provide more services, and acquire new and more sophisticated equipment. The Hospital Auxiliary was a major asset, giving their services and also raising money to donate equipment. They received permission to open a gift shop in 1975. Barbara Doan was director of volunteers. Mr. Parrish encouraged the formation of a Hospital Foundation to facilitate major funding projects.

By 1970, time and growth of the city had changed the way people were relating to each other. Nobody sat on the front porch talking to neighbors who strolled by; air conditioning and television kept them inside. Few people walked around Main Street on Saturdays to exchange greetings and news, but they did gather in homes and various meeting places to support the elements they wanted to see thrive in their community. Community spirit was generated in supporting causes, entertainment, special interests, community improvements, and various art forms. Meeting rooms in various types and sizes were made available.

Cafes had regular customers who exchanged information and opinions or socialized. The

With strong support from the Chamber of Commerce, John Boyle, former city attorney, was elected to the Texas Legislature in 1972. His first appointments were to Urban Affairs, School Districts, Public Health, Criminal Jurisprudence, and the Committee on Youth.

The Northgate Office Plaza was developed opposite MacArthur High School with a restaurant and a gazebo on an interior plaza. The Buena Vista Movie Theater on the front at the south corner became the most popular theater in town and a favorite place of children for Saturday entertainment.

best known and most often remembered are LeeLo's on Irving Boulevard west of Nursery, Farina's on Irving Boulevard east of the creek, Townsell's Grocery Store and Joe's Coffee Shop on Sixh Street, where Irving citizens first met and ate with Carol Wood, who worked for owner Joe Thompson when the shop had only forty-six seats. She later bought the business. The friendly service and down-home cooking were so popular that seating was expanded every four years until by 1980, there were 150 seats. Families also liked to eat at Los Ponces on Britain Road at Grauwyler, the first Mexican restaurant in town. They served the Tex-Mex food that had become popular in Dallas, but also offered steaks, fish, chicken, and hamburgers. The Ponce family were pioneers in Irving, having come from Leon, Mexico, in 1914. The number and type of eating places expanded rapidly as the city grew, but those establishments mentioned above were still favorites even when there was plenty of competition by the end of the seventies.

Many meetings were held in the Colonial Room, which was available for community use, in the Dallas Federal Savings and Loan building in Plymouth Park.

Loop 12 was connected from the south and continued north of Highway 183 in time for the opening of Texas Stadium, which brought crowds into Irving.

The Irving Symphony was a full orchestra with more than sixty musicians, Yves L'Helgoual'ch conducting and a very strong support group. The Symphony Ball, the largest and most elegant social event each year, was a major fundraiser for the orchestra. The first ball was chaired by Dr. Francis M. and Shirley Gilbert. In 1970, the officers of the Symphony Association decided they needed a league to increase financial support and boost ticket sales. Almost everyone who attended a tea at the home of Johnetta and Jim Ratteree joined the new Symphony League,

Jackie Townsell, who was chairman of County Precinct 179 for seven years and election judge for Irving Precinct 4, was a strong influence in the move to annex Bear Creek. She served lunch in the grocery store that she and husband, Jimmy, established. Jackie was the first black woman to serve on a Dallas County grand jury. Movers and shakers enjoyed her food and her ideas for improving Irving. She lost her first run for City Council by two hundred votes but filed again and was elected in 1977.

Right:
LeeLo's, east of Nursery in the Irvingate Shopping Center, survived many changes in Irving. It served breakfast and lunch for workers in the surrounding community and attracted both business and political leaders. A back room accommodated groups. Courtesy Paula Cobb

which brought boundless energy and imagination to ticket sales and financial development. The Red Stocking Follies brought almost everyone in town to see well-known leaders from the business, political, and social circles in a musical review on the Irving High School stage. The first one, chaired by Bette Hutchinson in 1973, was so popular that the Symphony League staged two sequels. Cargill Productions from New York came to town with script, music, costumes, and a director. Irving supplied the musicians and the actors.

Ben Carpenter, with the help of research, planning, and engineering firms, and a review by the Urban Land Institute, had created a detailed development plan for land that his family had acquired through the years and had buffered by donating pieces to desirable projects. They had even given land they owned east of the Elm Fork to the City of Dallas for a park. In 1973 Carpenter unveiled his vision of an integrated residential, commercial, and entertainment complex to a large invited audience at the Las Colinas Country Club. His plan included an urban center that was larger than downtown Dallas without the intrusion of traffic. Half the land area was planned as open space in the form of lakes, parks, golf courses, and other recreational uses. Some attendees were elated with the prospects; others said it was a pipe dream. Mr. Carpenter and his staff began building infrastructure. The creation of Dallas County Municipal Utility District No. 1 had made possible $12,500,000 of bond financing for the project.

Texas Stadium opened with the Greater Southwest Billy Graham Crusade September 17–26, 1971. The structure, covering ten acres, had 65,639 contoured seats boasting no sightline interference, topped by 170 Circle Suites and the Stadium Club. Suites sold for $50,000 unfurnished. Twelve Suites were reserved for lease at $15,000 per year, including tickets and one minute of scoreboard advertising. Clint Murchison was quoted in the *Houston Post* as saying, "It's the finest football stadium ever built. It will be the only modern stadium built primarily for football since World War II." Tourist and Convention Bureau Collection

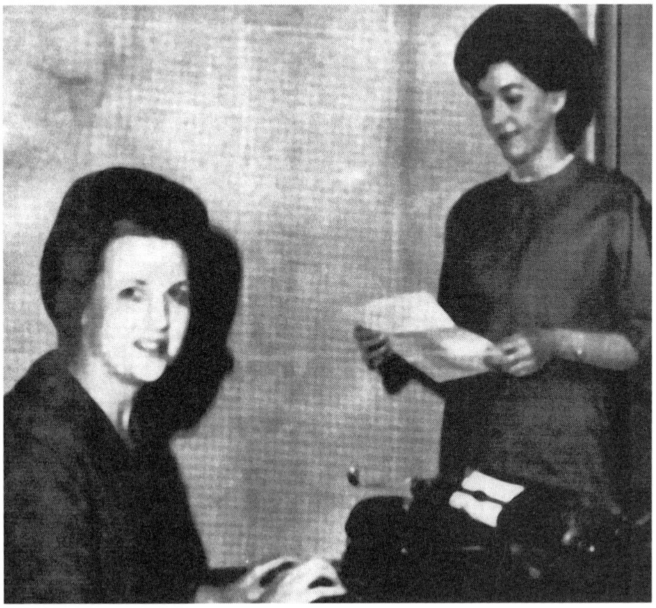

Above Left:
Naomi Laird, assisted by Margaret Southerland, typed (there were no computers) letters of admission to be mailed to persons who bought tickets to the Symphony Ball at Las Colinas Country Club.

Above Right:
Before there was a Symphony League, a Symphony Benefit Ball ticket committee was formed each year to plan and oversee sales.

Right:
When the Red Stocking Follies was produced, Twelve ladies of the Symphony League were billed as the Fandango Rockettes.

Above:
Advance advertising was colorful for the musical review March 30–31, 1973.

Above Left:
As the Vegas Dancers, community leaders got in the act to support the Symphony.

Left:
The costumes brought in by the producers were fitted with pins and basting stitches.

Ben Carpenter had the vision, the mentality, and the heart to conceive a whole city on mostly bare grazing land.

Top Right:
From the beginning, Dallas/Fort Worth Airport was a major income generator for the region.

When site preparation for the airport was completed, the equipment was moved to Las Colinas. Although the site was smaller, the dirt-moving task was much larger because of the 125-acre lake and canals, designed to manage potential flooding. The creeks and tributaries in the area had frequently overflowed during rainy weather. Mr. Carpenter said that from his home on a hill, he had seen boats where Williams Square was eventually built. They were able to do what old Irving had not done and plan ahead for drainage.

Darr Equipment, the Caterpillar franchise company that had arrived in Irving in 1954, provided equipment and maintenance for the mammoth projects. Arnold Martin, Darr vice president, and his wife, Alice, were already deeply involved in the civic and social life of Irving. Now Mr. Martin's hands-on involvement helped lay the foundation for the two biggest projects that affected the area's destiny.

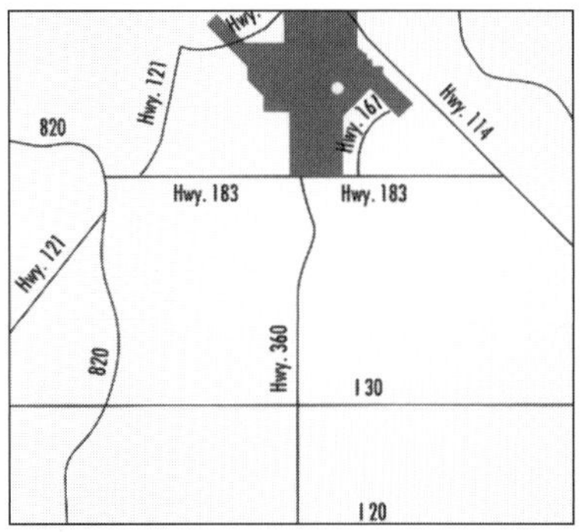

Right: Both major east-west routes to the Airport pass through Irving.

A new zoning category was essential to the success of the plan. After considerable debate, the City Council adopted a planned unit development ordinance that permitted multiuse development in units of thirty acres or more.

The City Council hired a new city manager who

The drawings of the Las Colinas plan were transformed into a three-dimensional model that was periodically used throughout the years to inform targeted groups of the history and future plans for the development.

was willing to work hard to help make the dream a reality. When he arrived, the Council was still working with the architect on the final plans for the new City Hall Complex. While he was involved in that project and the many challenges of a city that had outgrown itself, the Dallas/Fort Worth Regional Airport opened.

The Airport, the largest and most efficient in the world, was dedicated with great fanfare September 21–23, 1973, and opened for business on January 13, 1974. Irving residents attended the dedication along with officials from Washington, heads of international airlines, and diplomatic representatives of fifty nations. Willie Nelson and Doc Severinsen were among the entertainers at an evening charity gala. Attendance was estimated at 200,000. The supersonic Concorde made its first American landing. Nine miles long and eight miles wide, the Dallas/Fort Worth Airport was larger than Manhattan Island and three times the size of Kennedy International Airport. In its first year, DFW Airport served 6.8 million passengers and handled 105,000 tons of cargo with some 420 daily flights. The number and scope of services increased every year. With a neighbor like that, Irving could either benefit or be destroyed.

The Library Board had hired a new director who tackled the complex job with zeal. Shelah Bell joined Board members Garrett Sherman and Jerry Wright in executing a plan to almost double the size of the Library to 16,960 square feet by attaching a manufactured metal structure out of sight behind the existing Library. The project was finished and ready to be dedicated on the same day Irving was officially designated as a Bicentennial City, and the Library was officially named a depository for government documents.

When City Manager Morris Howard retired, Jack Huffman, a young, energetic engineer with city management experience, was the right man at the right time for a city growing rapidly while needing to catch up with infrastructure and services. For the next twenty years, he managed to prioritize and focus on the projects he knew were essential while responding to intense citizen participation and sometimes angry criticism.

On June 5, 1974, the City Council broke ground for a new and much larger City Hall.

On November 3, 1974, Irving was designated an official U.S. Bicentennial City at a ceremony in front of the Central Library at 915 O'Connor Road with Neill English, chairman of the Irving Bicentennial Commission, presiding. Members of the Irving High School Band played, and the Irving Boys Choir sang. Representatives from state and national Bicentennial administrations, the Daughters of the American Revolution, and the Color Guard of the 7th Bomb Wing, Carswell Air Force Base, participated. The official U.S. Bicentennial Flag was presented to the City of Irving.

The first official Bicentennial event of the 1976 year was the presentation of three one-act plays commemorating American history that were written by local citizens for a play writing contest. The plays were staged by the Irving Community Theater in the little original Presbyterian Church building at Lucille and Second Streets. Pictured are Stovey Stovall, Judge Lloyd Russell, and David Anderson in *British Tea is Not For Me*, written by MacArthur High School seniors Bobbi Griffith and Michael Bethard and directed by Dale Riley.

Irving citizens celebrated the anniversary of the American Revolution; it was almost impossible to live in the city and not be involved in some way. A Bicentennial Commission was organized by City Council resolution in June 1974 with Mr. and Mrs. Neill English as general chairmen. Mayor and Mrs. Dan Matkin were honorary general chairmen, and all living former mayors and their wives were honorary co-chairmen. The commission had twenty-nine members and seven ex-officio members. An official calendar of events was placed in the lobby of the Central Library and updated as events were added. Reference Librarian Linda Vaughn coordinated suggestions for newspaper notes on interesting events in 1776. High school students planted two hundred trees, donated by groups and individuals, along Irving Boulevard. Picnics, plays, essays, arts, crafts, parades, music, school history fairs, pioneer-food tasting, an ethnic food festival, street dances, and ceremonies kept the city lively for more than a year.

On June 15, 1975, the Municipal Historical Museum officially opened in a storefront at 308 Plymouth Park Shopping Center. It was a lively place during the Bicentennial celebration, housing various collections and artifacts depicting Irving history and also prize-winning projects by Irving students. Dr. Ben and Bobbie Thomas, who got involved at that time, tried to keep the museum open after the 1976 celebration. They are still involved in the effort to establish a museum in Irving. It may finally happen after the city's 100th birthday.

Both the mayor and the city manager were supportive of libraries and wanted senior citizens to have an adequate facility. They secured the funding to increase the book budget and also build a Senior Citizens Center. Since there were many demands on City funds, they used a building similar to the library. It was located on City-owned land across the creek from Senter Park. There was a parking lot, a croquet court, picnic tables, and enough space in the building for senior activities. The Southwest Branch Library opened in leased space on Shady Grove near Story Road, and Patty Landers was hired as the librarian

In 1977 Marvin Randle was elected mayor. After three terms on the City Council, he knew the problems, potential problems, and almost everybody in town. Astute in dealing with people, he was a strong positive leader but also knew how to maximize his colleagues' contributions.

The struggle to keep up with the infrastructure in the face of rapid growth was ongoing, but the city was growing in a good way and the outlook was good. The growth in Las Colinas was creating little burden on the city considering its potential benefit.

When in 1973 Irving needed a new library director, members of the Irving Library Board consulted with state administrators and leaders in both public and academic libraries and selected top candidates to interview. They hired Shelah Bell, who brought connections to the larger world of libraries and management skills to the Library that Irving had outgrown.

On July 3, 1975, Sister Mary Schulze and Mr. and Mrs. Charles Schulze gave the Schulze family home at 303 South O'Connor to the City of Irving. It was designated the Heritage House for the Bicentennial and was restored by the Schulze family and the Heritage Committee. The Heritage Society was organized at the house after a Valentine Tea in 1978 that was patterned after a tea given by Virginia Schulze when the house was just two years old.

Above:
There was no age limit for participation in the Commission-sponsored project.

Right:
During the celebration, many fireplugs were painted as a soldier of the American Revolution. Would-be artists applied for and were issued the right to paint specific plugs, which were judged for recognition.
Sam Akin Collection

Above:
In July 1976, the City Council officially opened the new City Hall Complex with a twenty-one-gun salute. The Complex had been in the planning and construction stages for seven years. A one-story Council Chamber was designed to accommodate an overflow crowd standing in an atrium behind the seated audience. It flowed into the four-story wing that housed the various City departments. One complete floor and parts of each floor were reserved for future build-out and furnishing, which allowed for phased funding and the growth of City staff.

Left:
The City was on the cutting edge of technology with a mainframe computer that filled a room in the basement of City Hall. The one pictured here was in the Irving State Bank. The Library was working with several others to develop a computer-based project for sharing information and materials, but the City computer lacked the capacity for the Library holdings. Microfiche was the best alternative at the time.

Irving residents were familiar with the resources of the University of Dallas, which not only offered citizens lectures, art exhibits, musical events, and other productions, but also opened its facilities for community meetings. With the familiar Braniff Tower in the background, students on the mall are approaching the William Blakley Library. Courtesy Sybil Novenski

The University of Dallas was a major asset to the community. Its reputation as a strong liberal arts institution was unsurpassed. Because of major gifts, the campus had grown, with buildings to house the expanded curriculum that now included graduate degrees in the liberal arts and a Graduate School of Management. As corporate headquarters moved into Las Colinas from various parts of the world, the MBA program met needs of the growing and diverse business community. Dr. Cherie Clodfelter, director of the Education Department and a former teacher in the Irving system, designed a teacher education program that drew praise nationally.

Irving seemed to be growing in a very positive way physically. Citizens were organizing and focusing attention on education, communication, the arts, and everything related to the quality of life in a larger city.

Marvin Randle, mayor 1977–1981, was rooted in the community as a third-generation citizen, a business owner, a three-term councilman, and an enthusiastic participant in a broad spectrum of community life.

Northlake College, the sixth college in the Dallas County Community College System, was expected to open in the fall of 1977 on a 276-acre site bounded by Story Road on the west and the proposed extension of MacArthur Boulevard on the east.

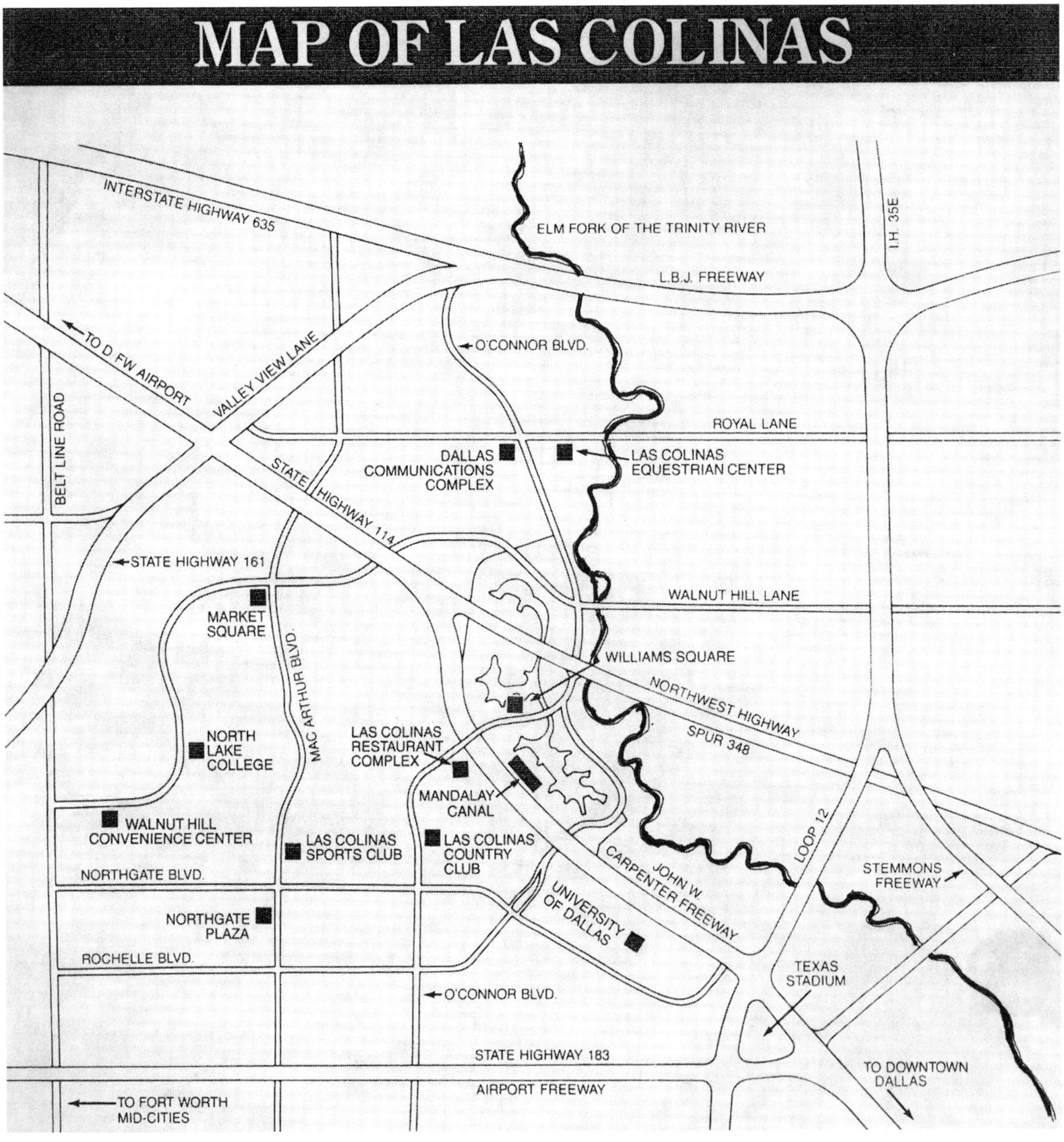

Attractions north of Highway 183 in the 1980s. The river is the city limit.

Chapter 9

Full-Grown

By 1980, Irving was full-grown in terms of physical boundaries. The Elm Fork of the River on the east, the West Fork on the south, the county line and Grand Prairie on the west, and city limits of neighboring cities to the north defined the ultimate size the city could become. However, the territory within the perimeters was not yet fully developed. From 1977 through the 1980s developers were rapidly filling in previously undeveloped land and thousands of citizens organized to focus attention on quality of life issues.

The founders had started Irving with a conventional city plan based on a business district connected to a rail service and surrounded by residences. After years of rapid growth, there was no recognizable design to the city. Developments were scattered in a way that fostered dependence on the automobile for daily activities. Traffic passing through was putting more of a burden on the city that was already straining to keep up with road improvements. Personal isolation could have been the result if Irving citizens hadn't been constantly involved in celebrating, fundraising for community projects, and various forms of entertainment.

It wasn't entertaining when a U.S. marshal served the members of the City Council with a demand that the landfill east of the old Singleton Road be removed. But some people were actually amused. After a few abortive attempts to fight back, the City began digging up and moving seven years of garbage. There had been requests for a municipal golf course, but it had not been a priority for City Government, although there had been some discussion. The thought occurred that now was the time to move forward. A plan was drawn for a golf course and land was contoured as the garbage was moved.

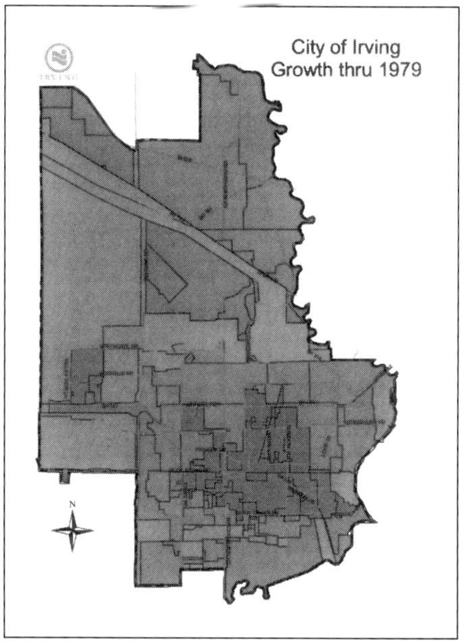

The shape of the map in 1980 reflected the final outline of Irving.

The transformation from garbage to golf took time and money when many basic services needed to be upgraded. A golf course became one of nine proposals in a 1982 bond election. The pitch was that three hundred acres, which the city already owned, could be developed for outdoor recreational purposes and preservation of open space. It also was noted that the golf course would be adjacent to a proposed greenbelt along the river.

The entrance to the golf course would be from Shady Grove Road not far from the bridge to Dallas that was built in 1931. It was estimated that the bridge was carrying fourteen thousand cars a day to and from Dallas when the State condemned and closed it. The City Council was surprised to learn that land on the banks of the river was in Irving. They decided to deannex that strip and let it revert to the County. Rebuilding the bridge was a long process. Fortunately there was another bridge in place from a new leg of Irving Boulevard.

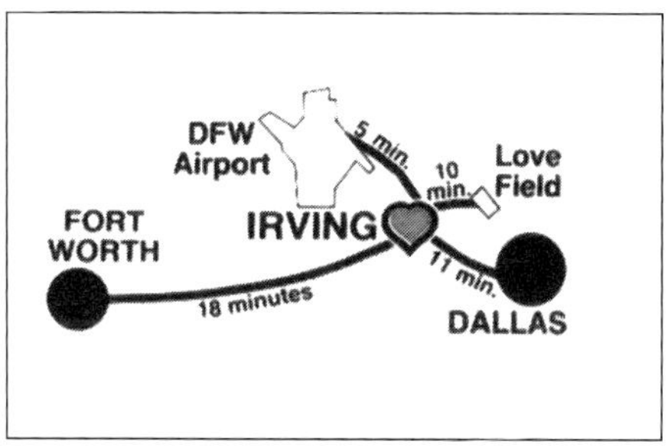

The city logo and slogan put a positive outlook on location. Traffic congestion came with connection to the resources of the metroplex. More importantly the attraction of major businesses improved the tax base. It was good to be the "heart of the metroplex."

A traditional Cherokee precept is that a leader thinks about the impact of decisions seven generations into the future. In 1974, Ben Carpenter wrote a letter to the personnel of Southland Real Estate Resources, Inc. and Affiliates. The letter was given to each new employee throughout the life of the corporation. He referred to the opportunity for the creation of an outstanding example of real estate improvement and issued a challenge. Excerpted from his letter: "Whether

As the golf course was developed, the Singleton Bridge just south of Shady Grove Road was closed and the road was converted to a jogging trail.

this opportunity is fulfilled . . . with a properly balanced community of diversified uses in a permanently pleasing and useful environment or instead . . . is missed through the mere extension of another series of typical commercial and residential subdivisions depends almost entirely upon the desire and dedication of the staff who make up these companies. . . . Remember that generations who will make Las Colinas their home (both business and personal) will follow us. Let them look back and reflect on the fine effort made by those who were its custodians during the development stage."

After fifteen years of careful planning the work on the Urban Center, which was to be the hub of Las Colinas, was progressing rapidly. The land that had been accumulated by the Carpenter family under the umbrella of Southland Financial Corporation was planned in land-use subareas and sectors based on categories of uses. The first two sectors of 110 and 154 acres were for office buildings and support structures such as hotels and conference centers. The developers had spent millions on streets and utilities to support the major buildings that they were

A map of the golf course, from which seven years of garbage was excavated, shows the original athletic fields that were built at Shady Grove and Singleton by volunteers in the 1940s and 1950s. The West Fork of the Trinity River wraps the south and east sides of the course with old Singleton on the west and Shady Grove on the north.

Back when this bridge on Singleton was new, it was the destination for a pleasant afternoon stroll.

From the bridge it is possible to view the creek and mid-levels of the golf course.

constructing. Allstate Insurance Company bought the first 22 acres in the 110-acre business park for a regional office building.

The third sector was dedicated to townhouses and apartment buildings. There were four residential subareas that would each have adjacent retail facilities. As these areas developed there were executive homes and mid-priced homes, fine restaurants, and shops. A wide range of housing alternatives was available near multinational corporate headquarters and open space amenities.

Skeletons of multistory buildings sprang up all at once in the planned urban center.

Allstate Insurance Company and Associates Corporation of America both completed major office buildings in 1976. Soon Caltex, IBM, Xerox, Zales, Kimberly-Clark, and Corry Jamestown moved in and UCCEL consolidated operations into a new twenty-story headquarters tower called 900 Las Colinas Boulevard. GTE and Exxon moved their corporate headquarters into the area. Roads in the original Urban Center were constructed prior to the buildings but some of the major corporations built and moved to surrounding sites before streets were completed. Darlene Williams, who came with the Zale Corporation in 1989, said that she had to take a little country road to get to their building.

The Urban Center was planned on three levels to separate pedestrian and vehicular traffic. The most interesting pedestrian walks are along the canal where festivals, art shows, and entertainment occur regularly. A fully automated train operated on the third level carries passengers

By the middle to late 1980s, many buildings were finished and occupied. Williams Square is at upper left. The twenty-seven-story Mandalay Hotel faces Las Colinas Boulevard and overlooks Lake Carolyn on the other side. Shops and loft apartments stretch along the Boulevard.

Right:
The pedestrian level along the canal is lined with shops and restaurants. Water taxis and a water bus navigate the canal and the lake.

Above:
In the first eight years the Studios of Las Colinas made seven feature films including *Silkwood, Trip to Bountiful, Streamers, Robocop, Problem Child, JFK,* and *Talk Radio.* Television productions like "Walker, Texas Ranger" were regulars at the studios.

horizontally through buildings as elevators move vertically through each building. The long-range plan projected a five-mile, two-lane dual track and twenty stations.

In 1982, a company founded by Trammell Crow created the Communications Complex on 125 acres at Royal Lane and O'Connor to provide a third coast for the communications and entertainment industry. One of the seven buildings was the Studios of Las Colinas with three sound stages and other fully equipped production spaces.

On the other side of O'Connor the Equestrian Center opened in 1982 when Irving was no longer a haven for those who had a place in the country to ride their horses. In a highly urbanized area the Center preserved the traditional values of horsemanship. It adjoins the Mustang Ranch and sixty-two acres of woods and grassland maintained by the City for parks and equestrian uses. The trail rides and other outings are family-oriented for casual pleasure. Both children and adults can enroll in classes to learn the various facets of horsemanship.

In Johannesburg, South Africa, Mr. Carpenter was impressed with a sculpted herd of impala antelope running through water. He commissioned Robert Glen, an internationally acclaimed wildlife artist in Nairobi, to create a magnificent herd of mustangs and had the plaza at Williams Square constructed with Texas granite to simulate a prairie. Moonstone on the bottom of the stream causes reflections both day and night.

In 1985, fifty thousand people worked in Las Colinas and twenty-five thousand lived there. This was a period when a downturn in the economy was having a devastating effect on developers, but during the first three-quarters of 1987 Las Colinas recorded absorption of 571,056 square feet of new office space. The theme seemed to be, "build it and they will come."

The development had a community antenna system, underground cables with capacity for two-way communication, television entertainment in homes, and data-sharing in offices. It was unique at the time. They also had their own security patrol.

Above:
There were show barns and outdoor and covered arenas. There was even a roping arena. On July 12–16, 1989, the Equestrian Center hosted the Mercedes Southwest Jumping Championship.

Right:
A unique example of landscaping is the Flower Clock on the east side of O'Connor at Highway 114. About one thousand seasonal plants are changed six times a year to create the twenty-five-foot-diameter clock face and the Las Colinas name. The minute hand is fifteen feet long and the clock actually functions.

Above:
The nine bronze Mustangs of Las Colinas running free across a four-hundred-foot-long watercourse on the plaza at Williams Square are an inspiring sight. They represent the historic free spirit and vitality of Texas where herds of wild mustangs were ancestors to the Texas cow pony. This is still referred to as the world's largest equestrian sculpture.

Against the skyline of the Las Colinas Urban Center, the Hackberry Ranch that John Carpenter established in 1928 was still a working ranch.

This float in the annual parade expressed the sentiments of citizens who wanted aesthetic improvements along Highway 183. Landscaping would be ideal, but a sign ordinance was the first priority.

Every detail of the environment was meticulously attended. Trees and flowers were planted and maintained by the Las Colinas Corporation. Some citizens in Irving thought the City was favoring the north area with spectacular landscaping and expensive maintenance, but the City wasn't doing any of that planting and watering.

One of the propositions in the 1982 Bond Election was storm drainage, which included lining Delaware and West Irving Creeks to provide security from high water in flood-prone areas.

Capital projects during the decade of the 1980s were possible because of the propositions passed in that 1982 Bond Election. Irving Community Television Network (ICTN) was operational in time to help with information and promotion. The process leading to ICTN began in 1979 when the airwaves and telephone lines were reaching a saturation point, as more and more uses evolved. Cable companies began approaching cities to obtain permission to build cable delivery systems. Since they had to use public right of way to lay or string their cables, the City could negotiate a franchise agreement or refuse to allow the service. The Irving City Council was heavily lobbied by several companies. The term "rent a citizen" was coined because some companies sought out influential citizens to help influence the elected officials. They even promised part ownership and participation in decision making to selected individuals or groups. Council members worked with Library Director Shelah Bell and City Secretary Lester Ford to research and observe the experience of other cities. They noted that promised equipment and production staffs for community programming were often placed in public buildings and subsequently removed to another city. They wrote a detailed Request for Proposal that listed every piece of studio equipment, a fully equipped van, a studio building, and some support for personnel that would be the base requirement to obtain the franchise.

Much of Delaware Creek had been deepened and concreted to improve the flow of water to its destination in the West Fork. Most of the time there was so little water that it was unbelievable that flooding could be a problem. Still a good rain could fill the channel.

The Library director vigilantly enforced the terms of the franchise requiring the cable company to build and equip a studio for the community network. It was placed on Rogers Road south of Rock Island, adjacent to what was then the Williamsburg Shopping Center. The crew occupied the building in March 1983.

The first studio was set up in the Library's little auditorium and part of the lobby. The first crew began producing television programs and covering City Council and School Board meetings as soon as the cable system was activated in late 1981. Left to right are Robert Watts, Heather Brown, Patty Landers, Cathy Whitman, Skye Gaskill, and Paul Wahlstrom.

After proposals were reviewed and debated a franchise was awarded to Teleprompter on April 3, 1981. On May 21 the City created the Department of Libraries and Communication by expanding the duties of the Library director to include contract administration, construction oversight, and community programming. Linda Lawler and Denise McKnight worked with Library Director Shelah Bell on the first two assignments and Patty Landers became administrator of telecommunications with a staff to produce local programming. A nine-member Cable Television Board and a seven-member Telecommunications Committee were appointed. The entire 5 percent fee from the cable company was dedicated to community programming instead of going into the general fund as it does in most cities. Through the years of programming ICTN has won many awards.

In 1982 the Hospital was already overcrowded and was in need of both space and equipment. The Foundation had been created with Pat Carnell as the director and the first TexasFest fundraiser had been successful in 1980. On August 4, 1982, a kickoff dinner for the Foundation's expansion fund drive was held to initiate the drive for funds from area businesses and individuals. Four groups affiliated with the Hospital: the employees, medical staff, auxiliary, and Board members had already completed their fund drives and raised $1.4 million.

Ronald Krause, president of Associates Corporation and chairman of the Development Council for the Hospital, said to the assembled business leaders: "Most of us have picked a particular community to live and work in and you can't just take from that community, you have an obligation to the community." Apparently most people in Irving felt that way.

When the new north wing opened in 1984, a week of tours brought thousands into the Hospital while the Board and staff were already making plans for other expansions. In 1985 the Board appointed their Hospital Administrator Morris Parrish to be CEO of a new hospital that was being planned. The Valley Ranch Medical Center opened in 1986. In November a contract was signed to build a 82,982-square-foot Medical Office Building adjacent to the original Hospital.

In 1983, Tom Landry and Tex Schram broke ground for a Cowboy Center at Valley Ranch in North Irving.

After the Irving Heart Institute and the Women's Imaging Center opened in 1986, and the Valley Ranch Medical Center and other projects mentioned above were well established, Morris Parrish retired in October 1987 leaving Michael O'Keefe to be the new administrator of the ever-growing hospital system.

The Valley Ranch development on the far north side of town took shape and the Dallas Cowboys moved into a new training facility.

The Police and Fire Departments were growing in numbers and in scope of services. Firemen were receiving extensive training covering fire fighting, emergency medical procedures, and fire prevention. Emphasis was on teaching residents about fire prevention and on inspections to find possible fire hazards and enforce fire code.

The annual TexasFest raises large sums of money for the Hospital and Irving participants have a roaring good time. The unique themes are a big part of the fun. These longhorn steers in front of the Hospital were great advertisers. Pictured are Pat Carnell, director of the Foundation, and Mary Jo Deatherage, chair of the 1984 event.

"Under the Big Top" was the theme of the carnival on the Hospital grounds celebrating the Silver Anniversary. Employees with families and friends enjoyed food, clowns, music, and games. Dr. George Susat and Morris Parrish were dressed for the occasion.

Bobby Joe Raper was mayor from 1981 to 1987. In that busy time he may have set a record for presiding over openings, celebrations, and tree plantings.

Under Chief Benny Newman, the Police Department was stressing personal contact with citizens. The motto was "to protect and serve." A computerized information system was evolving, the organizational structure included the patrol units, a division of criminal investigation, and a community service section for handling youth problems and teaching public awareness of police issues. A Youth and Family Counseling Advisory Board was established to work with the Police Department. Statistics had proved that counseling programs for juvenile offenders and their families was effective in improving lives and that it was cost effective for the justice system.

By 1989 the patrol fleet numbered one hundred vehicles including six motorcycles. The joint request for police and fire in the election had been $7,325,000.

Throughout the 1980s there was emphasis on education and the arts. By the end of the decade there were three public school systems within the Irving city limits. Much of the high-dollar development to the north was in either the Carrollton Farmers Branch or the Coppell School District. The Irving Independent School District with Jack Singly as superintendent served more than twenty-one thousand students in three high schools, six middle schools, sixteen elementary schools, and four special schools with a curriculum that included a variety of vocational classes. The purely academic classes achieved high ratings, but distributive education classes were also appreciated. Some people who lived through the furor that almost destroyed the school system in the 1950s couldn't help remembering that one of the biggest issues was the accusation that a printing lab and classes had diluted emphasis on the "basics."

At the University of Dallas the strong classical academic core curriculum was still in place bringing highly motivated students from around the country for undergraduate and graduate work. It was the youngest university to be approved for a Phi Beta Kappa chapter. A sophomore semester in Rome, Italy, was offered and encouraged.

On the other hand the very practical Graduate School of Management at UD was thriving and had gained an international reputation. The school was founded by Robert Lynch in 1966, when some faculty members thought the University should remain focused on classical education and leave practical education to other institutions. Dean Lynch was a Board member of TAGER, a closed-circuit television system that linked seven universities and fifteen industrial studios in the North Texas area. In his spare time, he lectured in Japan, Thailand, India, Pakistan, Germany, Netherlands, France, England, Switzerland, and Spain. The Graduate School of Management was important to the corporations that were coming into Irving during the 1980s. It was a training ground for employees who had come from all over the world and it attracted prospective employees preparing to function as managers in their varied fields. Eventually thirteen specialized programs were offered in flexible plans to meet career and working professional needs.

On September 9, 1985, Councilman Joe Bailey hosted a barbeque fundraiser for the Irving Youth and Family Counseling Services affiliated with the Police Department. Each year this event grew larger. Pictured are Nancy O'Teter, Mary Marks, Joe Bailey, Chief Benny Newman, Beth Wells, and Community Services Officer Leonard Carmack. Courtesy Nancy O'Teter

DeVry University, a nationwide system of universities that offer technology-based degree programs integrating general education with industry-specific coursework, located a campus in Irving. Its executives became involved with the business community and became leaders in the Chamber of Commerce.

The Public Library started the 1980s with education on a different level. In addition to the reading programs, puppet shows, story times, movies, and information services, an Adult Basic Education Program was added. Adults could prepare for the high school equivalency exam. Pat Nicks reported from the Southwest Branch Library that from July 1, 1980, through June 30, 1981, 3,152 persons enrolled and 1,463 received their high school diplomas.

North Lake Community College was community-oriented from the day it opened. The curriculum grew to offer not only the first two years of college courses, but also courses created to serve the business community and continuing education courses for adults. A five-hundred-seat

The Braniff Graduate Center on the University of Dallas campus with the Las Colinas Urban Center in the background. Courtesy Sybil Novinski

North Lake College sat on a 276-acre site with a lake lending a serene atmosphere to a very busy community asset.

auditorium was used for college programs, musicals, and plays and for community performances like the Irving Symphony before there was a performing arts facility.

From the beginning, Don Newport, the first president, and other administrators of the college appreciated the value of the arts in the life of a city and invited the newly formed Cultural Affairs Council (CAC) to get involved with the college. The CAC sponsored a two-week art festival on the campus culminating in the official dedication of the building October 23, 1977.

Without the CAC acting as a catalyst for the arts groups and the community that wanted a stronger presence for the arts in the city, a performing arts complex in Irving would not have come as soon as it did. Participation and support for the arts was strong and eclectic, but there was no suitable facility to house the many cultural activities. The City Government was struggling to provide basic services and solve the problems created by phenomenal growth. There was no way they could fund such a facility.

Irving citizens were part of a statewide effort to get House Bill 296 passed in the sixty-fifth session of the legislature. Representative Lance Lalor introduced the Bill to provide municipal funds for art programs by revising the "occupancy tax" law to allow Texas cities to increase the tax to 4 percent and use part of that hotel tax for support and promotion of the arts and for his-

Phase One of the area personal transit opened in 1989 with 1.4 miles of dual guideway serving four stations: Bell Tower, Lincoln Place, Xerox Center, and Cigna Tower. When it was built this was considered to be a very innovative service.

From 1982 to 1992, Gwen Shea represented Irving in the Texas House of Representatives. She was the first woman in Texas history to sit on the influential House Ways and Means Committee.

Below Right:
Music filled the air all day from a platform built in front of the theater.

Below Left:
The Irving Community Television van was on the road covering every event.

Below Center:
Mr. Carpenter was persuaded to make a public announcement that the ten acres next door would be donated for an arts complex.

toric preservation. Within a week after the Bill passed, civic leaders and representatives from the organizations that had been active in influencing the vote officially formed the Cultural Affairs Council. They perceived a clear path to funding the arts and providing appropriate housing. Volunteers staffed a donated office in the American Bank Tower on Highway 183. A comprehensive mailing list was developed by volunteers and computerized by the University of Dallas. Master mailing lists were provided to member organizations. A quarterly calendar and newsletter were initiated. The office moved to North Lake College and the calendar expanded to a monthly schedule. The office and use of rooms by arts groups was free. The *Irving Daily News* started an "Art Scene" column. Arts representatives were interviewed on television shows, and a speakers' bureau was created.

They applied to the National Endowment for the Arts for full participation in the City Spirit program for cities that could demonstrate pride in their community and an interest in the arts. Irving was chosen for a visit by a facilitator who would determine if the city qualified for a City Spirit Grant from the NEA. When Bruce Beers arrived in the spring of 1978, the city was alive with arts activities morning, noon, and night. Performances, exhibits, and demonstrations of every type were coordinated into his schedule. All of this activity coincided with political campaigning for the April elections. Irving Community Theater presented *The Music Man* in the ballroom of Villa Inn on the same night there was a rally for Ray Hutchison who was running for governor.

Irving was rated high on city spirit and received a grant from the NEA to help arts organizations help themselves. But there was no source of funds large enough or predictable enough to provide a facility. The major issue in the 1980 city election was carrying out the intent of the Lalor Bill, and after the election of candidates who pledged support for the concept, a formal proposal was delivered to the Council. On August 14, 1980, two items on the agenda proposed designation of the funds and differed only in how they would be administered. The decision was between the Convention and Visitors Board and a new Arts Board. The Council Chamber overflowed with supporters who stayed and participated in the discussion even though, on one of the hottest days of the year, the air conditioning at City Hall was not functioning. The vote was to appoint an Arts Board and it was done that same hot night.

The Buena Vista Movie Theater had been vacant for several years after the Irving public learned that the *Snow White* that was playing there was not for children but was an adult X-rated movie. Mr. Carpenter, whose company owned the property, terminated the lease and closed the building. The tenant took all of the equipment including the seats when he vacated.

When supporters of existing performing groups approached Ben Carpenter, he was willing to make the theater available for the community. He also confided to appropriate persons that his company owned the ten acres south of the theater, which they were willing to convey to the City for a building that would be adequate to the needs of the growing community. A limited time lease on the Buena Vista Theater was signed. Perennial critics read the lease and commented publicly on what they thought was a high price. They didn't know that the Southland Foundation

Above:
The first movie theater outside of Main Street was on East Irving Boulevard. Bill and Kathy Pecchi turned it into a complete movie studio by removing the seats, pouring concrete to level the floor, and creating a sound stage. Bill was a featured recording artist who had worked in the Hollywood film production business. From the Irving studio and surrounding locations they produced everything from TV commercials and shows to complete feature films.

Left:
Johnny Crawford was filmed at the studio.

was paying it on behalf of the City. With a loan from the Convention and Visitors Bureau facility fund and private donations the renovation of the theater began. Money to buy 536 seats was raised from donors whose names were placed on a plaque in the lobby. They could also have priority seating at the gala on opening night.

Anticipation was so intense that, three months before the theater was ready for use, the Special Projects Committee of the CAC put together the largest and happiest arts festival yet. In the morning a colorful parade kicked off the celebration. There were performances throughout the day in the Gazebo and in front of the theater. Every imaginable art form was displayed throughout the day in every space within the Plaza and in shelters on the vacant land to the south. There was a children's area with constant entertainment and involvement in various art forms. The Symphony played a rousing evening concert.

The gala opening night finally arrived in October 1983. The performing arts finally had their first home in Irving and serious planning of the permanent facility was begun. The Southland Foundation funded a conceptual design.

The library administration played a very early role in overall planning for the Bond Election. Using master plans from previous campaigns and lists of active and influential citizens,

Left:
Chuck Norris from "Walker Texas Ranger" with Kathy and Bill Pecchi.

Far Left:
Mickey Rooney was interested in starting a school in the area with acting and production instruction by professionals.

The Byron Nelson Golf Classic has been an annual event in Irving since 1982 when it was sponsored by GTE. It is operated by the Salesmanship Club of Dallas to benefit their clubs and camps for boys and girls with severe behavioral problems.

The senior citizens had a fine new home in the vacated Library on O'Connor.

The Main Library east of City Hall on Irving Boulevard.

they outlined a plan to ensure the success of the nine proposals. The proposition relating to libraries asked $7,225,000 for a new building because the twenty-year-old Library on O'Connor was miserably overcrowded. The Library Staff, Library Board, Friends of the Library, and other supportive organizations participated enthusiastically in promoting passage of the whole bond package and especially the library request.

When the bonds passed, the services and spaces needed to address them were already documented. Councilman Frank Skipper suggested a contest in which selected architects would, for a fee, submit plans and drawings based on the documented needs assessment and recommendations from a library consultant. One of them would be awarded the contract.

When Lamar Veach assumed the role of library director, the funding had been voted and the architect chosen. Construction of the Library began on the site east of City Hall.

A significant change took place at Texas Stadium in early 1985 when an eleven-member limited partnership headed by H. R. "Bum" Bright bought the Dallas Cowboy franchise for an estimated $80 million. The arrangement with the Murchison Company that had owned the Cowboys and the Texas Stadium Corporation was that for a fee they would operate the stadium for the City and the income would be used by the City to pay off the original bonds. "Bum" Bright took over Texas Stadium Corporation and leased the stadium. They paid a minimum $950,000 per year against 8 percent of gross revenue from the stadium. They paid off the outstanding bonds, spent about $26 million to improve the stadium, and built a new row of "crown suites." The City then owned a better stadium free of debt.

The new Main Library opened in 1986 and quickly became a center of activity with space for the collections, children's activities, microfiche readers, a Genealogy Department, an auditorium with a stage, and smaller meeting rooms.

The senior citizens were anxious to move into the vacated Library on O'Connor. There was a slight delay while other bids for the building were advanced. The IISD was the most vocal. The building and the land were adjacent to the Administration Building and could provide for consolidation of some related departments. They offered to trade the J. O. Davis School, which the City was currently using as a recreation center. The seniors prevailed and happily moved into the building.

The year 1986 and the following years were incredibly busy in Irving with new facilities and services and with celebrating and preserving reminders of the past. The Texas Sesquicentennial was observed all over the state. A wagon train was organized to follow as near as possible the routes of early trails around the state. About 150 wagons covered some three thousand miles in a six-month period. In Irving, Glen Courson was an honorary assistant wagon master. He provided an office on Rochelle, a wagon, supplies, and sometimes drove a wagon that picked up travelers who just wanted to experience the ride without investing six months in the adventure. The wagon train entered Irving via the California Crossing. They used the bridge instead of the muddy low water crossing that the pioneers had. On July 28, 1986, they arrived in Valley Ranch at 10 a.m. and made camp. That evening Triland sponsored a barbeque dinner for the travelers and invited Irving guests. During the day the campers were offered free access to the ice skating rink.

On the Fourth of July the Symphony presented a patriotic concert at Williams Square followed by a fireworks show over the lake. This is an annual event still observed in 2003.

Heritage Park was conceived after the organization of the Heritage Society. The land on Main Street north of the old Library was in a neglected state when Carol Susat was elected president of the Historic Society in 1984. She learned from John Everett, who had moved into a house on Main Street, that the land passed to Home Savings of America in California when they bought out Civic Savings. The City bought the property and an intrepid group of people who wanted to preserve reminders of Irving pioneers went to work. Pete Fernandez had the Main Arterie at 135 South Main where she promoted the work of Texas artists. She had a gallery for showing artwork and studios for local artists. She organized the first art festivals on the park land and found an old depot that was similar to the one that had been at the north end of Main Street. The permanent structures in Heritage Park were found and installed and celebrated in 1986 and 1987. Multiple annual celebrations bring people from all over Irving to the original town and Heritage Park every year. The Downtown Association organizes the Heritage Festival. The City sponsors the annual Fourth of July parade and antique automobiles are regularly displayed. The Christmas parade, the music, and the lighting of the tree at City Hall remind one of the downtown Christmas during the Depression.

The Gilbert house, in which Dr. Franklin Monroe Gilbert and Dorothy Brandon Gilbert raised their family and generously proffered medical help to whoever needed them, was recognized by the Heritage Society with a historic marker. The Gilbert house was later recognized with a state historic marker. Left to right are Charles Schulze, Dr. Clay Gilbert, Dorothy Gilbert, Dr. Francis M. Gilbert, Shirley Gilbert, O. D. Bates presenting the plaque, and Estelle Bates. Courtesy Dr. Clay Gilbert

The Irving Homebuilders Association donated materials and built the gazebo in Heritage Park. The old depot came from Fate, Texas.

Above:
Edmund Caster helped his father build this cabin near Shady Grove and Beltline before Irving was founded. His daughter, Mabel Miller, moved it to a lot on Pioneer. Jaycee members, along with Carol Susat, George Edwin, and Pete Fernandez, got it dismantled and moved to Heritage Park.

Right:
Louise Henderson donated this windmill to Heritage Park. When she and "Dub" Henderson opened the Great Outdoors sporting goods store on a lot that had been part of Himes City, the windmill was in the parking lot. Though it had to be removed, Louise couldn't give it up and stored it until she found it a good home.

Avove:
The little 1950s Library was already on the property at Heritage Park.

Left:
The water tower, which was preserved by Lloyd Smith at his home in Union Bower, originally stood in the middle of the intersection of Main and First Streets. Smith was once elected mayor of Union Bower, but they didn't have enough population to incorporate, so he was always a mayor without a city. The tower is now preserved in Heritage Park.

This charming bronze sculpture named *Family Outing* is at Victoria Park. Several similar pieces can be found around town.

Chapter 10

Maturing and Reminiscing

The 1990 census recorded a population of just over 155,000 in Irving. During the 1980s there had been a very conscious effort to preserve the history of the area. The Heritage Society actively accumulated and preserved artifacts, structures, and information. Interviews with longtime residents were recorded. A recurring sentiment among those who recorded their memories was that Irving was a good place to grow up and a good place to raise a family. There was a strong sense of community when everybody knew everybody and everybody cared. Every adult was a parent to every child. Obviously it had been several decades since it was possible to know everybody in town, but some residents were clinging to the thought that there was still a sense of community. They felt it and many newcomers agreed.

The town had grown rapidly to the north and northwest. New people coming into town and upwardly mobile residents had filled each new subdivision as it was built. At first *south* was defined as south of the railroad tracks. Then later South Irving was south of Highway 183. Then there was South Irving, Central Irving, North Irving, and Las Colinas. The twelve-thousand-acre master-planned community of Las Colinas was vastly different from any other part of Irving. There were nine hundred business firms in the development with sixty thousand employees. There were five single-family subdivisions, some of which were behind walls, and seventy-five hundred apartment units were 95 percent leased. Employees were more than double the number of residents. There were more than fifty restaurants in the area and six hotels.

Dr. Robert Pierce, mayor from 1987 to 1991, was on the first medical staff of Irving Community Hospital where he served twice as chief of staff. Though he was a busy and popular physician, he somehow found time to serve on the School Board and two terms as mayor.

The difference in the master-planned development and the rest of Irving was dramatic because it had happened so quickly and more people worked there than lived there. But the rest of Irving had changed too. A large percentage of residents were employed in Irving, so it was no longer a bedroom community for Dallas.

In the town that had once been described as a mass of truck farms, only one truck farm was still in operation. West of MacArthur Boulevard at Oakdale, Doug LePori was still raising vegetables and supplying Tom Thumb groceries. His father, Cyril, had bought the ten-acre farm adjacent to Vilbig Lake from the Miliara family. His niece used vegetables from the farm in dishes served at Traci's Restaurant, which she owns and operates at 2403 Thomas Avenue in Dallas.

About the only thing that hadn't changed was the constant need to improve the road system and the concern for ensuring an adequate supply of potable water. Older streets were deteriorating and the thoroughfare system needed to be expanded. While he dealt with immediate problems, City Manager Jack Huffman never let his staff or his City Council forget that Highway 161 was going to be extremely important. He once described highway 183 as a Model T upgraded to a 1950 Ford and said 161 would be a Cadillac. The completion of that highway was absolutely essential to serve the growth that was rapidly taking place and he never let it rest. After twenty years and many success stories, Jack Huffman retired in 1993, leaving many grateful admirers. A statement in 1990 by Ralph Ellis, the very conservative assistant city manager for finance, says a

Roy Brown was mayor from 1991 to 1993. He had served four terms on the City Council.

Before Carpenter Road crossed Irving Boulevard and was renamed MacArthur Boulevard, St. Luke's Catholic Church was on Perch Hill. Before the address became 200 North MacArthur, the congregation had grown enough to warrant the construction of a new sanctuary, which was recognized with a historical marker from the State of Texas on April 10, 1988. The St. Luke's congregation built and occupied the first church in Irving in 1904.

lot about why Huffman was successful during a volatile time in the history of Irving. "Jack has a unique ability to relate to all of his employees. It's easy to feel comfortable with him. He seeks out our opinions and considers them before he has to make his own. It is a mutual relationship of trust and respect and that works for everyone."

An important success story was the connection of a central thoroughfare from the northern to the southern city limits. The names of what had been unconnected segments were dropped and the entire corridor was named MacArthur Boulevard. This connection provides access to significant places that serve to bring residents of north and south Irving together. South of the tracks it passes the Ratteree Career Development Center, Townley Elementary School, and the South MacArthur Church of Christ at Shady Grove Road, which is recognized with a State Historical Marker. That large bilingual church is the direct descendent of the second church in Irving, which was originally on Delaware at Irving Boulevard. John Haley Elementary School, St. Luke's Church, School, and Family Life Complex, and the City Hall Complex, which includes the Main Library, are also on MacArthur Boulevard south of the tracks. Between the tracks and Highway 183, MacArthur passes the original Irving Community Hospital, now renamed Baylor Medical Center at Irving, where the volunteer auxiliary still donates many hours of valuable service and raises money for the Hospital. Entering Las Colinas, it passes North Lake College and the site of the annual Byron Nelson Golf Classic, pro tennis tournaments, and the year-round Byron Nelson Golf School, then MacArthur goes on through the many retail, restaurant, and commercial entertainment developments. But in the middle, between Las Colinas and Highway 183, there is MacArthur High School and the Irving Art Center. The Center for the Arts is the product of community effort that brought together citizens from every part of the city and from the various strata. They worked in unison to create a funding source through legislation and to secure the first interim facility for the visual and performing arts. They organized and participated in celebrations that generated enthusiasm. When it was time to plan the permanent facility there was a broad base of citizen input. Business leaders and attorneys worked free for the cause. Arts groups were working together in the temporary facility and had gained the benefit of experience and access to experts in theater and gallery design. Every detail of the proposed facility was studied, argued, and reviewed publicly so that by the time the architect was engaged the general plan was clear. There had been a strong lobby for a two-to-three-thousand-seat auditorium adjacent to Texas Stadium. The feasibility study by Theatre Projects Consultants, Inc., confirmed what the large majority of volunteers had concluded with regard to optimum size, location, and functional design. During the planning process Rob Pocklington, the executive director hired by the Arts Board, kept the temporary theater running, worked with the Board and the organizations and reported findings and conclusions about the proposed permanent facility to the city manager.

When Jack Huffman retired March 31, 1993, his assistant city manager, Stephen McCollough, assumed the position of acting city manager for eight months before being confirmed as city manager.

Michael Riffkind demonstrated Venetian stained-glass art techniques at the Grand Generation event. He was one of the artists who worked and exhibited at the Main Arterie which Pete Fernandez, Merriam Kokojan, and Noni Chance operated at 135 South Main in the old downtown. Courtesy Mary Higbee

When there was enough agreement the chairman of the Arts Board, Marge Korkmas, presented the conclusions of the Arts Board to the City Council. That report cleared the way for confirming the land donation, hiring the architect, establishing funding sources and building the visual and performing arts complex at 3333 MacArthur Boulevard.

Phase I was completed and occupied while plans for the theater funding were still being finalized. This first phase provided offices for the Convention and Visitors Bureau, the Chamber of Commerce, and the Arts Board. The Cultural Affairs Council, Heritage Society, and nonprofit Irving arts organizations shared a common office. There were meeting rooms and a visual art gallery. The inclusion of the Chamber of Commerce on a lease basis brought another strong presence that spanned the entire city.

In the interim between the completion of the first phase and beginning the construction of the theater phase, the Arts Board led by Mary Higbee brought the Smithsonian Institution touring exhibit to the site for a month. Titled "The Grand Generation: Memory, Mastery, Legacy," the exhibit showcased examples of the skills and artistry of early Americans. In Irving the exhibit was brought to life by local citizens demonstrating most of the same skills and in workshops where young people were taught to emulate the creative accomplishments of their ancestors. A special postal cancellation was used in the region during the exhibit period.

Phil Dunn, an Irving fireman, was an expert saddlemaker. He brought the art back to life for visitors to the Smithsonian exhibit. Courtesy Mary Higbee

The successful Sesquicentennial Celebration had been chaired by Joseph Rice who became the author of a Heritage Society–sponsored history of Irving titled *Irving: A Texas Odyssey*, which was published in 1989.

In the fall of 1990, Irving celebrated the opening of two highly functional theaters built back to back and connected to a large rehearsal hall and a shop for scenery building. The lobby of each theater is connected to the two visual art galleries and each lobby offers additional exhibit space. The lobby of Carpenter Hall is graced with an elaborate chandelier that was a gift from GTE Southwest, one of many corporate supporters of the arts in Irving.

The opening of this facility was particularly poignant to a very large and diverse army of

The building at the Irving Art Center faces east to MacArthur Boulevard with the offices on the front side. The window in this picture is on the north side where one can look into the lobby of the 712-seat Carpenter Performance Hall. Courtesy Jo Trizila

The Carpenter Performance Hall is a dream home for the Symphony, the Ballet, and musical shows of all types. An orchestra pit with hydraulic lifts can be raised to extend the apron of the stage. The second tier of seats includes boxes on either side. Attention to acoustics and sightlines ensures that every seat is good.

citizens who shared the vision and worked to make it reality. The necessary government involvement was evoked and shaped by the cooperation, enthusiasm, and persistence of arts and civic organizations, individual supporters, educational institutions, businesses, and elected officials. Most of the people involved never did and never will see their names or pictures in print, but they have a sense of pride in the building that is the embodiment of true City Spirit and in the community-enriching performances, exhibits, and programs that it houses.

After the 1990 Gala Opening, chaired by Rosalie Jensen, a full month of performances and exhibits organized by Mary Oberlin and executed by the arts and civic groups of the city filled every space in the complex. In 2003 that facility still vibrates with activity that involves and represents the entire spectrum of the Irving population. There's always something going on there every day of the year. The theaters are booked by the beginning of each season. In 2002 it was estimated that over one hundred thousand persons visited the building. More that three thousand youths participated in Kids Arts. Thirteen performing organizations, including three symphonies, called the Center home and claimed performance and rehearsal dates in the two theaters and other parts of the building.

In 1989, Jerry Jones bought the Dallas Cowboys and Texas Stadium Corporation with the lease to operate the Stadium and started making some changes. He fired manager Tex Schram and legendary coach Tom Landry, and hired Jimmy Johnson to work with him as coach. In 1990 he opened the question of liquor at the Stadium. It had been ten years since the ordinance to allow liquor to be served in restaurants had caused such public controversy that most people still didn't want to talk about it. The election on that subject generated a voter turnout that has still not been matched in Irving. In answer to Mr. Jones, the City Council decided that there could be a restaurant adjacent to the Stadium that would operate under the City ordinance which required that 60 percent of revenue be derived from the sale of food. Security guards would be posted to prevent drinks from being carried into the Stadium. Strangely, at that time fans were allowed to carry coolers with beer into the Stadium, which caused problems that the Council agreed they should address. But before the zoning ordinance to allow a restaurant with a liquor license outside Texas Stadium was finalized, City Attorney Don Rorschach pointed out that there was a loophole in the existing agreement that would allow a third party to operate a concession without paying the 8 percent of proceeds that the Texas Stadium Corporation was obligated to pay to

When a symphony performs a portable shell improves acoustics for this type of musical performance. The New Philharmonic Symphony, organized in 1988 from members of the original orchestra, is a full orchestra made up mostly of music lovers who are eclectic in their ages and their "day jobs." They play for the sheer joy of making music together. The original Irving Symphony has become a professional orchestra.

The 263-seat Dupree Theater, named to honor Betty Dupree Carpenter, is accessed from the south side of the building. Meeting rooms and a small art gallery are also on this side. Courtesy Jo Trizila

The Irving Community Theater chose the musical *Follies* as their first production in the new Dupree Theater. It was fun for the cast and for the audience. Courtesy Jill Stephens

For the first time the Irving Ballet had a suitable stage for their performances. The size of the stage, the wing space, the orchestra pit, and the floor made the staging of classic or modern ballet a wonderful experience. Irving Art Center

Like the larger performance hall the Dupree Theater is fully equipped including an orchestra pit with hydraulic lift. It is the ideal size for plays, recitals, and multiple other uses. There is no center aisle but entrances on either side provide good access. The curved arrangement of the seats, space between rows, and the rake of the floor add up to the fact that there isn't a bad seat in the house. Courtesy Jo Trizila

The art gallery, accessible from either theater, hosts many exhibits in the course of a year including professional, special interest, and student winners from the schools. A small new talent gallery is adjacent.

The courtyard in the center of the building can be viewed through glass walls. The children are participating in the Kids Art program, which is an annual feature at the Center. It grows each year to the delight of the children who participate.

the City. An amendment to the existing agreement became a condition for passing the ordinance.

When Mr. Jones appeared before the City Council in February 1991 to ask for permission to sell beer and wine at the concession stands inside the Stadium, the public was aroused. The crowd overflowed into the atrium and the meeting lasted eight and a half hours. It ended with a unanimous vote against the proposal. The existing alcoholic beverage zoning ordinance was not appropriate for the stands at Texas Stadium. It was agreed that the Council would discuss a plan and probably appoint a committee to study the matter.

The Cowboy home games were a small part of the activity at the Stadium. It was a busy place throughout the year with concerts, festivals, graduations, high school football playoffs from across the state, and a broad variety of special events. By spring 1991, there was a Texas Stadium marketplace with six hundred vendors and amusements operating every weekend, except when the Cowboys were playing or other events in the Stadium were scheduled. Zales Jewelers opened an outlet store with over $500,000-worth of sterling silver items at 75 percent off retail. Proceeds benefited the local Junior Achievement programs.

The excellent Irving school system has progressed along with the changes in society. Time and technological advancements increased the body of knowledge that must be learned, and at the same time provided tools to help master the learning process. Computers and the training to use them were included in the curriculum, and at the turn of the century a long-range plan to issue laptop computers to high school students began and parents were brought into the loop to ensure proper use and benefit from the tool. That's a long step from the time when students had to provide their own books and the nearest place to get them was in Dallas where Reverend Barcus, Netta Brown's father, had a bookstore.

A large part of the success of the schools is the result of the active involvement of parents. And again the interaction of parents in PTA and the activities of schools bring people together in communities.

All of the schools now have libraries, media centers, and gymnasiums. Air conditioning is taken for granted. When the program to air-condition schools began in the late 1960s, the PTA

A restaurant authorized to serve alcoholic beverages was opened about fifty feet from the east gate next to a concession and souvenir stand that was equipped for food preparation. Named the Corral, it was enclosed by a wrought-iron fence and covered by a tent-like roof. There was a large-screen TV. Fans could gather before and after the games. A few stayed during part of games.

Tom Landry was memorialized at the entrance to the Stadium, along with the record of Super Bowl Championships won by the Cowboys. The first two were won while he was the coach.

Barbara Cardwell, standing in front of Superintendent Jack Singly, has set a record for length of service on the School Board. To be "Recognized," schools and school districts must have at least 80 percent of each population group pass each section of the TAAS. The dropout rate must be 3 percent or less at the secondary level.

Lamar was the first school from Irving to receive the most prestigious education award in the country. It recognizes excellence in leadership, teaching, curriculum, student achievement, parent involvement, and community support.

presidents engaged in a drawing to determine which schools would get that improvement first. There wasn't money to do them all at once. It took several years to complete the program.

All elementary schools now start with kindergarten. In 1999, the district became a Recognized District by the Texas Education Agency. Individual schools have been awarded status for high achievement. In 2000, Irving schools began receiving national recognition as Blue Ribbon Schools. Lamar Middle School was the first, followed by John R. Good in 2001. MacArthur High School is the latest to receive the honor. Representatives from the schools go to Washington, D.C., to accept the awards.

From the early days, Irving teams excelled in sports. Competition proved how good they were. At the turn of the century every imaginable sport is represented in Irving through the schools, the Park Department, and various associations. All ages from kindergarten to senior citizens can be involved in sports.

Academic competitions have proved that Irving also produces high-achieving scholars.

The High School Academy opened in August 2001 on the southeast corner of the North Lake College campus along MacArthur Boulevard. The instructional model incorporates rigorous academic expectations with career awareness to prepare the student with potential for higher education along with experience in the real world of a chosen career area. Students who are accepted at this school may pursue extracurricular activities in their "home" schools as long as they can meet all requirements of the Academy experience.

Irving students have won numerous academic competitions. Probably the most comprehensive is the Academic Decathlon. Teams are composed of three each with A (Honors), B (Scholastic), and C (Varsity) grade averages. Over a two-day period they compete in ten categories: essay writing, speech, interview, math, social science, science, economics, language, literature, and fine arts. Nimitz High School has won this competition in the region fourteen times in sixteen years.

After a successful bond election in 2001, more campuses were planned. Lorenzo de Zavala Middle School opened in 2002. The Academy of Irving that opened in August 2001 is a different type of school. The stated aim is to achieve "effective integration of business, community, and education resources to provide students with . . . academic and career preparation." The school actively seeks employment for students in their chosen career field during the summer before their senior year and for fifteen to twenty hours per week during the final school year. A number of Irving companies participate as partners in the concept by hiring interns who are still finishing their high school studies. The students have made a career choice and have had three hundred hours of class instruction before being recommended to an employer as skilled in their specialty. The areas of specialty cover a broad spectrum including education, legal, medical, dental, applied technology, visual arts, and communication. Partnerships have been established with companies like Nokia, Texas Instruments, NCH, the Medical Centers, Head Start, and others.

This 2001 team from Nimitz not only won first place in the Region X Decathlon, they took first place in the Super Quiz Relay for the fifth consecutive year and the team brought home sixty-seven medals which was thirty more than any other team.

The basic concept is not new. Irving schools have a long history of career-oriented programs. The houses built by students in building trades classes are testament to the early success of one of them. The Academy concentrates the concept and raises it to a new level and broader scope.

The Irving Schools Foundation, an independent nonprofit corporation, is an avenue for large and small businesses to benefit the schools by funding projects and activities for which tax dollars cannot be spent. Since 1985, the foundation has given more than $1,000,000 in teacher

The Robert Pierce School at Britain Road and Union Bower accommodates about 250 four-year-old students for a half-morning session and another 250 for a half-day afternoon session. ESL instruction is available for adults in the evening.

grants and student scholarships. Presentations are made at an annual "Breakfast with the Stars."

The Partnerships in Education program is aimed at involving business people with schools. Talking to classes, mentoring, and sharing knowledge and insight is encouraged. Student tours of work sites have been organized to help students decide on career paths. The Chamber of Commerce is most instrumental in making this program work for Irving.

The Irving School District is the first educational institution in the nation to be designated the Microsoft Center of Excellence recognizing the district as an innovator in the use of technology to enhance teaching and learning.

The district has expanded in the other direction to reach children in their early formative years. Three Early Childhood schools opened in 1999–2000. The Clifton School on Pleasant Run, the Kinkeade School on Cameron, and the Pierce School on Britain Road accept prekindergarten students. The HIPPY program expands the effectiveness of early childhood intervention. It's not about the sixties generation but is Home Instruction for Parents of Preschool Youngsters. Funded by Title 1 federal money, AmeriCorps grants, and the National Council of Jewish Women, the instruction is open to any applicant but targets families with limitations in English proficiency and income. The emphasis is on parental involvement in teaching. Parents are taught how to use educational software and to encourage learning at home. They make a two-year commitment to home visits, field trips with the children, meetings with other parents, and becoming teachers to their own children. The Nissan Corporation donated three hundred used computers to the district and every HIPPY family was issued a computer and trained in basic computer literacy and educational software. The experience makes a difference in the future of the children and their parents.

The Robert Pierce Early Childhood School at 901 Britain Road at Union Bower is near the historic Union Bower Community where Professor Steele taught all grades in one room. The Twelve Oaks Retirement Village across the street is an interesting juxtaposition of our youngest and oldest citizens. The Joffre and Dorety homeplaces were once here. Britain was the earliest road that extended from the original town to beyond what became Highway 183. Britain Road is now broken up by the freeway, and many old landmarks are gone, but a trip north from the Pierce School is interesting. Older homes are in various states of repair until just south of the railroad track that crosses Britain at an angle where the Raible Place condominium complex is well maintained. This was the first subsidized housing in Irving and was the subject of bitter controversy when it was built.

As soon as we cross the tracks the relatively new Salvation Army Building is facing Britain Road and backing to a renamed street that now ends without the connection it originally had to Grauwyler Road. A new underpass and a wider road are responsible for the change. In the late

The old Salvation Army Building has been replaced by this much larger and more impressive building. It houses all of the services provided by the organization and the Jean and Jerry Jones Early Childhood Center. The Jones family and the Dallas Cowboys are strong supporters of this facility and the services it provides.

1930s, Louis Ponce traded a hog and $75 he saved in the bank while he was in high school for land on that corner. His father, Marcelino, had come from Leon, Mexico, during the revolutions in 1914, when Louis was just four months old. Marcelino worked for the railroad and raised four boys and five girls right in the original town of Irving. Louis was sent to his grandparents' home in Mexico for school in the summers. He came back to school in Irving during the regular school term. His parents had high respect for education.

The two-lane section of Grauwyler Road that bumped up over the railroad track was rough, sometimes a bottleneck, and it was not pretty. Knowing they couldn't depend on the railroad to remedy the problem, the City tackled the job and created an attractive and functional underpass east of Britain Road.

Recent statistics indicate that the population of Irving is now over 30 percent Hispanic, but the Ponce family was the first in what was then, and is now, a city with families from many countries speaking a number of different languages. In 1996, Irving established a formal Sister City relationship with Leon, Mexico, through the Irving Friendship Foundation.

Paul Keyes Elementary School is on the northwest corner of Britain and Grauwyler Roads, and the Hindu Temple is just north of the school property. On the southeast corner of Britain and Highway 183 a car dealership has replaced the popular drive-in movie of the 1960s and 1970s.

Ethnic diversity has become a popular topic of conversation and government concern with growing community recognition of its reality. Like the rest of America, Irving was founded by people who came from many countries and spoke different languages. When they intermarried, families sometimes spoke two or three languages at home, but they spoke English in business and civic relationships. Carl Althoff, the first jeweler in Irving, is an example. His mother came from the French part of Switzerland. She spoke French and German. His father was from Vienna, Austria, and spoke German. They spoke German at home and young Carl spoke German before he spoke English. Carl married Pauline Miliara whose parents both came from Italy. It has always been true in Irving that a large percentage of schoolchildren come from families where languages other that English are spoken.

The Irving School District offers five language programs. French, German, Latin, and Spanish classes follow the tradition of language instruction. The fifth offering is Introduction to a Second Language, which introduces Spanish, French, Italian, Latin, German, and Japanese.

The large numbers of Spanish-speaking residents who do not speak English has prompted many programs in the schools, libraries, parks, churches, and social service providers to teach English as a second language. Teachers in elementary schools take courses to learn how to communicate with parents who do not speak English. Irving Community Television has added Spanish programming on Channel 74.

Census data in 2000 indicated that one of three residents speaks a language other than

This building, hidden now behind the Salvation Army structure, has an interesting history. It housed the first Mexican restaurant in Irving, but before that it was home to the L&M Spice Company and the L&M Grocers. Louis and Manuel Ponce created the company, which imported spices and sold wholesale to restaurants and other bulk users. Later they established the drive-in grocery stores that were scattered around the area. When they sold the stores the buyers kept the name. It was after they retired from those businesses that Louis and his wife opened Los Ponces Restaurant in this building.

The Dallas/Fort Worth Hindu Temple at 1605 North Britain Road is nestled between the back fo the Keyes Elementary school campus and an apartment complex. As the name indicates it serves a broader area than just Irving and it does it so quietly that it would be unnoticed were it not for its pristine beauty.

English at home. In recent years estimates of the number of languages spoken in Irving have ranged from forty-seven to sixty. That seems impossible because most of us don't even believe there are that many languages. But when we look around, it is surprising how many we find.

The three-screen Chateau Theater in the Plymouth Park Shopping Center became less popular as larger movie houses competed for audiences. It is popular again as the Everest Theater, which shows Indian films in Hindi, Tamil, Malayalam, and seven other Indian languages. Families come from as far away as Plano to enjoy being transported to their native land by the movies. Some have said that they use the films to reinforce cultural values in their children. The snack bar has spicy potato samosas and sweet masala tea, along with popcorn, candy, and soft drinks.

The Chateau Theater in the Plymouth Park Shopping Center was the first multiscreen movie house in Irving and gradually lured audiences from the less modern and less centrally located theaters. In turn larger multiscreen theaters and larger shopping centers lured audiences. It is now the Everest Theater where Hindu films draw audiences from all over Irving and the surrounding metropolitan area.

Major corporate headquarters that moved into Las Colinas brought international business associations and employees. The Dallas/Fort Worth Freeport, Foreign Trade Zone, and Dallas/Fort Worth International Commerce Park brought employees from around the world. Six industrial parks and four office parks have the potential for supporting international companies. Gradually stores and restaurants reflecting different cultures opened and employed immigrants from other countries. In 2002 the Irving Chamber of Commerce listed Belgium, Canada, Finland, France, Germany, Italy, Japan, Korea, Saudi Arabia, Switzerland, and Taiwan as countries with companies that have local offices in Irving/Las Colinas. In 2003 the two top graduates from MacArthur High School were first-generation Americans whose parents came from China. Mingming Ma made perfect scores on the SAT and the PSAT tests. She is a National Merit Scholar and a Presidential Scholar. Both of these top graduates speak fluent English and Mandarin. Bincheng Wu also speaks Cantonese. Maria Seppy, a longtime Park Department employee who now works at the Senter Park Recreation Center, came from Brazil and earned degrees in Rio de Janeiro and Philadelphia. She speaks English, French, Spanish, Portuguese, Italian, and two Brazilian tribal languages. We are beginning to realize how little we really know about the breadth of diversity in our city. It is a fact that Irving is an international city and most citizens enjoy the richness that diversity brings.

Some ethnic groups brought together by their culture become communities in spirit and

The Black Arts Council can always be counted on to bring traditional dancers and drummers to the festivals at Heritage Park.

share traditional celebrations. The Academy of Bangla Arts and Culture produces a complete season of elegant dance and traditional music. Its purpose is to preserve a common culture and to foster awareness and appreciation of the creative work of the people with roots in Bangladesh and West Bengal, India.

The Irving Black Arts Council shares the African culture by hosting visual art exhibits, theatrical performances, festivals, and workshops. Young people can learn the traditional African dances and music in the dance and drumming clinics. They also encourage the cultural development of African American talent. In the spring they award scholarships to Irving students in their annual oratory contest.

Several times during the year the parking lot on O'Connor Road and Pioneer, which many residents remember as Gibson's lot where carnival rides were brought in twice a year, is transformed into a staging area for traditional observances by Hispanics. The grocery store now there and Danal's Restaurant are popular among those who have discovered them. They sponsor the traditional observances. Christmas is a special time with several colorful performances. Every year, the Virgin of Guadalupe celebration is observed on December 12. On December 15 the parking lot is transformed to represent the journey of Joseph and Mary as they seek shelter. October 12 is Dia de la Roza, and of course Cinco De Mayo is a lively and colorful celebration.

When Morris Parrish became mayor in 1995, he was faced with an ongoing controversy about a proposal to expand two runways at the Dallas/Fort Worth Airport. Citizens who were adamantly opposed to the plan had formed ICCAN—"Irving Concerned Citizens Against Airport Noise."They fought fiercely against the proposed runways. In December 1990, the City, on behalf of the City Council, staff, consultants, and citizens, issued and circulated an eight-page publication presenting conclusions concerning the Draft Environmental Impact Statement generated by Airport officials. It covered errors, omissions, misleading statements, inconsistencies, and false conclusions. The controversy continued with litigation and no solution. The Airport was a major contributor to the economy of the region, with twenty-three hundred flights daily connecting to

Everybody gets in the act for a tortilla-making contest at Heritage Park. Courtesy Kirk Stricklin

The Ballet Folklorico de Irving, founded by Florine Jaime, celebrates Cinco de Mayo. Courtesy Kirk Stricklin

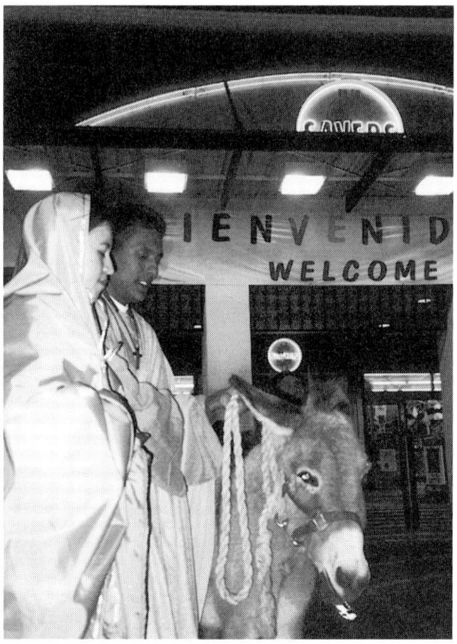

December 15: Representing Mary and Joseph they journey from shelter to shelter around the lot seeking a place to rest. Courtesy Kirk Stricklin

Dia de la Roza, October 12: An employee in the Cost+Plus store celebrates by representing Christopher Columbus. Courtesy Kirk Stricklin

over two hundred destinations worldwide. There was direct access to Canada, Mexico, Europe, and Asia. Two-thirds of all Texas air cargo was handled at that airport.

Soon after he was elected, Mayor Parrish began working with the chairman of the Airport Board and the Airport and City staffs toward an agreement that would bring closure to the controversy and litigation. The result didn't please everyone but he said: "It enabled the city to move ahead to other matters."The next issue he had to deal with was a highly emotional division of the city over an election to pull out of Dallas Area Rapid Transit. He stood firm.

The need for public transit had come up periodically through the years. The Council of Governments had produced a plan for the mid-cities in the 1960s. Representatives from Dallas and Tarrant Counties met in the 1970s at the Airport to work on a plan to connect the region with public transit. Jim Widener, an Irving representative in the planning said: "It would be a tragedy if we missed this opportunity." Irving voted favorably to create the Lone Star Transit Authority, but the proposition failed in the counties. Cities in Dallas County then formed an Interim Regional Transportation Authority to create a transit plan. Hundreds of meetings were held to gather input from citizens and develop a plan that would serve the area. Irving had a large task force that analyzed the probable needs for bus service based on points of interest and employment. Kurt Baden and John Danish worked enthusiastically to draw the lines on a map. Based on input from cities, the Interim Transit Authority, with Dan Matkin as one of the Irving representatives, developed a plan for immediate bus service and later rail service. It was supported by a finance plan based on a 1 percent limited sales tax. Irving was one of the cities that approved the plan to create the Transit Authority in August 1983. Legislation was passed to define the transit agency and permit the sales tax. Collections began in January 1984, and bus service was on the streets of Irving before the end of the year. Para Transit service was initiated to provide portal-to-portal service for certified handicapped individuals. In spite of the economic crisis of the 1980s, the service grew with added routes and transit centers until a hard-fought pullout election plunged the city into controversy again. The popularity and mystique of the Dallas Cowboys and large sums of money were used to convince Irving voters to pull out of Dallas Area Rapid Transit, but in August 1996 they voted to remain with the program, and in

Morris Parrish, mayor from 1995 to 1999, had already served two terms on the City Council before he ran for mayor. He came to the office knowing the problems he would face.

Bus shelters on opposite sides of O'Connor Road are connected by a tunnel under the road.

December the Trinity Railway Express brought passenger rail service from Dallas back to Irving, right where the city was founded in 1903. A stop at the Medical/Market Center was a convenience for many Irving residents who were employed there. Connections to the network that served the combined service area were also important to commuters.

The goal of the Trinity Express was to connect the rail service from Dallas to Fort Worth just as this corridor had done when Irving was founded. Stations were opened in Richland Hills, Hurst/Bell, CenterPort/DFW Airport, and West Irving at Esters Road. In December 2001, passenger service between Dallas Union Station and the T&P Station in Fort Worth was connected for the first time since 1969. The added element was access to the Airport from the CenterPort Station by connection to circulator buses. Plans for a light rail connection through Las Colinas from Dallas to Dallas/Fort Worth Airport are in progress. The total DART system connects Irving to Dallas and Fort Worth, the mid-cities and to eleven other suburban cities in the DART service area.

At the 2003 Transportation Summit, hosted by Irving for the sixth consecutive year, national, state, regional, and local representatives seriously discussed the possibility of developing a regional transit system to provide seamless connections in north Texas.

Mayor Parrish was interested in the aesthetics of the city. He led the City Council in planning some amenities such as pocket parks and sculpture. Councilman George Susat had promoted tree planting for years. He was sometimes called Mr. Crepe Myrtle. The staff was asked to add five miles of neighborhood sidewalks each year. This program was aimed at both aesthetic appearance and livability. Sidewalks encourage pedestrian traffic and neighborhood integrity. The creation of pocket parks that Morris Parrish started continues with the cooperation of the Public Works Department and Public Art Irving. A linear park on Story Road between Highway 183 and Rochelle is the latest example.

Marge Parrish was very active in the Heritage Society and played a major role in the development of Heritage Park. The Heritage Society established the tradition of the Bracebridge Dinner in 1990. Every year in December they organize a seven-course dinner recreating the

Left:
Hundreds of enthusiastic Irving citizens gathered to welcome the arrival of the Trinity Railway Express in December 1996.

Above:
In December 2001, representatives from Dallas, Fort Worth, and the mid-cities along the rail corridor drove the ceremonial golden spike symbolizing the connection of the DART and the T service areas by the Trinity Express.

Left:
In December 1997, VIPs took a special ride on the train with Santa to celebrate extended hours of operation.

This monument faces O'Connor Road north of Northwest Highway and backs to the trail between the Bird's Fort and California Crossing Parks. The North Irving Transit Center is on the other side of O'Connor.

Christmas dinner at Bracebridge Hall as Washington Irving wrote it. Attendees are encouraged to dress in period costumes and join in preprandial conviviality and the promenade to dinner in the Great Hall. Guests are typically entertained by madrigal singers, Renaissance dancers, and bagpipe, harp, and trumpet interludes.

After years of continuing arguments concerning the origin of the name of Irving, the Heritage Society met and voted to take a position that there was enough evidence to determine that the town was named for Washington Irving, America's first man of letters, who was a storyteller, historian, humorist, biographer, and a distinguished diplomat. He was Netta Brown's favorite author and J. O. Schulze had been a member of the Washington Irving Literary Society at the University of Iowa. On October 22, 1998, the Irving City Council made it official by passing an ordinance declaring the origin of the name.

The type of fiscal conservatism promoted by Mayor Matkin in the 1970s and perpetuated by the director of finance and subsequent City Councils led to a AAA bond rating that was sustained until 1996 when Irving received a double AAA rating from both Moody's and Standard and Poor's. This is the highest possible rating and is held by only seventeen other cities in the nation. Of course the Airport and the Las Colinas development are major contributors to the economy of the city, but prudent management is ultimately the key to the financial soundness of the City government.

Irving assumed a leading role in the development of the Trinity Greenbelt with the creation of Campion Park and trails along the Elm and West Forks of the river. For more than forty years improvements along the banks of the Trinity River and access to trails had been discussed. Finally, the Trinity Trails Coalition of sixteen counties, which are members of the North Central Texas Council of Governments, formalized a comprehensive plan for a 250-mile trail system that would link cities in the Metroplex. The Irving Parks and Recreation Department took the initiative, and a Master Plan for a 22-mile project along the frontage of the Elm and West Forks of the river in Irving was approved in 1995. This local trail that will connect to the regional trail system is the first officially adopted section of the regional "Trinity Trails System." The Irving Park Department has already led the development of trails and parks along the Elm Fork from Keenan's Crossing Park north of Royal Lane to California Crossing Park east of the Urban Center near the intersection of Rochelle Road and Highway 114. These parks along with Spring Trail Park and Bird's Fort Park between Northwest Highway and Royal Lane are reminders that early riders on horseback and wagon trains forded the river and passed through long before the land was anything more than wide-open space.

The police functions had been spread out in three separate buildings at the Civic Center Complex. The new Criminal Justice Facility on ten acres was built on O'Connor Road south of Pioneer. It houses the city jail, police personnel, and the municipal courts.

Development of the southern portion of the trails started along the West Fork with access from Twin Wells Park on the eastern portion. On the west, the sixty-acre Mountain Creek Preserve can be accessed via East Hunter Ferrell Road or Nursery Road. This was the first park built along Campion Trails and was a joint effort of the City of Irving, Dallas County Open Space Board, and Texas Parks and Wildlife Department. George Edwin, who has given freely of his time and talent to Irving projects, is chairman of the Dallas County Trails and Open Space Board. Within the Mountain Creek Preserve there is fishing access and a pedestrian canoe launch that will allow limited navigation of the West Fork of the Trinity. There are area picnic shelters, playground equipment, a basketball court, horseshoe pitch, nature trail, mountain bike trail, practice sandlot ball field, and an equestrian meadow. Families are again drawn to the river as they were from the 1800s to the 1920s, but now they have more amenities at their disposal.

When the 250 miles of planned trails are completed, Irving will be right in the middle at the intersection of the Elm and West Forks of the Trinity River.

The Kiosk at Spring Trail Park is adjacent to a twelve-foot-wide paved section of trail that invites hiking, bicycling, roller-blading, and even wheelchairs. It is possible for residents in Valley Ranch to go to the North Irving DART Transit Center or to workplaces in the Urban Center on the trails.

City services have constantly expanded through the years. Both the Police and Fire Departments are fully staffed and equipped. On-board computers provide vital information to help police with background information about offenders they encounter. Firemen can call up the floor plan of a building they are about to enter. Many other uses of computer databases enhance the ability of our protectors to do their jobs. Policemen in Irving are trained to project the attitude that every individual deserves respect and consideration, which makes them different from many officers we see depicted on television shows. Irving people like it that way.

Both policemen and firemen engage in programs with young people. Some of what they do is on their own time. The Irving Police Athletic League is a vehicle to reach out to at-risk youngsters with structured activities that interest them, instill pride, and engage their time to keep them out of trouble. Their building has a full-sized boxing ring and physical fitness equipment. In 1996 about two hundred at-risk youngsters participated in weekly recreational activities with the Police League. Probably the most important aspect of the program is interaction with policemen who serve as role models who care about them. Policemen also devote off-duty time to teach fourth and fifth grade students about drug awareness and self-esteem.

The Police Department interacts with and receives help from citizens who volunteer for Irving Citizens on Patrol. The Citizen Police Academy has a waiting list and there is a Citizen Police Academy Alumni Association. A new Hispanic Citizen Police Academy is for those who

The 26,400-square-foot Lee Park Recreation Center has two gymnasiums, three racquetball courts, a fitness center, locker rooms, showers, a multipurpose classroom, a kitchen, crafts area, and a teen center.

speak little or no English. The purpose of the ten-week course is to acquaint these residents with police functions and civil and criminal law.

The police and courts outgrew their quarters in the City Hall Complex and moved into a new building on O'Connor Road. There are stations that provide police presence in outlying areas and densely frequented places. The storefront station in the Irving Mall is an example. A mobile command post, tactical unit, and K-9 unit enhance the efficiency of the officers. In April 2002, a North Irving Police Station was opened to reduce response time to the northern portion of the city and provide convenience for citizens who need information or services. The basic intent of dispersal is to have officers acquainted with neighborhoods and their inhabitants before any incidents occur.

In 1996, a domestic violence unit was formed with state grant funds and 2,421 cases were handled the first year. This was one of the steps toward the creation of a Family Advocacy Center.

The Teen Court has been a successful learning experience for fourteen- to seventeen-year-olds. For misdemeanor cases, the peers of the defendant volunteer to act as jurors, bailiffs, and attorneys. Convicted offenders are sentenced to hours of community service. Repeat offenders are referred for family counseling. Teens who volunteer for positions in the court receive orientation and training and must commit to serve each Tuesday for four months. In 1996 this court heard 842 cases, resulting in the contribution of over seventeen thousand hours of community service.

The Senter Park Recreation Center and the park behind it have been enlarged several times since the high school sociology class planned it and spearheaded the drive to build it as a youth center in 1954. It is one of the centers that sponsors Saturday night jams. These supervised multiactivity sessions are similar to the first ones. The Garden Art Building across the street that belonged to the ladies who helped with that early project is still in use, but the Park Department now operates and maintains it.

With the great variety of programs available, every young person should find constructive, interesting, and fun things to do all the time. The Library has an ongoing series of interesting and informative events for all ages, interests, and levels of education. The *Hennan's Public Library Ratings Index 2000* named the Irving Library the best public library that serves a city of more than 170,000. A $225,000 grant from the Melinda Gates Foundation was used to purchase computers for patron research.

The parks are alive with sports, classes, and programs throughout the year. There are nine fully equipped and staffed recreation centers. The Art Center involves young people in every imaginable art form. The schools have a variety of extracurricular activities. The Youth Action Center provides an innovative and interesting alternative, which brings teens from all over Irving to interact in very positive activities. A tremendous amount of enthusiasm is generated, a lot of learning in fun ways takes place, and the sense of belonging is enforced. It is another example of grassroots initiative that is characteristic of Irving.

Concerned citizens approached the City Council with little red wagons filled with letters and petitions requesting that funding be allocated for a program under the national America's Promise initiative. Volunteers worked with Parks and Recreation staff to develop leadership training programs, to organize teen summits, and to equip a teen center. The initial location was in a four-thousand-square-foot leased office space on Highway 183 and Story Road. It was

The Whistle Stop Plaza has become a popular place in old Irving. The weekend farmers' market reminds one that this area was once a mass of truck farms. The soil is still good for gardens and people bring produce from small gardens to sell. It seems to be more pleasure than profit.

equipped with a computer lab, conference room, study rooms, game room, lounge, and a teen newsroom. A news magazine is produced quarterly by teen writers and photographers. An appointed Youth Council works with City staff in the ongoing development of teen-based activities. The Youth ACTION Council of fifteen-to-nineteen-year-olds represents the voices of teens in all Irving high schools. They have conceived and helped organize many events and have represented their peers on "Open Line" on Irving Community Television. Teens not only plan fun social events, they are involved in community service projects. They donate service to the community and help show that teens can and do made a difference. New leaders are developed through this program. According to the Youth ACTION Council mission statement: "They are responsible for the identification of issues and problems facing the City's youth and for developing activities and creating solutions to unify the community as a whole." In 2000, their talent shows for their own enjoyment culminated in a Friday Nite Live event at the Art Center with singers, dancers, individual musicians, and bands competing. The occasion provided a large audience for the presentation of the Spirited Youth Awards.

By 1996, the Fire Department had 272 firefighters and 113 of them were trained paramedics. With five ambulances and a pool of paramedics, the average response time was less than five minutes. There is a Hazmat team that receives constant training to answer calls related to hazardous materials.

In 1997, the City purchased the First National Bank Building on Nursery Road south of Irving Boulevard and named it the Human Services Building. The building had been part of Irvingate, which was the first shopping center outside of the original downtown. It had been vacant for several years but was in excellent condition. A cross-section of services is brought together in this building.

DART funds an art project at each transit center and works with a local committee to choose and plan something that characterizes the community surrounding the station. The Irving committee chose the trails map that is on the floor of the transit center. Some residents wanted a more visible landmark. The clock tower at the end of Main Street in front of the location of the original train station was planned and executed on DART land by the Downtown Association,

The former bank building in southeast Irving is well located for accessibility and large enough to bring an array of needed services to an aging area of the city.

The City owns the building and shares it with County, State, and nonprofit agencies for the convenience of Irving citizens.

Seeing the office/bank tower come down was almost traumatic to some residents who surrounded it with fond memories and to others of a frugal nature who couldn't understand ruining a perfectly good building. Irving Archives

the Heritage Society, and the Preservation and Redevelopment Board working together. It has become a gathering place for various events from fiddlers' contests, cakewalks, square dances, and a weekend farmers market to Super Saturday with contemporary entertainment and a chili cook-off. Whistle Stop Plaza features a seventy-foot tower sitting on a granite base with a clock and a computerized chime. It is in front of the location of the original depot where earlier settlers stood when they attended the auction of the first lots in Irving. This tower was finished in time to fill a void when the ten-story bank tower was demolished in 1999.

The bank tower on Irving Boulevard and Main was more than a physical landmark in a historic location. It had brought people who worked in the offices, visited the bank, or attended meetings and social functions into the original town. In 1999, the owners faced a citation because the building did not meet city building codes. The cost to remedy was prohibitive when office rentals and other activities had waned, and so the owners decided to simply demolish the building. A new one-story bank building was erected.

Attorney Joe Putnam, who was elected mayor in May 1999, had offices in the bank tower for many years. He was forced to move when the City cited the owners of the building for building code violations. Mr. Putnam was not new to City government. He had been a councilman from 1973 to 1982 and again from 1995 to 1997. Many of the issues he and the City Council dealt with at the approach of the city's one-hundredth birthday have been on past agendas. The opening of the Hackberry Pump Station in July 2003 was the culmination of a plan to ensure an adequate supply of water for future needs in the ever-growing city. The plan was conceived in the 1950s, and in 1968, Mayor Robert Power and City Attorney John Boyle signed the contract for construction of a nineteen-thousand-acre reservoir outside of Cooper, Texas. The progress of the plan to bring water to Irving was followed year after year as Lake Chapman was completed and the sequence of facilities required to bring treated water to Irving were placed in operation. When the last thirty-three miles and the Hackberry Pump Station were complete, the project was debt free because each phase had been paid as it was constructed.

The census count for Irving population in 2000 was 191,615. The two proven essentials for a city to be established and to survive are transportation and communication. Irving didn't need a newspaper to know what was going on in town when people met face to face regularly, but it had one on the day it was founded. Through the years there was always a newspaper, and sometimes two or three. But on November 12, 2000, the last *Irving News* was circulated. Publication of the *News* had previously been reduced to two issues a week by Dallas/Fort Worth Suburban Newspapers Inc. It has become an insert in the *Dallas Morning News* on Thursday and Sunday. But communication has changed. The City has a first-rate website with information about every

Joe Putnam, mayor since 1999, is well acquainted with Irving history. He presided during the Irving Centennial Celebration.

The Hackberry Creek Pump Station on Ranchview Drive is the primary center for receiving Lake Chapman water and distributing it to other pump stations throughout Irving.

function of the City. The Chamber of Commerce has an excellent website. The school systems and almost every organization have developed informative websites. The City publishes the *Spectrum* and distributes it to every postal patron six times a year. ICTN televises meetings, informative programs, and news of activities. Neighborhood organizations have newsletters. There are ethnic community newspapers, and events beyond the Irving city limits are reported in the Dallas and Fort Worth papers, on television and the Internet. We aren't really out of touch.

The City has taken the initiative to keep residents in touch and enjoying a sense of community with shared values in many ways. The promotion of Keep Irving Beautiful, the formation of neighborhood organizations, the sponsorship of parades and festivals, programs at the art centers, the parks, the schools, and the libraries bring residents face to face and promote a sense of belonging.

In 1996, Irving hosted the Keep Texas Beautiful Conference and was recognized for outstanding beautification efforts. By 1998, 125 spots had been adopted by Adopt a Spot volunteers. Eighty residents, businesses, and City staff were honored at a Keep Irving Beautiful Proud Partners Awards Banquet in 2003.

Neighborhood associations have been formed in every part of Irving from Valley Ranch, Las Colinas, Plymouth Park, and the Arts District to Southwest Irving. The projects and ways of relating are as varied as the neighborhoods. All participants are encouraged to keep abreast of city affairs and become actively involved in the solutions to problems as well as visions for improvements.

In September 2001, the *Dallas Business Journal* reported that Las Colinas had more than two thousand major companies, more than twenty Fortune 500 corporations, and four hundred corporate headquarters. There were more than ninety-eight thousand employees and twenty-five thousand residents within the development. As amenities it listed four eighteen-hole golf courses, three private country clubs, seventy-five-plus restaurants, a wide range of hotels, and retail developments ranging from neighborhood centers to power centers. They also listed ten miles of hiking and biking trails, an equestrian center with two polo fields, and forty-five-hundred acres dedicated to open space.

Multifamily housing was part of the planned development from the beginning and accounted for much of the population. The first luxury high-rise multifamily building opened in June

People of all ages come together to keep Irving beautiful by adopting a spot and committing to keep it clean. They also participate in landscaping. The payoff is valuable intergenerational friendships and pride in the community.

Graffiti doesn't last long enough in Irving to gratify the perpetrators. In 1995, City crews removed 200,000 square feet of graffiti from public and private buildings. In 2000, they removed 43,519 square feet from 347 properties as soon as it was reported.

Left:
At the Environmental Learning Center, the Public Health and Environmental Services Department worked with master composters, volunteers, and elementary school children to grow a vegetable garden. They donated the crop to the local food pantry.

2002 on Las Colinas Boulevard adjacent to the Mandalay Canal. The seventeen-story, 247-unit project was rapidly leased adding to the ever-increasing population of Irving. The developers built a gondola dock and walkway adjacent to the canal. This will be part of a pedestrian promenade that is planned to ring the lake. Gondola service on the canal is another addition to the ambience of the canal area with its water taxis, below-street-level shops and restaurants, festivals, and concerts.

Mixed-use projects are in various stages of planning and development along the projected route of a light rail line, and City Council is considering plans for a convention center.

During this forward-looking planning and development, the Boy Scouts of America Museum and Family Research Center moved to a site next to the National Headquarters of the Boy Scouts of America in the midst of one of the Las Colinas office parks. The fifty-thousand-square-foot facility opened in October 2002 with, among many other things, the largest collection of Norman Rockwell's Scout paintings anywhere. It includes the first Scout painting he created in 1918 and his last work created in 1976. In addition to artifacts and exhibits, there are virtual reality adventures and learning experiences that provide a journey through the ninety-two-year history of the Scouting movement.

The neighborhood coordinator from the Community Affairs Department works with neighborhood organizations and citizens groups to facilitate communication and generate help for targeted projects. Pictured at an informal meeting are Elvia Martinez and Platon Lerma from the Hispanic organization "Believe in Yourself"; Richard Gilmette, active in Family Advocacy; Holly Smith, neighborhood coordinator; and Jan Killen, chairman of her neighborhood organization.

The Equestrian Center on forty-two acres adjacent to the Elm Fork provides lessons in all aspects of horsemanship and recreational riding for whole families. Stalls for boarding are available. There are two polo fields and both outdoor and indoor arenas. It attracts some of the leading riders and horses in the country and hosts national and regional competitions and events.

The official Museum of the Boy Scouts of America at 1329 West Walnut Hill Lane is a place to explore and enjoy and also a center for primary and secondary research projects and studies of the role of the Scouting movement in social issues.

Mustang Canyon, on a portion of Lake Carolyn, covers thirty acres with permanent ski jumps, easy access for boats, and viewing areas for spectators. It has served as the site for the USA Water Ski Association's South Central Region Show Ski Tournament and the Wakeboard National Championships. It is the home of the areas' only professional water ski team.

The National Museum of Communications at 6305 North O'Connor Road is one part of the seven-building Communications Complex that includes the largest production center between Florida and California. Major motion pictures, television programs, and commercials are produced at the studios, which have complete music, film, video, and multimedia capabilities. A collection of sets and props from many movies including *The Hunt for Red October*, *Wayne's World*, *The Sound of Music*, and the Oval Office set from *JFK* are displayed. Over one hundred thousand visitors tour these facilities each year.

The Libraries are still popular places for information resources as well as leisure reading material. The programs that started in the early days with storytelling and book reviews are now so multifaceted that there must be something for everyone in town, if they notice and choose to attend. In July 2002, the sixth Library branch opened on the North Lake College campus. This two-story, fifty-nine-thousand-square-foot facility is a joint public/college Library that meets the needs of the college students and faculty and all of the Irving community. By combining their strengths, the County and the City saved the taxpayers several million dollars. This wasn't the first collaboration of the City and the college. The natatorium at North Lake was a joint venture, which adds a year-round swimming pool to the six seasonal pools in the Irving park system. The pool with a retractable roof is particularly suitable for aquatics instruction and the Irving synchronized swimming team. A third joint use is the location of a branch of the college in the City-owned Human Services Building on Nursery Road.

Mandalay Canal festival site.

Irving City government and caring citizens have never forgotten the need to nurture and protect families in every way possible. The Family Advocacy Center Building that opened in January 2002 is the result of at least twenty-five years of progressive work by Irving policemen and concerned citizen volunteers to deal with problems of juvenile offenders, dysfunctional families, and victims of abuse or crimes. When the legislature passed the revised penal and family codes in the 1970s, counseling became an alternative to prosecution for juvenile offenders. The police chief and a group of citizens from a cross-section of the city began working together to discover potential offenders and to analyze the causes. It became obvious that family counseling was needed and parents were brought into counseling programs. The Subsequent Offender Program is for juveniles who have been arrested more than once. Parents and children commit to four weekly sessions focused on positive skills and controls.

The Irving Neighborhood Youth Services Agency with a thirteen-member Board of

The joint college and City Library at North Lake College serves as a resource for the community and for the students and faculty of the college. It is in a location that qualified for a city branch Library. All of the players congratulated themselves on the success of the project.

On January 11, 2002, City officials cut the ribbon and invited the community to tour the new Family Advocacy Center.

Directors opened in January 1980. It served 138 adolescents and 150 adults in the first year. The name was changed to Youth/Family Counseling Services. The early funding for the agency was largely dependent on community fundraisers until the City began including it in the budget and grants became available. The interrelationships with other agencies led to the conclusion that for the sake of efficiency and comprehensive service to offenders and victims they should come together under one clearly identifiable roof. That's what the Family Advocacy Center provides for Irving. The building has offices of the Youth/Family Counseling Services and space for the Domestic Violence Unit, Sex Crimes and Child Abuse Units of the Irving Police Department, the Texas Department of Protective and Regulatory Services, and the Dallas County District attorney. It was made possible by the bonds approved in 1999.

Research reveals that even before there was a town of Irving, inhabitants of the Forks celebrated the Fourth of July with picnics, music, dancing, and entertainment. People who grew up in the original town of Irving remember the current location of Heritage Park as a place for

impromptu football games, short horse races, revival tents, community picnics, and celebrations. The annual Fourth of July parade is a longstanding tradition in the Irving Heritage District. Since exuberant citizens love parades, it isn't the only one each year, but it was the first one. The route follows Second Street and Irving Boulevard in the Heritage District.

The Irving Symphony's tradition of a Fourth of July concert at Williams Square, followed by fireworks over Lake Carolyn, started when Irving celebrated the Sesquicentennial. The Symphony Association has faithfully sought funding for the occasion, and its three successive musical directors have led the orchestra in rousing performances for the celebration. Some of the large crowds that show up for the concert in Las Colinas have been celebrating all day, starting with the Heritage District Parade followed by festivities in Heritage Park.

Of course there have always been Christmas celebrations and more of them every year. People who lived in Irving in the early years remember the annual tree on Main Street and the year that Santa arrived on the bus. Those who were children in the early 1960s remember Santa arriving at Plymouth Park in a helicopter, and in the 1980s the ceremonial lighting of the Christmas tree east of City Hall heralded the start of the season. That tree lighting and the accompanying program are still observed in the twenty-first century. For the past sixteen years the Downtown Association has organized a parade followed by a celebration in Heritage Park. The theme for 2002 was "The Sights and Sounds of Christmas." The parade started and ended at Whistle Stop Plaza. Trophies were awarded in Heritage Park, where there were activities for children, a visit with Santa, and hot cider was served.

The many wonderful productions by resident arts groups and visiting artists are thoroughly appreciated by Irving audiences, but *The Nutcracker* is a tradition. Before there was a performance hall, the Irving Ballet accompanied by some members of the Symphony began annual performances of this Christmas favorite. Tiny ballerinas get their first stage experience and both younger and older audience members are delighted year after year.

One of the oldest continuously observed celebrations is Juneteenth. Longtime residents of the Bear Creek community remember when they went to Reverend Morton's house to sing and dance, play games, and have homemade ice cream and barbecue. Now the celebration is held at

The Family Advocacy Center, a twenty-two-thousand-square-foot building on the corner of Sowers and Pioneer, brings together under one roof in a non-threatening atmosphere a variety of resources to protect and strengthen families.

Above:
The young people with the flags represent the Irving Sister Cities associated with the Irving Friendship Foundation. They are Merton, England; Marino, Italy; Boulogne-Billancourt, France; Leon, Guanajuato, Mexico; and Espoo, Finland.

Right:
There are always horses and buggies to honor the Fourth of July and to remember Irving heritage.

the large fully equipped West Park and Recreation Center. There is a Bear Creek Heritage Society that helps organize the event. Some of the members are also active in the Irving Heritage Society. Gloria Oliver is a former Ms. Mature Irving. Elmer Sweat, Luther Steadham, Dixie Caraway, and Gladys Scales are well known in Irving. Marquette Stevenson is a bright young man who is becoming involved in Irving affairs. Many observers expect him to move into expanding leadership roles.

Uncle Sam usually shows up in some form for the downtown parade on the Fourth of July.

Above Left:
Organizers of the parades encourage participants to get together and create their own floats.

Jackie Townsell has of course made a deep mark in Irving history. The Bear Creek Heritage Center bears her name. Two early homes of African American leaders, J. O. Davis and Sam Green, have been moved to the park and rehabilitated. The homes and the entire park are devoted to preserving the history of the community in a way that will let future generations understand where they came from and appreciate with pride the courage and accomplishments of their ancestors. A $75,000 donation from the Mobil Oil Corporation, presented on the June 19th anniversary of the day Texas slaves learned they were free, helped fund the project.

The career of Jackie Townsell as a civic leader, public official, compassionate friend to those who needed help, and strong advocate for community services to benefit all of Irving is legendary. She was the second woman and the only black person elected to the Irving City Council, and she served eighteen consecutive years which is the record for that service. The first event at Texas Stadium was the Billy Graham Crusade in 1971. On October 17, 2002, the Stadium was filled when his Crusade returned to the area for the first time in thirty-one years. Jackie was there in 1971 and again in 2002. It was the last thing she did. A heart attack before she left the parking lot ended her life. The Jackie Townsell Bear Creek Heritage Center, dedicated in 1995, is a memorial she enjoyed while she lived. The Black Arts Council, which she founded, dedicated their 2002–2003 season to her. On February 2, 2003, the Irving School Board voted unanimously to name the nineteenth elementary school Jackie Mae Townsell Elementary School. The way she lived her life, her positive attitude, and her many accomplishments should be an inspiration to all young people.

The Nutcracker **is repeated every year, but it never grows old for Irving audiences.**

Jackie Townsell at the center that bears her name. Her own words explain best why her service to the city was so effective. "I'm for the entire city, all of Irving, not just West Irving. I have no hang-ups about black or white, rich or poor. I serve all."

After redistricting, Linda Harper-Brown was elected to the Irving seat that was created in the House of Representatives. She was the first representative in ten years to live in Irving. She immediately assumed positions of leadership and was recognized for outstanding performance by her colleagues. Courtesy Bill Brown

On January 7, 2002, busloads of proud supporters from Irving traveled to Austin to see Gwen Shea sworn in as secretary of state. Between 1982 and 1992, she had represented Irving in the legislature, and from 1993 until her appointment to one of the highest offices in the state she was the Dallas County constable for Precinct 2, which includes Irving. The constable job required some training, and, although there is no record of her using a gun to perform her duties, she made a perfect score her first time on the firing range. Redistricting was the cause of her being forced out of the legislature in 1992. Irving was divided among five House Districts, and not one of them covered enough of the city to elect a representative from Irving. For the next ten years none of the five legislators who represented Irving lived in the city. Irving was the largest city in the state without its own seat in the House of Representatives.

Redistricting in 2002 created District 105, which was all in Irving from Rock Island to the northern city limits and gave the city a representative who lived in Irving and was already active in City government, as well as regional and statewide issues that affected the city. Linda Harper-Brown left the City Council and was elected to the new seat in the House of Representatives. She made her supporters proud immediately by becoming president of the House of Representatives Freshman Class and treasurer of the House Republican Caucus and by appointments to the Transportation Committee, the Select Committee on State Health Care Expenditures, and the Elections Committee. She was elected chairman of the Freshman Caucus. On July 24, 2003, Representative Harper-Brown was recognized at a ceremony in San Francisco during the National Conference of State Legislators as the "Freshman of the Year." Recipients of the award must have demonstrated leadership legislatively, politically, and in their communities. They must possess the qualities of dedication, conviction, fairness, and integrity. In response to the award, House Speaker Tom Craddick called her the perfect candidate for the award and referred to her leadership as key to the seventy-eighth session of the legislature. He said, "We are very proud to have such an outstanding freshman in the Texas House of Representatives."

In this year of celebrating the birth of Irving, it is interesting to know that our legislative representative is a direct descendent of Ike Story who was so prominent in the early history of the "Forks" and who was the first to bid at the auction which marked the founding of Irving.

The shopping strip that had replaced the school buildings was demolished in 2002.

He bought two lots on First Street at Britain Road, built a house, and brought the first mail into town.

In 2002 the City was stepping up the revitalization of the original town in anticipation of the one-hundredth anniversary on December 19, 2003. A Centennial Task Force was planning activities and recreating the history of the town. Streets and bridges were being improved. Attention was focused on the original town, which was officially the Heritage District.

A tour of the district reveals activities that are enhancing the area, commemorating the past, and bringing attention to the oldest part of Irving.

August 8, 2002, members of the Lively Advisory Committee participated in the groundbreaking for a new Senior Citizens Center on the old school site. Photo by Jerrold Johnson

The most active and attention-focused project is the transformation of the land bounded by Second, Jefferson, Fourth, and Delaware Streets, which was the original school complex and later became a shopping strip. Seniors who grew up in Irving have fond memories of their first schools with "Old Red" and the "best gym ever" on that land. Many of them shopped there as adults after the schools gave way to commercial development. In December 2000, after considering eight sites for a new Senior Citizens Center and receiving nine hundred signatures on a petition, the City bought the strip shopping center and began preparations for the superb new Senior Citizens Center scheduled to open in the Centennial year.

Young people at the Youth Action Center are anxious to move into the Lively Park Center when the seniors move to their new quarters.

A tour of the core of the commercial and residential original town reveals that many of the buildings have been preserved by individual business owners and residents. Most of the houses on Main Street were built in the 1920s. The children who grew up there experienced the Depression years and had a good time playing games, riding bicycles, fishing or swimming in creeks or gravel pits, and walking to school. Downtown with movies and stores and drugstores with soda fountains were just a few steps away. The First Baptist Church is right where it has always been since the town founders donated the lot. It has just gotten bigger and bigger with multiple buildings and an artfully designed sanctuary.

Senior citizens are engaged in numerous activities at their Lively Park location, including a dance every Tuesday evening. They will have an even better dance floor at the new center.

By August 2003, the new Senior Citizens Center was nearing completion. People who went to school here as children, and shopped here as adults, will enjoy numerous activities here as senior citizens. It represents a full circle in the Heritage District.

Across the street on the northwest corner of Jefferson and Second, the Community House that was built by the WPA during the Depression has been reconstructed to house the Preservation and Redevelopment Office and a community meeting area.

The building that was the Water District Office became the first City Hall and grew to house the Police and Fire Station. It is still standing but no longer houses any of those functions.

Across Fourth Street at 327 South Main the house built by C. J. Range Sr. in 1919 has been altered and enlarged, but the basic house which had a Delco system for electricity is there and occupied by "Shorty" and Martha Russell who were actively involved in Union Bower politics before they moved into the old town. The next house at 321 was home to Frank and Velma Haley and their five children. Attorney Tally Parker grew up at 309 Main. In a recorded interview he described the year-round activities on the vacant lots that are now Heritage Park and noted that kids could roam all day and nobody worried about where they were.

Louis and Laura DeHaes lived in the only brick house on Main Street. Years earlier, before there was an Irving, William DeHaes, who came from Belgium, built the first brick house in the area on what later became Highway 183 near Wingren. It was Louis who set up the first movie on North Main in 1919 and was visited by hooded men who told him they didn't want any Catholic shows in town. He built the house on Main Street in 1939 and paid it out at $52.50 a month. His father and mother, William and Octavia, maintained a "Sunday house" at 304 South Main, although they still had the large two-story house in what was then "out in the country." Neighbors were charmed when Octavia sat with a child in the porch swing singing softly in French.

In 2003, the houses on Main Street seem to be in good condition. All of the residential streets in the district are tree-lined and clean. Walking to the commercial blocks or to the train station would be simple. The old town has some of the earmarks of what planners are calling livable cities. But you won't walk to the movies like the early residents did. You won't run up to the "town" on Main Street for groceries, dry goods, or hardware, but you will have a choice of places to eat right in your backyard. Most of the businesses seem to be run by the people who own them, and they know their customers just like the merchants did fifty or sixty years ago.

Gradually the houses that have fallen into disrepair or lack functionality are being replaced. Two projects on Third Street led the way. The house on the corner of O'Connor Road and Third Street across the street from the Heritage House was beyond repair when Fran Bonilla bought it. Historically it had been the home of Charlie Lucas who owned Banner Mercantile on the southeast corner of Main and First. He moved the old wooden building and built the brick one that housed B&H Dry Goods before Big State Drug was there. Mrs. Bonilla removed the old house and built a new one in an architectural style that was contemporary when the town was new.

The house next door where Ione Jackson, Charles Lucas's daughter, lived was also removed and replaced by Patsy Bryant.

On the south side of Third Street and facing O'Connor Road, the house that Charles

The Baptist Sanctuary at 403 South Main Street.

The Parker house at 309 South Main still has a swing on the porch. It's like being transported back to the pleasant neighborhoods of the 1930s and early 1940s when people actually sat on the front porch.

Frank and Velma Haley raised their five children at 321 South Main Street. Sue Haley Huffman, the youngest, and husband John are renovating the house and plan to move back in.

The building at the southeast corner of Main Street and Irving Boulevard has a long and colorful history. The citizens who are living and talking about it in 2003 are most enthusiastic about the time when R. J. Byrd owned it and it was a high school students' hangout. Mr. Broach, the pharmacist, and his wife, Clara, were not the owners, but they ran the place, hired the soda jerks, and seemed to enjoy the kids who kept the place busy. After several years without food or drink services, the doors are again open as a coffee shop and the owner is just down the street.

Top Right:
Louis DeHaes built the brick house at 314 South Main for his young bride, Laura.

Bottom Right:
Hans Smith's theater, once so popular, is still a good building, but instead of entertainment it now houses shops and offices.

Schulze Jr. built for himself when he returned to Irving to help his father in the lumber business is in good condition. Dr. Robert and Sandy Fong bought the house in 1972.

The Heritage House across the street is maintained by the City and managed by the Heritage Society, which meets there and sometimes opens the house for tours. Dr. Clay Gilbert still lives next door in the historic home of his father, Dr. Monroe Gilbert.

The original town is alive and well and getting better every day as the Senior Center is about to bring even more activity back home.

The one-hundredth anniversary of the founding of Irving was December 19, 2003, commemorating the day the first lots were sold by auction. Celebration of that event was not a spur-of-the-moment affair for Irving citizens. They started serious planning in 2001 when the mayor appointed a twenty-seven-member Centennial Task Force of dedicated citizens to make everybody in Irving aware of Irving history and involve the resources of the community in actively celebrating the Centennial. Marvin Randle and Shelah-Bell Andrews, co-chairs, immediately set up nine committees and started intensive planning.

Big State Drugs is still remarkably like it was in the 1940s. The owners are pharmacists and they know their customers. The old-fashioned hamburgers are cooked on the grill when they are ordered, and there's a genuine soda fountain for malts, sodas, or shakes. A friendly waitress serves the counter and the booths. Early birds can get a hearty breakfast. It seems the only thing that has changed is that the juke boxes are gone and the customers are not teenagers.

Here on Irving Boulevard, J. O. Schulze opened the first business in Irving. C. P. Schulze ran it until Charles Schulze Jr. came back home to help. He turned it into Handy House, a building supply store, and now it houses a few offices and the Culinary Improv where the owners know their customers and diners always see someone they know.

Looking south across Irving Boulevard, the corner lot on the east was the site of the first house in Irving, built for Otis and Netta Brown and enlarged for Chaney and Sarah Miller. On the right is the building that housed Peck's Office and School Supply and Bookstore, which displaced Etta Williams Roberts' Boarding House where schoolteachers stayed. In the center, on the other side of Second Street, the spire of the new sanctuary of the First Methodist Church can be seen from anywhere in the Heritage District. The third church in Irving never moved from the original site. It just kept growing.

On down Irving Boulevard, just east of Delaware Creek, the slogan is "Where Irving meets and eats." It was Joe's Coffee Shop on Sixth Street where Carol Wood worked and then owned the growing business. The business has moved to the building that was originally Farina's, but the service and down home cooking still attract repeat customers where there is a feeling that "everybody knows your name."

A strong advocate of the preservation and redevelopment of downtown Irving, Fran Bonilla practiced what she was preaching when she replaced a deteriorating house with a new one in a turn-of-the-century style.

Patsy Bryant had the old home and office of Dr. John Haley moved from Second and Ohio to 315 West Third.

Special historical markers and plaques were planned. Permanent art in the form of a painting and a sculpture was commissioned. The schools were invited to provide and develop artwork and a video featuring Irving's history with curriculum plans for use in history and government classes. Junior historians were involved in tours. Videos for and by students were developed through the drama teachers. A centennial logo and various types of memorabilia were created. A Centennial Choir was initiated. A neighborhood grants program encouraged planting trees, shrubs, and flowers. Large and small events were planned. The Water Utilities Department even produced a manhole cover with the Centennial logo to be used in the downtown area.

When the Haley house was in place on Third Street and refurbished, it was an asset to the neighborhood and a boost to the redevelopment effort.

The official celebration was scheduled to involve special events over a fifteen-month period beginning with an official kickoff on October 3, 2002, and climaxing with activities on December 19–20, 2003. The planned highlight was the arrival of a train from Dallas and a reenactment of the lot sale and barbecue at the end of Main Street.

The Opening Ceremony at the Irving Art Center was a festive occasion attended by a large crowd, most of whom were dressed in versions of period costume. The Irving Symphony played an original composition written for the Centennial. The life-sized bronze sculpture of two surveyors, by celebrated artist Paul Tadlock, was unveiled. An oil painting depicting the town auction was lowered onto the stage. The artist, Guy Deel, grew up right where that event took place. He was the youngest of the six children whose parents brought them to Irving in 1939. They bought the famous hotel at the end of Main Street and turned it into their home. Guy has been a highly successful professional artist for more that fifty years. Most people remember his work with Walt Disney Studios. His sister, Louise Gill, is a member of the Centennial Task Force. Brothers George, Burnis, and James and sister Burnise also have roots in Irving.

This house on O'Connor Road at Third Street, built for Charles and Catherine Schulze in 1948, is used as an office by Dr. Robert Fong.

April 5, 2003, more than forty thousand people were counted at a big birthday bash for Irving at Texas Stadium with music, food, carnival rides, arts and crafts, children's games, and a long list of professional entertainers, some of whom were homegrown.

The gateway to the Heritage District is greatly improved by Millennium Park, which is a symbol of Irving entering the twenty-first century. It sits in a triangle formed by Sowers Road at the base and the convergence of Irving Boulevard and Second Street.

New manhole covers for downtown. Photo by Jerrold Johnson

On May 4, over two hundred people enjoyed "Murder on the Irving Centennial Express." They enjoyed a train ride complete with dinner, a mystery drama, and clues to help them solve the case. Then on June 14, 2003, it was time for the annual Heritage Festival sponsored by the Downtown Association. This year it had added excitement and participation because of the Centennial involvement. In fact it started Friday evening with a Front Porch Music Tour with musical groups performing on porches on Third, Second, and Ohio Streets, followed by a square-dance demonstration on the parking lot at Second and Ohio. The Shady Grove Ramblers played on the Main Stage followed by the annual Old Time Fiddlers Contest.

Saturday was a full day with all of the usual exhibits and vendors. The emphasis was on the early pioneer arts, skills, and way of life on the one hand and the arts and foods from different countries represented in the population of Irving on the other. The International Stage on International Boulevard (100 South Main) showcased entertainment from thirteen countries.

Centennial Park and Founders Plaza was dedicated on October 4 when the sculpture of two surveyors representing J. O. Schulze and Otis Brown was permanently installed in Founders Plaza. This location next to Delaware Creek was first scheduled to be developed as a park in 1932.

The next day on October 5, the citywide Centennial Church Choir celebrated at Calvary Temple. Then on October 18, a Cub Scout Family Historic Trail Hike convened at the Boy Scouts of America National Office at 1325 West Walnut Hill Lane where there is a Bird's Fort Trail Marker.

The Irving Art Association opened a monthlong Centennial Show at the Jaycee Center for the Arts on November 30.

A Holiday Extravaganza, Parade, and Tree Lighting occurred on December 6. Then on the ninth, revelers feasted at the annual Bracebridge Dinner. The finale on December 19–20 closed the Centennial celebration. But probably the new acquaintances who joined in the festivities during the Centennial will continue to participate in some of the annual festivities that are traditional in Irving. And maybe they will help establish some new ones, too.

During the first years of the twenty-first century, attention has been directed to the oldest and most southern part of Irving and overdue improvements have begun. But vision is not so

Many fans of the Shady Grove Ramblers don't know that they have won numerous prestigious awards and have a national reputation. They think the Ramblers belong to Irving and it's not a festival or any celebration without their pickin' Kevin Kirkpatrick, David Miller, Tom Uhr, Loyd Hinch, and Chris Burkhalter.

myopic that the value and many contributions of every part of this complex city go unappreciated. Most citizens view the city and its inhabitants as a whole and feel a part of the entire complex community. Contrary to some popular propaganda, it is possible to celebrate individuality and at the same time appreciate a common thread of values and humanity. Maybe in 2023 Irving will celebrate the Golden Anniversary of the announcement of the plan for Las Colinas. The promenade around Lake Carolyn will be finished and would be a great place for festivities.

Irving is a collection of communities that can come together in one big community when there is an occasion to do so.

Co-Chairs Marvin Randle and Shelah-Bell Andrews presided at the Kickoff with Mayor Joe Putnam and his wife, Jan Hart, senior archivist for the City. Photo by T. J. Friedel

Prominent citizens involved in making and preserving the history of Irving were seated on the stage where the commemorative artworks were displayed. Photo by T. J. Friedel

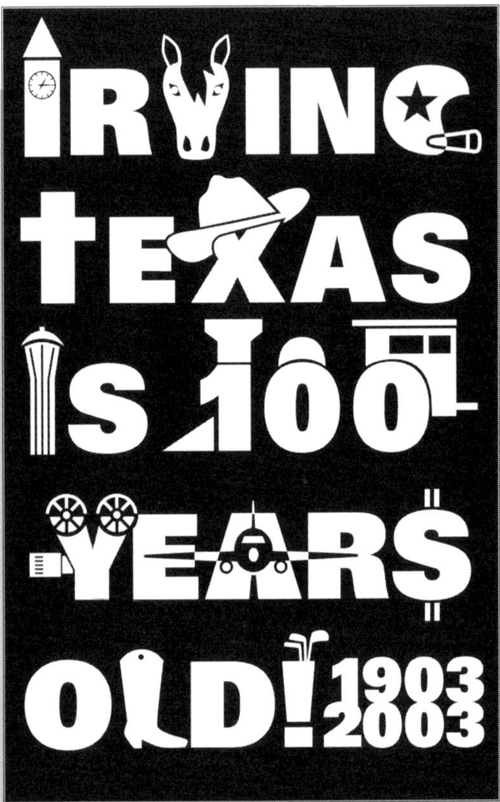
IRVING
TEXAS
IS 100
YEARS
OLD! 1903
2003

YESTERDAY
TODAY
TOMORROW
International Blvd.
Rock Island Stage
Third St. Stage
Gospel Singing
Food & Drinks
Rest Rooms
Crafters
Children's Games
Children's Activities
Home Show Vendors
Sidewalk Sale
Quilts & Art Show

RENT TO OWN

AL'S RENT TO OWN NO CREDIT CHECK
TV · Stereo · Furniture · Appliances

It has been more than seventy years since a Schulze Park was planned along Delaware Creek. In June 2003, the Delaware Creek Park was almost complete between Second and Sixth Streets. Next to the footbridge, Founders Plaza features the life-size bronze sculpture representing J. O. Schulze and Otis Brown.

IRVING TEXAS 1903 2003 CENTENNIAL

CENTENNIAL CELEBRATION TASK FORCE

CO-CHAIRS
Shelah-Bell Andrews
Marvin Randle

TASK FORCE MEMBERS
Gloria Agyemang
Jo Armstrong
Sharon Barbosa-Crain
Elena Blake
Pat Bolger
Juanita Britain
Charles Brown
Kathy Burke
Bob Curtis
Pete Fernandez
Paula Flatley
Louise Gill
Sunny Gray
Steve Hillier
Donna Hoskins
Rosalie Jensen
Arnold Martin
Bob Nelson
Robert Power
Marquette Stevenson
Jim Street
George Susat
Bobbie Thomas
Gary Tong
Chris Wallace
Mickey Watson
Velma White

CITY LIAISONS
David Cardenas
Assistant to the City Manager

Kim Sutter
Mayor's Assistant

CITY COUNCIL LIAISON
James Dickens

IRVING

Bibliography

Allen, Tom. *Journey Toward Excellence*. Irving Independent School District, 1984.

Anderson, Sherwood. *Home Town*. Alliance Book Corporation, 1940.

Barton-Aschman Associates. "Mid-Cities Area Public Transportation Plan". March 1974.

Baskett, Sam S. *The American Identity*. Lexington, Mass.: D. C. Heath and Company, 1962.

Bessler, Betty Beauford. "Six Generations in Irving." Unpublished history. 2002.

Board of Commissioners of the Town of Irving. Minute Book. April 14, 1914–November 29, 1930.

Brown, Dee. *When the Century Was Young*. Little Rock: August House Publishers, 1993.

Brown, Mrs. Otis. "A History of Early Irving." Irving Heritage Society.

Burgess, Tommy, ed. *The Irving Fire Department*, Commemorative Edition. 1983.

Carpenter, Ben H. *Las Colinas: Reflections from Its Founder*. New York: American Society of Civil Engineers, 1993.

Clower, Terry. "Assessment of the Film/Video Industry in Irving, Texas." University of North Texas, 1998.

Connor, Seymour V. *The Peters Colony of Texas: A History and Biographical Sketches of the Early Settlers*. Austin: Texas State Historical Association, 1959.

Dealey, Ted. *Diaper Days of Dallas*. Nashville: Abingdon Press, 1966.

Dunkin, J. T. and Associates. Irving Land Use and Heritage Preservation Plan. 1985.

Durham, Floyd. *The Trinity River Paradox*: *Flood and Famine*. Nortex Press, 1976.

"Goals for Irving." Essays for discussion at the Waco Conference. May 1968.

Greene, A. C. Dallas: *The Deciding Years*. Austin: Encino Press, 1973.

Hazel, Michael V., Ph.D. *Dallas: A Dynamic Century*. Sulphur, La.: Wyndham Publishing Company, 1998.

Irving Department of Parks and Recreation. "Master Plan for Parks and Recreation." 1970.

Irving Department of Community Development. "Eight Planning Studies, 1970–1976."

Kahn, Molly, coordinator. "The Dawning: Irving Performing Arts Center." GTE/Creative Printing Services, September 1990.

League of Women Voters. "Open Space Report." October 1972.

Leipziger, Hugo-Pearce. "Irving, Comprehensive Development Plan." July 15, 1960.

Mallon, Thomas. *Mrs. Paine's Garage and the Murder of John F. Kennedy*. New York: Pantheon Books, 2002.

Moore, Robin. *Compulsion: Psychiatric Analysis by Robert Custer*. New York: Doubleday, 1961.

Parrish, Morris. Paper on his years as mayor, 1995–1999.

Peterson, Peggy. "Growth of Irving Symphony." Manuscript. January 28, 1963.

Pruit, Dr. Thomas, ed. *The Cistercians in Texas*. Mix Printing Company, 1998.

Randall, J. G. *The Civil War and Reconstruction*. Lexington, Mass.: D. C. Heath and Company, 1937.

Rogers, Mary Beth. *Texas Women—A Celebration of History*. Austin: Texas Foundation for Women's Resources, 1981.

Santerre, George. *White Cliffs of Dallas*. The Book Craft, 1955.

———. *Dallas, First 100 Years, 1856–1956*. The Book Craft, 1956.

Schafer, Mike. *Classic American Railroads*. MBI Publishing Company, 1996.

Scott, Stanley. *A Giant in Texas: History of the Dallas–Fort Worth Regional Airport Controversy, 1911–1974*. Nortex Press, 1974.

Seeber, Martha. "Irving, Town Between the Forks of the Trinity River." Typescript.

Shirer, William L. *20th Century Journey, 1904–1930*. Simon and Schuster, 1976.

Strong, Ann Louise. *Planned Urban Environments*. Baltimore: Johns Hopkins Press, 1971.

Stowe, Estha. "Irving's Golden Year, Historical Script."

Theatre Projects Consultants, Inc. "Irving Theatre Feasibility Study." September 1986.

"The Journal's Corporate Guide to Las Colinas & Greater Irving." AGF Company, 1984.

Werner, George C. "Railroads." *The Handbook of Texas Online*. Austin: Texas State Historical Association, 1997–2001.

Media

Adair, W. S. "Dallas Was an Island in 1866." *Dallas Morning News*, September 3, 1922.
Brown, Otis. "Autobiography" (written for his own use). *Irving Herald*, August 19, 1932.
"Carpenter to Tell Why Navigate the Trinity." *Irving News*, January 28, 1962.
"Chamber of Commerce Sponsors Made in Irving Exhibit of Manufacturers." *Irving Herald*, April 23, 1948.
"Churches in Irving Reflect Spirit of Progress." *Irving Daily News*, February 26, 1967.
"Eagle Ford, Rip Roarin' Town of 1875." *Dallas Times-Herald*, September 29, 1946.
Fulton, R. E. "T Model Ride Began Happy Story." *Daily News-Texan*. April 16, 1964.
Harden, Josephine. "Irving Pioneer Recalls." *Irving Daily News*, January 7, 1974.
Irving Daily News-Texan. Anniversary Edition, April 16, 18, 1964.
———. "Parade of Progress—History Section." February 23, 1975.
Lewis, Charles. "Our Town at Her Best." *Daily News-Texan*, December 12, 1962.
"Officials, Arts Groups Mark Theater Top Out," "Main Event Slated for Heritage Park," "Irving to Host Arts Council Convention." *Art Times*, November 1989.
Shaughnesay, Ann. "GTE Announces Move to Las Colinas." *Las Colinas Weekly*, November 17, 1988.
Schulze, J. O. "Irving Co-Founders Believed in Growth." *Irving News-Record*, October 30, 1958.
"Schulze Park." *Irving News*, December 22, 1933.
Shannon, Pierce. "Irving Orchestra, Choir to Give Concert." *Dallas Times-Herald*, November 25, 1963.
"Sowers Name Seemed Destined for History." *Daily News-Texan*, April 16, 1964.
"Uncle Ike," "The New Rock Island Town in the Forks of the Trinity," "The Passing of Kit—Some Reminiscences." *Irving Index*, July 1904.

Between February and October 1955, newspapers across the state carried frequent reports on the Irving school controversy.

Acknowledgments

The Mayor and City Council of Irving appointed Co-Chairs Marvin Randle and Shelah-Bell Andrews and a twenty-seven-member Task Force to plan a major celebration of the one-hundredth anniversary of the founding of the city. This book about the history of Irving is one of the many projects launched by that group of dedicated citizens. When they gave me the opportunity to research and write the history, I had no idea how interesting or how challenging the assignment would be. Personal conversations with more than two hundred people individually or in groups of three to twenty convinced me that there are a million stories to be told but not enough pages allowed to record all of them.

The first help toward understanding the early years came from Betty Miller who made available information and pictures she had used for presentations on behalf of the Heritage Society in the 1970s and 1980s. Joseph Rice was chairman of the Sesquicentennial Committee in 1986 and later wrote *Irving: A Texas Odyssey*, published in 1989. My quest for primary sources took me to some of the same resources he had used for that excellent book. These were interviews with pioneer citizens that Estelle and O. D. Bates began recording in 1974.

When the interviewing project began, there were people still living who could recall events and experiences from the time Irving was founded and earlier. Various volunteers continued conducting interviews. These oral histories are especially useful when they preserve the actual words of people who were involved in the events that shaped Irving and provide firsthand information unfiltered by media summaries and unaltered by the retelling. Under the direction of Senior Archivist Jan Hart, interviews are still being conducted, and they are transcribed to hard copy and entered to computer programs for easier access. She made it possible for me to hear or read the words of ninety-seven people who lived in Irving at different times during the hundred-year history. Many others are available.

The Irving Archives is an amazing storehouse of historic documents and artifacts crowded into limited space. It seemed magical to me that if I could phrase the question about Irving history, Ms. Hart or Kevin Kendro could find information somewhere on the floor-to-ceiling shelves. I am most grateful for their help. Eleanor Corry Bell, who volunteers in the Archives, shared her research on several key subjects and provided pictures from her own collection. Collections donated by organizations and by families proved to be valuable for facts as well as atmosphere.

Librarian Sara Vance helped me access the considerable resources of the Local History and Genealogy Section of the Irving Public Library.

Garfield Andrew organized the first large group that came together to recall for me their experiences in Irving. They were growing up and attending school in the 1930s and 1940s. The remarkable thing about this group was that they all seemed to have a very positive attitude about a period that is often characterized as painfully grim and they all conveyed a very real affection for their former school and the city of Irving. Later Louise Henderson arranged a meeting with four Irving natives who became well-known owners of businesses in the old Irving area. Their conversations about working as young boys, their wages, and sleeping out where Centennial Park is now gave life to the demographic facts we had gathered.

Mrs. Henderson also brought in information and pictures and gave me a copy of the *Directory of the Forks*, which was assembled and published by R. E. Fulton in 1938. This directory was a valuable source of information because of the numerous advertisements and the listings of residents and businesses within and beyond the city limits. There were street names in town, but no house numbers at that time. Frank Hamm III, son of the second owners of the Irving Hotel, delivered the *Irving News* to every house in Irving, and he was the one who went out to record the location of homes and businesses in the town of Irving and surrounding territory for the *Directory of the Forks*. Names of men, women, and children were listed with each location. Juanita Britain made an appointment with Frank Hamm III so that I, along with representatives from the Archives and the Centennial Committee, could talk with him. The interview with Mr. Hamm added insight to the life that we had not seen recorded.

Betty Beaufford Bessler compiled the story of the six generations of her family beginning with Henry Eugene and Catherine E. DeBeaufford who came to the area in 1883. She wrote the history and included pictures, deeds and newspaper clippings in an unpublished booklet. This factual information was extremely helpful in sorting out the many stories about the early land uses and relationships.

Raymond Story shared the fruits of his extensive research of the Story and Farine families. His research and his own memories were interesting and informative. They clarified some issues that were otherwise clouded with confusion.

Pat Carnell, longtime director of the Irving Hospital Foundation, was the best source of information and access to pictures about the creation and growth of Irving Community Hospital.

Morris Parrish gave us a wealth of information and some pictures not only about his tenure as mayor but also about the Community Hospital and about the house at 321 South O'Connor and its first inhabitants. This was the second home of Otis Brown who was the first mayor of Irving. Lynn Brown, the fourteenth mayor was born there. Morris and Marge Parrish restored it and lived there while he was the twenty-second mayor of Irving.

C. J. Range proved to be a storehouse of information about the Heritage District. He was able to give clear verifiable dates, ownership, and uses of buildings. The location of post offices was particularly helpful.

Sue Haley Huffman gave us well-documented information about the Haley, Miller, and Duckworth families through the years beginning long before the founding of Irving. She also wrote insightfully about what it was like to grow up in Irving during the Depression years.

Carol Susat wrote for us an account of the first attempts to clarify and record the history of Irving, the development of Heritage Park, and the sequence of efforts that led to the establishment of the Family Advocacy Center.

Edgar Brown gathered information and pictures about the Estelle community and created an excellent unpublished history of the area. Without his efforts, much of that information would have been lost.

Dr. Clay Gilbert shared his own memories of growing up in Irving as well as documentation of the lives and influence of his parents and grandparents who provided the first medical services in the area. He has restored and preserved the home at 309 South O'Connor where Dr. Franklin M. and Dorothy Gilbert welcomed patients at all hours.

The house next door at 303 South O'Connor, built in 1912 for C. P. and Virginia Schulze, was donated to the City by Charles and Catherine Schulze. It became the official Heritage House managed by the Heritage Society and helped spur preservation projects. Members of the Heritage Society still keep the social traditions of early Irving alive with tours of the home and reenactments of the Valentine Tea staged by Virginia Schulze in 1914. Catherine Schulze continues to be a source of information about the social life and mores of the early years.

Help came from so many people that I have hesitated to start naming all of them. I can only hope that they will be pleased that they had a part in making this book possible.

Index

About the Author

Norma Stanton. Photo by T.J. Friedel

Norma Stanton has followed the history of Irving for forty-six years. After ten years on the faculty at Southern Methodist University and simultaneous teaching assignments at the downtown evening extension known then as Dallas College, she retired and moved to Irving with the intention of quietly raising a family in a small town. In less than a year after the birth of her first child in 1957, she was teaching at the University of Dallas in Irving, and before the second child she was also teaching classes for the American Institute of Banking. In 1963 she retired again to care for her four children who eventually were educated in Irving schools. For the next forty years she was deeply involved in the development processes of Irving.

As president of an elementary school PTA, Norma was introduced to Irving citizens who were promoting improvements in the school system. As president of the League of Women Voters, she was introduced to the numerous issues facing both Irving and the state of Texas. She moderated public meetings on subjects such as Public Health Imperatives, Water Planning for Texas, Transportation Planning for North Central Texas, Child Care Concerns, and the Effects of Noise from the Proposed Airport. For twenty years she was coproducer and moderator of "Voters Digest," a weekly panel-format program on Channel 11 that addressed issues affecting the region.

Norma represented Irving in the Goals for Dallas program, the Regional Transportation Council, the County Tax Advisory Board, the Lone Star Transit Authority, and the Dallas Area Rapid Transit Authority. She represented cities with populations of 100,000 to 500,000 on the Municipal Waste and Resource Recovery Advisory Board to the State Department of Health. She chaired the Irving Library Board, the Northeast Texas Library Systems Advisory Board, the State Library Services and Construction Act Advisory Council, and the State Library Trustees Round Table, and she was elected four times to the Irving City Council. Long-range plans that she wrote for libraries, the arts, and community television were eventually implemented.

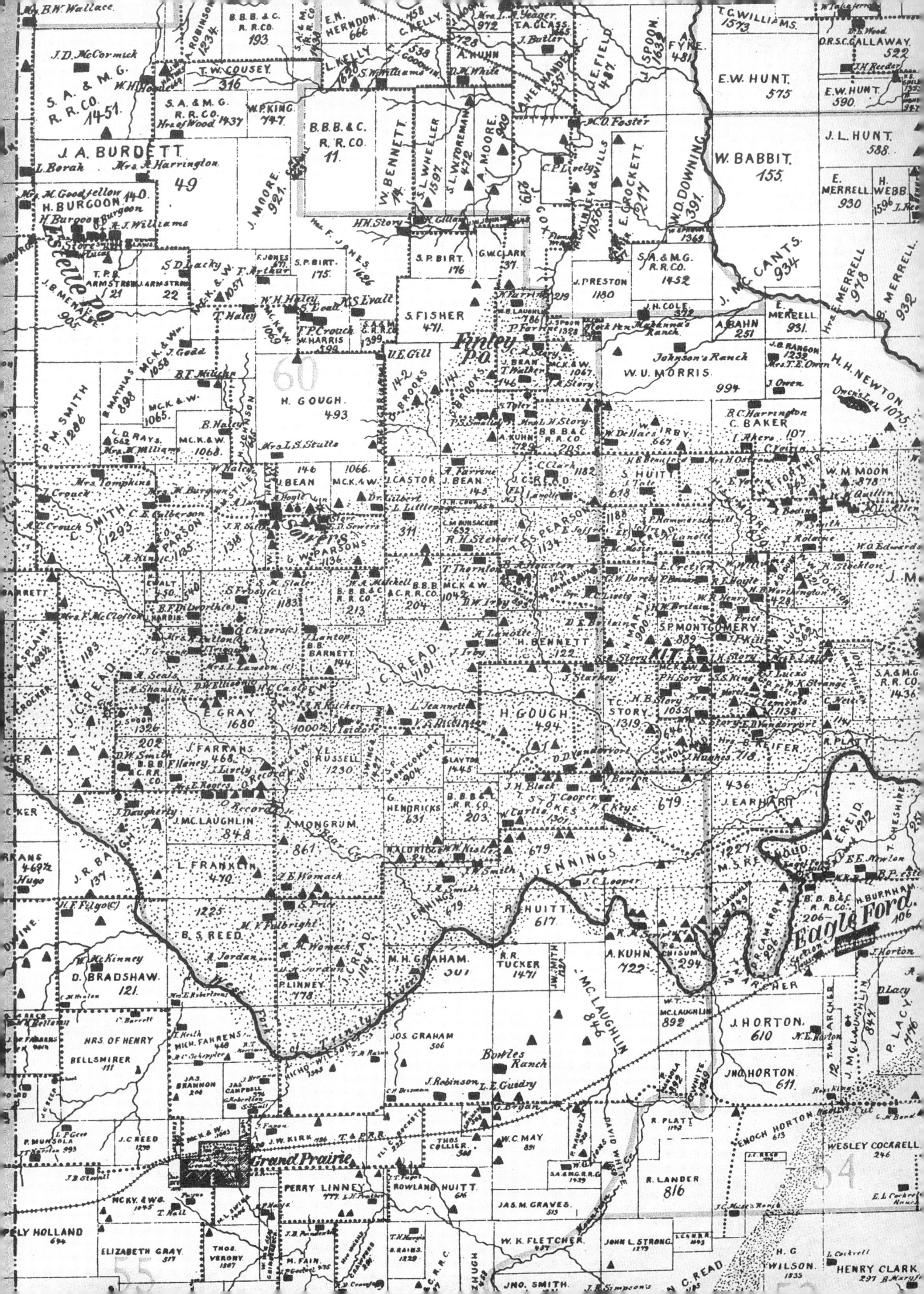

B.B.B. & C. R.R.CO. 193
E.N. HERNDON 666
C. KELLY
A. KUHN
J. SPOON 1632
A. FYKE 481
T.C. WILLIAMS 1573
J.D. McCormick
S.A. & M.G. R.R.CO. 1451
T.W. COUSEY 316
W.P. KING 747
E.W. HUNT 575
E.W. HUNT 590
J.A. BURDETT
49
B.B.B. & C. R.R.CO. 11
W. BENNETT
S.L. WHEELER 1597
A. MOORE
J.L. HUNT 588
W. BABBIT 155
H. BURGOON 140
J. MOORE 921
W.D. DOWNING 391
E. CROCKETT 217
E. MERRELL 930
H. WEBB
Estelle P.O.
T.P.B. ARMSTRONG 21
22
S.P. BIRT 175
S.P. BIRT 176
G.W. CLARK
S.A.&M.G. R.R.CO. 1452
J. PRESTON 1180
J. McCANTS 934
S. FISHER 471
A. BAHN 251
E. MERRELL 931
Finley P.O.
Johnson's Ranch
W.U. MORRIS 994
H.H. NEWTON 1075
60
H. GOUGH 493
P.M. SMITH 1286
C. BAKER 107
S. HUITT 618
W.M. MOON 878
T.E.S. PEARSON 1134
Sowers
C. SMITH 1293
G.W. PARSONS 1136
S.P. MONTGOMERY 889
H. BENNETT 122
J.C. READ 1181
J.C. READ 1183
E. GRAY 1680
H. GOUGH 494
S.A. & M.G. R.R.CO. 1436
Y.E. RUSSELL 1230
G. HENDRICKS 631
J.H. BLACK
679
J. EARHART
E. REID 1212
J. McLAUGHLIN 848
J. MONGRUM 861
L. FRANKLIN 470
JENNINGS
M.S. REDMOND
J.R. BAUGH 137
B.S. REED
R. HUITT 617
Eagle Ford
D. BRADSHAW 121
M.H. GRAHAM 501
R.R. TUCKER 1471
A. KUHN 722
J. HORTON 610
HRS. OF HENRY BELLSMIRER 111
JOS. GRAHAM 506
Bowles Ranch
J. McLAUGHLIN 846
JNO. HORTON 611
P. LACY 1146
Trinity River
West Fork
Grand Prairie
T. & P. R.R.
PERRY LINNEY 777
ROWLAND HUITT 616
R. PLATT
R. LANDER 816
ENOCH HORTON 613
WESLEY COCKRELL 246
JAS. M. GRAVES 513
ELIZABETH GRAY 517
W.K. FLETCHER 457
JOHN L. STRONG 1279
H.G. WILSON 1335
HENRY CLARK 237
JNO. SMITH
54
55